MW01196289

BROWN SKIN, WHITE MINDS

ᜊᜒᜇᜓᜏᜒᜈ᜴ ᜀᜒ | ᜐᜒ᜴ᜐ᜴ ᜋᜒᜈ᜴

FILIPINO -/ AMERICAN POSTCOLONIAL PSYCHOLOGY

(with commentaries)

E. J. R. DAVID, PH.D.

DEPARTMENT OF PSYCHOLOGY
UNIVERSITY OF ALASKA ANCHORAGE
UNIVERSITY OF ALASKA JOINT PH.D. PROGRAM IN
CLINICAL-COMMUNITY PSYCHOLOGY

INFORMATION AGE PUBLISHING, INC.
Charlotte, NC • www.infoagepub.com

Library of Congress Cataloging-in-Publication Data

A CIP record for this book is available from the Library of Congress
http://www.loc.gov

Printed in the United States of America

To My Wife Margaret, and our Works of Art –
Malakas, Kalayaan, and Kaluguran

BROWN SKIN, WHITE MINDS

ᜊᜓᜇᜓᜈᜒ ᜃᜊ | ᜎᜒᜉᜒ ᜃᜏ

*   *   *

TABLE OF CONTENTS

FOREWORD

By

Sumie Okazaki, Ph.D.

Like many books, this book is a labor of love. It is a culmination of a programmatic research in psychology carried out with scientific rigor but also born out of passion. Now, many mental health scholars – including myself – do care deeply about the subject matter and the population that we study. Our scholarship is motivated in part by a belief that our work has some positive impact on the little corner of the world that we study and write about. However, more than any other scholar with whom I have had the privilege to work, Dr. E. J. R. David has carried out his work out of deep love and commitment to the community. Dr. David's work is passionate to the extent that it arouses many collective emotions – anger at the centuries of historical oppression of Filipinos, sorrow for the lives lost to suicides and depression, dismay at the insidious and long-lasting nature of the legacy of colonialism, and the urgency to right the course for the community's psyche.

Dr. David was one of my doctoral students at the University of Illinois at Urbana-Champaign. As with many students who gain admission to a selective doctoral program in clinical-community psychology, Dr. David's undergraduate advisors at the University of Alaska Anchorage endorsed his scholarly potential with enthusiasm. His mentors at Alaska raved about his intellect, his work ethic, and his commitment to psychology as a scientific enterprise. And his time at Illinois proved not only that his undergraduate advisors knew a gem when they saw one, Dr. David was indeed a rare scholar who is inordinately capable and productive yet also extraordinarily grounded.

Dr. David brought his research ideas about Colonial Mentality – the subject of this book – to Illinois. Upon arriving in Illinois, he hit the ground running and has been running fast and steady ever since. My task as his research mentor was to slow him down just enough at the beginning to theorize about the nature of colonial mentality before plowing ahead full-force with the research program. In retrospect, this step was perhaps more for my edification as an Asian American mental health scholar who knew so embarrassingly little about dialogues within the Filipino American community.

The series of studies that Dr. David carried out under my guidance during his graduate career are systematic and rigorous. He first worked to present the theoretical framework for colonial mentality, next to develop and validate a questionnaire on colonial mentality, then to develop tools to examine colonial mentality at the implicit or subconscious level, and to demonstrate the relationship between colonial mentality and psychological distress among Filipino Americans. Whatever scientific tools he needed to accomplish the next step, Dr. David mastered with ease and speed; the rest of us watched in awe at his productivity and singular commitment to his scholarship. Yet I knew that Dr. David's work was driven not by ambitions for academic glory but by his wish to "give away" psychology to the community – a principle that is essential for any community psychology scholar. During his graduate school years, Dr. David devoted his effort to outreach to the Filipino American community through media appearances, teaching, and the development of an intervention to reduce colonial mentality among Filipino Americans. At the same time, he quietly toiled for years to bring first his brother and then his mother from the Philippines to the United States. He also managed to keep up the long-distance relationship with his high school sweetheart, now his wife.

And to this day, Dr. David continues to be a prolific scholar, as evidenced by the very existence of this book. In an academic discipline that does not necessarily value book publications, the initial edition of this book - *Filipino -/ American Postcolonial*

Psychology: Oppression, Colonial Mentality, and Decolonization -
was written by a junior assistant professor with a full set of teaching,
service, and research demands and a new father to a baby boy. Now,
this revised version – *Brown Skin, White Minds: Filipino -/ American
Postcolonial Psychology* – was accomplished while Dr. David was
raising three very young children with his wife. I write all this not to
embarrass E.J., as he is known to many, but as a testament to the
notion that academic productivity does not necessarily mean
shortchanging other important life commitments. When a scholar
engages in a work that has the potential to really mean something to
the community, as Dr. David has done and continues to do, there is
an urgency to disseminate the work as widely and effectively as
possible. And this book fully realizes that potential to make a
difference in the Filipino -/ American community. The book also
teaches us – Filipino or non-Filipino – the sheer importance of
understanding the historical context for our contemporary
psychological experiences. It is, then, not at all surprising that the
first edition of this book has already achieved critical praise as well
as a large community support. I am happy, not only for Dr. David for
his success, but also for the larger community of scholars, students,
and community members who will now be able to access this
important work.

Finally while I have this forum, I would like to take the
opportunity to set the record straight. As his graduate mentor, I have
benefitted quite a bit myself from the reflected glory of Dr. David's
scholarship. It is not unusual for me to have students and scholars
that I do not know contact me to tell me how much they have liked
my work on colonial mentality. However, as much as I would love to
claim credit, the credit belongs to Dr. David. I am just pleased that I
was invited on the ground floor for this important ride.

Sumie Okazaki, Ph.D.
Professor of Applied Psychology
New York University

Preface*

I was born and raised in the Philippines during the 1980s. My father began working in the United States when I was around four years-old, and as I was growing up, he regularly sent me VHS tapes of recorded shows from various children TV stations such as the Cartoon Channel. My mom would sit me in front of the TV to watch these tapes as she cooked, cleaned the house, or did other errands. What my father did was press the record button on his VHS player every morning before he went to work, and the machine continuously recorded countless different shows until the tape ran out. While spending hours watching these gifts from my father, I remember seeing the advertisements that were recorded in such tapes. I saw blonde- or brown-haired, blue-eyed, light-skinned kids playing with the coolest toys I had ever seen. It made me want to have what they had. I remember seeing those kids having the time of their lives in Disneyland, Universal Studios, or other theme parks. I wanted to go where they were.

When I was around six or seven years-old, I loved G.I. Joe toys. I remember my mother would take me to a local store about once a month to buy a G.I. Joe action figure, vehicle, or other accessories one at a time. Before I knew it, I accumulated more than 60 G.I. Joe action figures and about six different tanks, jets, jeeps, and whatever else. One of the things I remember most from these monthly shopping trips though, is that every time we went to the store to buy these toys, my mother always asked the store clerk if the toys were "orig." In trying to bargain for a lower selling price, she always said "Orig ba 'yan, baka local lang 'yan?" (Are you sure these are original? Are you sure these are not locally made?) To this, the store clerk always said, "Yes, ma'am. They are made in the USA." Upon hearing this, my mom would gladly pay for the marked price,

XIII

validating its value. I heard this every time we bought a G.I. Joe toy. So about once a month, I went home with a new, "orig," and Made in the USA G.I. Joe toy that I showed off to my friends and playmates. I was very proud of them.

As far back as I can remember, relatives and friends always talked about ways to make their skin color lighter, or at least, ways to prevent their skin from getting too dark. Many of them used bleach or skin-whitening soap on a daily basis. Others were so afraid of the sun that they would not come out of their homes until the sun is already beginning to set around dusk. For a tropical island country where the sun is out for most of the day, all year round, I found these vampire-like behaviors odd. The celebrities or "beautiful people" in the country who were supposed to be role models and the ones many people idolized and tried to emulate were all light-skinned or were mestizos/as (mixed Filipino and White). It was also these celebrities who the masses see as role models who regularly endorsed the use of skin-whitening products or procedures in television commercials and other media advertisements. They also endorsed, and proudly shared their experiences with, countless skin whitening clinics that are abundant in the Philippines. On the other hand, celebrities who often portrayed the villains in movies or the comedic relief characters that people make fun of, tease, or berate were often dark-skinned. They were also often regarded as ugly. I also often heard people, when asked if someone is good looking, respond with "aba, maputi yun!" (of course, he/she is light-skinned!).

I remember going to school in the Philippines and in all of our classes, except for "Sibika at Cultura" (Civics and Culture), we were required to speak English during class discussions, answer exam questions written in English in English, and read books that were written in English. Our teachers also used English for instruction. I remember being reprimanded by teachers for speaking the language that came naturally to me – Tagalog – instead of speaking the English language they were trying to train us with. Whenever I happened to watch the evening news and got a glimpse of our government officials speaking and conducting official business, I heard them speak English. Even government officials who obviously looked like they were struggling to find the right English words and pronounce them correctly were speaking in English. I remember hearing people remark that certain politicians were not smart enough to be leaders because they could not speak English. English seemed to be the language of the educated, of the higher class, of the cultured, of the successful. Tagalog or any other local language like Bisaya seemed to have been associated with being lower class, especially Bisaya or other non-Tagalog languages, which were usually associated with naiveté, lack of education, and lower socioeconomic class. Folks who speak such languages and could not speak Tagalog – let alone English – properly were often derogatorily labeled as "promdi" ("from the province).

These behaviors and attitudes became so normal and frequent to me that I never really gave them much thought. To me, that was just the way things are and how they are supposed to be. I thought being dark-skinned is not such a good thing, and that being light-skinned is better and more attractive. I thought anything made in the USA is better than anything made in the Philippines. I thought everything in the USA and about the USA was better than anything in the Philippines and about the Philippines. I thought being able to speak English well is a sign of intelligence and success. It seemed like the less Filipino you are, and the more American you are, the better of you will be.

When I moved to the United States when I was 14 years-old, I held these beliefs strongly. I was excited to leave the Philippines and see Disneyland, Universal Studios, and the Statue of Liberty, among others. It was a fulfillment of a dream. I tried to fit-in with my American-born cousins, tried to dress like them, speak accent-free English like them, and enjoy the same things as them. However, no matter how much I tried, many other Filipinos still had a long headstart than me in terms of being American. They have been here longer, some were even born here. So I still struggled with my accent, my Ps and my Fs, my "he" and "she." I still wore tight Levi's 501 button-up jeans that were cool in the Philippines at that time but was "so five years ago" in the USA. People made fun of me, teased me, called me a FOB (Fresh-off-the-Boat), laughed at my mistakes, the way I looked, and the way I acted. The message I received was that for me to be accepted, I needed to do a better job with being American and I needed to change a lot of things about myself; I needed to change my Filipino self.

Soon enough, after watching many *Save by the Bell* and *Boy Meets World* episodes, and after reading countless *Archie* comic books, I began to change the way I spoke, the way I dressed, and the way I acted. Also, I began to distance myself from other Filipinos, especially those who arrived to the United States after I did, for fear of being associated with them. Vicariously, I heard other people – including other Filipinos – make fun of their accents and how they are "so Filipino." Other Filipinos even made fun of their own parents' inability to speak English and pronounce English words properly, and how their parents' values were too Filipino and "old-fashioned." I was aware of what people said and felt about Filipino foods like dog and dinuguan (pork blood stew), both of which I happen to really like by the way. Hey, I just worked really hard to improve my English, change my mannerisms, and get rid of what these FOBs have (Filipino-ness), so why would I want to hang-out with them – the Filipino-ness might come back to me. I degraded them, avoided them like they had a disease or virus that I did not want to catch again. I heard people say "F#@!NG FILIPINOS, THEY COME HERE AND TAKE ALL THE JOBS!" I even got to the point where I denied I was Filipino. I did not want other people to see me as being part of a group that take jobs away! I felt uncomfortable around other Filipinos and did not want to be associated with them. I was not sure why, but I just felt like speaking Tagalog or other Filipino languages, or talking about Filipino-specific things, were inappropriate. When I saw them act like Filipinos I knew in the Philippines or tell jokes only Filipinos would understand, I felt very uncomfortable. My attitude was "Hey, we are in America so act like Americans." And in my mind at that time, Americans equaled White. Without me noticing at that time, all of my friends were White. My best friend in 8th grade, an awesome dude from a very Mormon family, was my constant companion. We spent almost every minute together, including the weekends during which I stayed over in his house. As I interacted and fell in love with this large, blonde, and blue-eyed family, I remember thinking to myself, "Why can't this be my family?" This continued on until my junior year in high school, when one day I saw these words written on my school locker: "SELL-OUT! COCONUT! YOU'RE FILIPINO, ACT LIKE IT!"

I was confused about my cultural and ethnic identity for a while. Questions about why people made fun of me and why I eventually made fun of other people were bugging me. Why do many Filipinos make fun of FOBs, and how did I end up discriminating against FOBs myself, turning from "victim" to perpetrator? Relatedly, why do some Filipinos become coconuts (brown on the outside, white on the inside)? Why did I feel ashamed of being Filipino? Why did I try to get rid of my Filipino accent? How come my American-born cousins never learned to speak Tagalog or Kapampangan, or other Filipino languages? Thinking of my cousins, why were they treated as being more special than me when they visited the Philippines as balikbayans? Why did it embarrass me that I held certain values and beliefs? Was it wrong to hold Filipino values and beliefs – or in the words of others – to be "old fashioned"? Why was I reluctant to admit that I enjoy eating dinuguan? Living in Alaska, I saw many of my Alaska Native friends living off the land by fishing, and I realized that I didn't know how to fish! So why did I not know how to fish, or no one told me that it was important to learn, especially given the fact that the country that I came from is surrounded by water? Why did I and many other Filipinos prefer anything that is "Made in the USA"? Why did I and many other Filipinos dream of coming to the United States or other Western countries? Why do many Filipinos desire to be lighter-skinned?

Psychology

Introductory Psychology taught by Dr. John Petraitis at the University of Alaska Anchorage was the course that began to provide explanations for some of the questions I had throughout high school. I learned plenty about why human beings think, feel, and do the things they do. However, I learned early on that many theories and research in psychology were conducted by, with, and for the dominant White population. Given the dominance of American and European psychology on Global Psychology, even the psychological discipline in other parts of the world are based on and are influenced by Western theories, concepts, and methods. There was definitely a large disparity between psychological research on non-White populations and the fact that the majority of people in the world are not White.

It was not until about the last 50 years that psychology as a field has paid increased attention to the role of culture on the psychological experiences of various ethnic and cultural groups that compose our highly diverse world. In the United States, psychological research focusing on the cultural characteristics of African Americans, Latinos/as, and Asian Americans, among others, have experienced remarkable growth (David, Okazaki, & Giroux, in press). Asian American psychology, for instance, has investigated acculturation, identity, multiraciality, spirituality, parenting, stereotypes, racism, mental health, coping, mental health help-seeking behaviors, and biculturalism, among many other important topics (Leong, Okazaki, & David, 2002). Indeed, psychology's understanding of the Asian American experience has definitely improved. However, many findings of such research cannot be appropriately generalized toward the Filipino and Filipino American population due to the different physical, cultural, historical, socioeconomic, and health characteristics of Filipinos and Filipino Americans.

There are a number of ways in which Filipino Americans differ from other Asian American ethnic groups: (1) the Philippines was colonized by Spain for approximately 350 years and, consequently, Filipino Americans are predominantly Catholic while other Asian American groups are not (Agbayani-Siewart & Revilla, 1995); (2) Filipinos were regarded as United States Nationals until 1938, the Philippines was a United States commonwealth until 1946, and United States Military Bases were maintained in the Philippines until 1992 (e.g., Agoncillo, 1974; Brands, 1992; Espiritu, 2003; Karnow, 1989); (3) Filipino Americans have generally lower socioeconomic status than other Asian Americans, and their levels of educational attainment yield the lowest socioeconomic returns with respect to jobs and salary levels among all racial/ethnic groups (Okamura & Agbayani, 1997; United States Bureau of the Census, 1993); (4) American-born Filipinos continue to be underrepresented in higher education and have lower educational achievements than their Philippine-born and other Asian American counterparts (Okamura & Agbayani, 1997); (5) Filipino American adolescents have one of the highest rates of suicide ideations and attempts in the country (President's advisory commission on Asian Americans and Pacific Islanders, 2001); and (6) Filipino Americans have depression rates that are significantly higher than the rates of the United States general population (David, 2008; Tompar-Tiu & Sustento-Seneriches, 1995). Furthermore, alarming statistics on other health issues such as rates of HIV/AIDS, unintended pregnancy, eating disorders, STDs, and drug use are also reported for Filipino American communities across the United States (as cited in Nadal, 2000 and Nadal, 2009). Indeed, with so many different characteristics and needs from other Asian ethnic groups, one cannot accurately understand and appreciate the Filipino American experience based on the experiences of other Asian Americans.

Among Filipinos in the Philippines, the legacies of Spanish and American colonialism continue to propagate the message that anything Filipino is inferior to anything American or Western (David & Nadal, under review). Indeed, the "beautiful" people are mostly light-skinned or someone who has European ancestry. Skin whitening products and clinics are abundant. English is the language used in schools, government, business, and science. Pretty much anything that is imported or "Made in the U.S.A." is automatically regarded as of better quality than anything made locally. Thus, the over 92 million Filipinos in the Philippines are barraged by Western and American cultural influences on a daily basis, messages that inferiorize the Filipino culture and ethnicity, and lead to many Filipinos wanting to become as Americanized or Westernized as possible. Therefore, it is not surprising that many Filipinos in the Philippines desire to immigrate to the United States to further their level of American-ness, and many of them do so. Today, the yearly immigration rate of Filipinos in to the United States is behind only to that of Mexicans and Chinese, which makes the majority (about 60%) of the large and growing population of Filipinos in America (3.4 million) immigrants from the Philippines (Hoeffel, Rastogi, Kim, & Shahid, 2012). To this end, it can be suggested that a large proportion of the alarming mental and behavioral health statistics presented above about Filipino Americans may have their roots in the highly Americanized or Westernized postcolonial Philippines. The historical and contemporary fusion of both Filipino and American culture in the Philippines that has been going on for over a century is the primary reason why I use the terms "Filipinos and Filipino Americans," or "Filipino -/ Americans" in this book. While I acknowledge that there are important differences between Filipinos in America and Filipinos in the Philippines, the undeniable fact that Filipinos in the Philippines are also influenced by American culture on a daily basis, the fact that many Filipinos in America today are immigrants from the Philippines (and many of them still refer to themselves as Filipinos and not Filipino Americans), and the fact that many Filipinos in America regularly visit the Philippines or at least regularly stay connected with family and friends in the Philippines are the reasons why I believe the contents of this book are equally relevant to Filipinos and Filipino Americans.

However, despite their unique characteristics, their long and significant history with the United States, the contemporary influences of American culture on modern day Philippines, the large annual influx of Filipinos into the United States, the alarming health statistics reported for this group, and their rapidly increasing numbers (2nd largest Asian subgroup in the United States; Hoeffel, Rastogi, Kim, & Shahid, 2012), it is surprising that psychological research focused on understanding the Filipino and Filipino American psychological experiences is relatively sparse. Indeed, a search in PsycINFO (by October 23, 2012) – the largest database of psychology-related studies – using the five largest Asian American ethnic groups as keywords returned 1054 published works for "Chinese American," 358 for "Asian Indians," 786 for "Japanese American," 622 for "Korean American," and only 202 for "Filipino American." Even a much smaller Asian ethnic group than Filipinos – "Vietnamese American" – produced virtually the same number of published works (190). Thus, it is not surprising that Filipinos and Filipino Americans are often regarded as the "forgotten Asian Americans" (Cordova, 1983) by society or the "invisible minorities" (Cimmarusti, 1996) by the psychological community.

So, returning to the questions I had about Filipino inferiorizing attitudes, thoughts, and behaviors, I initially did not find much in psychology that provided me with direct and satisfying answers. Given the lack of psychological research on Filipinos, it was very easy for me to arrive at the conclusion that it was just normal for Filipinos to have such odd thoughts, feelings, and behaviors; that perhaps there was something inherent about Filipinos. Maybe Filipinos were just born that way; they were born to believe that light skin is better; that American or Western things and culture were better; that the English language was better and is the language of the successful and educated; that discriminating against other Filipinos who were too Filipino is just part of life. However, one major area in psychology that provided me with hope for a different set of answers was Learning and Cognition. In essence, learning and cognition theories suggest that human behaviors, thoughts, and beliefs about the world are learned and are the results of our experiences. Thus, I began to think about the possibility that Filipinos as individuals may have had various experiences throughout their lives that influence them to hold such attitudes and feelings that lead to certain behaviors. Given how widespread these inferiorizing attitudes, feelings, and behaviors are among Filipinos, I began to entertain the possibility that Filipinos as a group may have had past experiences that led them to believe that anything Western is better than anything Filipino. This is when I began looking at the historical and contemporary experiences of Filipinos and Filipino Americans with a more critical eye, and my conclusion is that the Filipino inferiorizing attitudes, thoughts, and behaviors many Filipinos and Filipino Americans display today are not in-born characteristics – they were learned and someone or something had to be the teacher. And because it is something that is learned, it is possible to unlearn it. Put another way – if we can learn to hate ourselves, we can also learn to love ourselves.

Brown Skin, White Minds: Filipino /- American Postcolonial Psychology

It was disheartening for me as I was growing up and was experiencing both the Filipino and the American educational curricula, to see that the experiences of Filipinos were often ignored, forgotten, or if it was discussed, it was presented in an incomplete manner. Even when I was attending school in the Philippines, American occupation in the late 1800s was portrayed as a much-needed, positive, liberating, and enlightening experience. This dissatisfaction of mine regarding how little and distorted Filipino historical and contemporary experiences are explored and portrayed continues to this day. There are plenty of discussions of Western colonialism on other cultural groups and its consequences. For instance, Harold Napoleon's (1996) *Yuuyaraq: The Way of the Human Being* is an excellent and passion-filled exploration of the effects of colonialism and oppression among Alaska Native Peoples. My experiences growing up in Alaska surrounded by Alaska Native family and friends, and my continuous exposure to Alaska Native Peoples to this day primarily through my Koyukon Athabascan wife and her network of family and friends (as well as through our *Filibascan* children), have given me the opportunities and desire to attend and participate in numerous events, gatherings, and community programs that directly tackle the negative cultural, mental, and behavioral health consequences of colonialism among Alaska's First Peoples. Similarly, the colonial and postcolonial experiences of Native Americans or American Indians and their psychological consequences are also relatively well-documented and widely discussed, with Eduardo and Bonnie Duran's seminal book *Native American Postcolonial Psychology* (1995) being a prime example. Reading Duran and Duran's work was actually an enlightening experience for me, and their book served as a major inspiration for this book. I am sure Duran and Duran's work has inspired change and guided awakening among many Native Americans or American Indians who were searching for answers.

There is also an abundance of literature documenting and exploring the historical and contemporary experiences of oppression experienced by Africans and African Americans, and even more products inspiring change and empowerment in these communities. I am sure many Africans' and African Americans' lives were influenced and enhanced by such works. Even the United States' presence in other Asian countries such as Vietnam and Korea and the consequences of America's involvement in such wars are also often remembered and given their due acknowledgement. However, Filipinos' experiences of colonialism under Western nations, including the United States, are largely unknown to many. The fact that the United States were also involved in a war against the Philippines, during which thousands of Filipinos and Americans suffered death, is never remembered. The fact that there was a strong United States military presence in the Philippines until very recently is often unexplored, if not unknown, by many. Filipinos' and Filipino Americans' experiences of oppression with and in the United States, both historically and contemporarily, are often disregarded as

XXIII

Filipinos and Filipino Americans are inaccurately thought of as a *voluntary immigrant* group and a *model minority.* To this end, I hope to add the Filipino experience and example when we think about the consequences of historical and contemporary oppression. It is hoped that this book may serve as a tool for remembering the past and as a tool for awakening to address the present.

There are other recent works that attempt to address the lack of attention on the oppressed history and present of Filipinos and Filipino Americans, as well as to serve as tools to empower the community such as Yen Le Espiritu's (2003) *Homebound: Filipino American Lives Across Cultures, Communities, and Countries,* Maria P. P. Root's (1997a) *Filipino Americans: Transformation and Identity,* and Leny Strobel's (2001) *Coming Full Circle: The Process of Decolonization Among Post-1965 Filipino Americans.* These works analyzed in detail the inferiorization of Filipinos under Spanish and American rule. Although these works were not intended for the psychological field and the discussed contents were not connected to psychological constructs, theories, research findings, and applications, such published materials are definitely inspiring and enlightening for many Filipinos and Filipino Americans, myself included. A more recent publication, Kevin Nadal's (2009; 2011) *Filipino American Psychology: A Handbook of Theory, Research, and Clinical Practice* was a timely and seminal contribution to the field of ethnic minority psychology, connecting the complex array of Filipino American experiences to various psychological constructs such as cultural values, ethnic and racial identity, gender and sexual orientation, multiraciality and multiethnicity, acculturation and enculturation, and mental health. It is clear from Kevin Nadal's discussion of all of these psychological constructs that it is impossible to understand them without acknowledging the effects of colonialism and contemporary oppression. I hope to further extend what these inspirational scholars have started, and provide a more detailed and comprehensive discussion of how colonialism and oppression has significantly impacted various aspects of Filipino and Filipino American psychology.

In general, this book proposes that psychological research concerning the consequences of colonization among Filipinos and Filipino Americans are necessary, and we need to take into account colonialism and its impacts when thinking about the psychology of Filipinos in order to accurately understand and appreciate the psychological experiences of these individuals. More specifically, this book attempts to put forward a vital psychological construct among Filipinos and Filipino Americans, one that many scholars (e.g., Root, 1997a; Strobel, 1997; 2001; Tompar-Tiu & Sustento-Seneriches, 1995) have argued to be a psychological consequence of their colonized histories: Colonial Mentality. Although colonial mentality has been discussed quite extensively in other scholarly disciplines, the field of psychology has devoted very little attention to it. This is especially surprising given that the field of psychology is supposed to have people's *mentalities* as one of its major areas of interest. Thus, in addition to this book being written in a way that is understandable to anyone who may be interested in the psychological consequences of oppression and colonialism, it is also presented in a way that is palatable to psychological researchers and service providers as I attempt to connect colonial mentality with commonly-known psychological theories and concepts. This book attempts to blur the boundaries between cultural studies, ethnic studies, history, postcolonial studies, sociology, and psychology, with the intention of increasing the integration of larger historical and contemporary sociocultural factors in the psychological study of cultural and ethnic minorities. With such a presentation, this book may serve as a re-introduction of colonial mentality to the field of psychology, with the hope that it will spark the scientific exploration and therapeutic incorporation of this construct when working with Filipinos and Filipino Americans. I also hope that this book will shed some light on some questions many Filipinos and Filipino Americans may be asking about themselves.

This book is divided into three parts. Part I involves a discussion of the Tao who inhabited the islands we now know as the Philippines and of Filipinos' experiences under Spain and the United States. I am not a historian, so these historical discussions only include pieces of history that are relevant to contextualizing and understanding colonial mentality. The bulk of the book is in Part II, which begins with an explanation of colonial mentality as a psychological construct. Then, it is followed with an elaboration of how colonial mentality may influence and contribute to various aspects of modern Filipino and Filipino American psychology, including the loss of the indigenous Filipino core value of Kapwa, and many others that are alarming concerns in the community. The book concludes with Part III, where I make some suggestions as to how we can move forward and address the effects of colonialism in an adaptable manner, both in the individual and community contexts. Also in Part III, I discuss how the field of psychology in the Philippines and the rest of the non-Western world were colonized, and it was not until around the 1960s when the decolonization of psychology in the Philippines began and gave birth to Sikolohiyang Pilipino (Indigenous Filipino Psychology), which now serves as a model for decolonizing the field of psychology all over the world.

The book ends with five commentaries from other scholars and community leaders from various disciplines and social groups. Their perspectives, influenced by both their professional training and personal experiences, provide some insight into how this book's approach to analyzing the phenomenon of colonial mentality or internalized oppression may go beyond the discipline of psychology and the walls that typically surround the academic community. Given the multidisciplinary contents of this book, I hope students, teachers, researchers, service providers, and professionals from various disciplines such as psychology, psychiatry, mental health, social work, education, ethnic studies, postcolonial studies, and counseling, among many others, will find it useful. I also hope that the contents of this book may shed some light on questions Filipinos and non-Filipinos may have in their own efforts to understand themselves and the people they love.

In conclusion, I would like to acknowledge that the contents of this book may be difficult for some to accept. The possibility or fact that the reader or someone close to the reader may have colonial mentality is difficult to accept. The possibility or fact that many in the Filipino community may have colonial mentality is difficult to accept. However, I hope that by sharing my own personal stories about colonial mentality, and by providing empirical evidence that many in the Filipino community do experience colonial mentality, that at least some individual and community awareness, if not acceptance, is sparked by the book. Being aware that a concern exists is the first step to facilitating both individual and community change, and change is what I hope to come as a result of this book. The change I want to see happen is not a complete rejection of anything American or Western. I believe it will not be practical nor adaptive for Filipinos and other colonized peoples to make such a change. In fact, it is ethnocentrism that got us into this mess to begin with. In our highly globalized and diverse world, I believe it is necessary for us to understand that there are both good and bad things about our heritage culture and those cultures that may be having an influence on us. We need to integrate them. Besides, for many of us (especially Filipino Americans and those who are of mixed race), the new or other culture (most times, it is the Western or American culture) is an important part of our identity, an essential part of who we are. Thus, the change I want to see is not the kind where we love only our heritage culture – we cannot be ethnocentric or in the case of Filipinos, *Filcentric*. This is because we will still be hating or ignoring the other important part or parts of our selves. Instead, what I want to see happen is for us to be Bicultural (or perhaps multicultural) – love both cultures, appreciate both cultures, value both cultures, respect both cultures, know both cultures, be competent in both cultures…EQUALLY.

Maraming maraming salamat po and I hope you enjoy the book!

E.J.R. David

ᜐᜒᜎᜒᜏᜈᜒᜎᜈ ᜇᜁᜉ

*Parts of the Preface were previously published in David (2010a), which is a chapter in Nadal, K. L. (2010). *Filipino American Psychology: A Collection of Personal Narratives*. Bloomington, IN: AuthorHouse.

ACKNOWLEDGEMENTS

First and foremost, I would like to especially thank my mother, Leonora Manarang Ramos David – otherwise known to many as Ning-Ning (shine), for taking care of me, guiding me, and supporting me my entire life. Maraming salamat sa mga payo mo sa akin at sa iyong pagtitiyaga sa lahat ng mga kamaliang nagawa ko. Ikaw ang nagsabi sa akin na "edukasyon lamang ang maipapamana ko sa iyo." Sana ay nagampanan ko ng mabuti ang aking tungkulin bilang iyong anak. Mahal na mahal kita. Your ning-ning has definitely brought light to my life, Nanay.

Special acknowledgement goes to: my brother Bonz, my sister Ate Ellen, and my nieces Jass and Alex for always backing me up; my wife, Margaret Olin Hoffman David, for loving me, encouraging me, and at the same time keeping me grounded - negadesta; my Filibascan children – Malakas David, Kalayaan David, and Kaluguran David – for enriching my life in ways that I never could have imagined; my father, Leonardo (Ronnie) Mercado David for loving me in his own unique way; Jayson Vinas, Donovan Danner, Pumiaq Nageak, Dominic Barrera, Justin Espinas (Rest in Peace homie), Jesse Vinas, and Jarrod Vinas for being my brothers and for showing me different perspectives; Auntie Dolores Vinas and Uncle Jesse Vinas for giving me a home when I was homeless, and for giving me a family when I had none – I am not sure I will be where I am right now if it were not for your help; the Vinas, Ebue, Concepcion, Rochon, Danner, Morse, Olin, Hoffman, Shaw, David, Clemente, Pangilinan, Ocampo, Dimson, De Leon, and Abad families for being my family; Dr. Sumie Okazaki for her mentorship, support, and for writing the foreword; Drs. Anne Saw, Matthew R.

Lee, Noriel Lim, Brenda Hernandez, and Jennifer Manongdo for their friendships and peer mentorships; Dr. Kevin Nadal for being a brother, a role model, and for writing the afterword; Dr. Alvin Alvarez for his encouragement and support; the Alaskero Partnership Organizers – Christine Marasigan, Mariecris Gatlabayan, Dr. Gabriel Garcia, and Dr. Joy Mapaye for their support. Special thanks also go to Leny Strobel, Martin Manalansan, Nilda Rimonte, James LaBelle, and Andrew Paves for being role models, leaders, and for writing commentaries to this version of the book; Jacob Ira Azurin Vijandre for helping me learn and write the baybayin scripts in the book; and to George F. Johnson and Information Age Publishing, for seeing the value in my work and for allowing this book to break boundaries.

I also would like to thank: Choi Ortiz, Eddieboy Montero, Ferdinand Litang, Pocholo Niebres, Boy Bernal, Jaan Infante, Lloyd Salimbao, Cynel Cruz, Wranny Verame, Justin Crisostomo, and the rest of the Busko Boys for always being there for me, with me, and behind me; Elsie (Che-Che) Janes and Caryn Baksis (Ostermann) for being my sisters; Drs. John Petraitis and Claudia Lampman for getting me started in the field of psychology; the amazing and awesome Anissa Hauser for her patience, support, and guidance in my day-to-day work; the Departments of Psychology at the University of Alaska Anchorage, the University of Illinois at Urbana-Champaign, and the University of Alaska Fairbanks for nurturing me; the Nageak, Harcharek, Fuller, Baksis, and Prociw families for seeing something valuable in me when it seemed like no one else did; Barrow High School Whalers and the entire community of Barrow, Alaska for giving this lost boy a chance and some direction – you will always have a special place in my heart - Quyanakpak; the Philippine Student Association at the University of Illinois at Urbana-Champaign for welcoming me; the Asian American Psychological Association, the American Psychological Association Minority Fellowship Program, and the American Psychological Association's Division 45 (Society for the Psychological Study of Ethnic Minority Issues) for being my professional community; my undergraduate and graduate students, especially the Culture, Race, Ethnicity, and Minority Status (CREaMS) research group for their help; and Sam Aquino, Rachel Castillo, Phyllis Ferrera, Keisha Guangko, Mark McArthur, Cheryl Santiago, Allison Saulog, Laura Simone, Christine Gonzalez, Mike Maravilla, Alberto Villamiel, and to thousands of other Filipinos and Filipino Americans for letting me into their lives and sharing their experiences with me.

Mabuhay kayong lahat at maraming salamat!

E.J.R. David

PART I:

IN THE BEGINNING

The first part of the book provides a broad description of the history of Filipinos – beginning with an account of indigenous Filipino culture, followed by a discussion of Filipinos' experiences of colonization under Spain and the United States, and ending with a presentation of their more contemporary experiences of oppression both in the Philippines and in the United States. The presented histories in Part I of this book are only those parts of history that are deemed necessary to understand the concept of colonial mentality or internalized oppression. A more in-depth and comprehensive discussion of such histories are provided elsewhere. For instance, noted Filipino historian Renato Constantino's (1975) critical discussion of Filipinos' pre-colonial and colonial histories is excellent and eye-opening. Also, Yen Le Espiritu's (2003) and Ignacio, de la Cruz, Emmanuel, and Toribio's (2004) books are brilliant analyses of Filipinos' experiences under the United States. Lastly, Rimonte's (1997) paper is an awe-inspiring discussion of Filipinos' lives under Spanish rule.

My brief overview of the lives and cultures of the indigenous peoples of the Philippines in this section of the book is limited in the sense that I am not discussing the complexities and key differences between the very diverse groups of indigenous peoples that lived on the islands prior to Western colonialism. Instead, for brevity (and perhaps as a political and psychological tool that highlights the similarities and, thus, may contribute to unified efforts toward a common goal), I will be discussing the indigenous peoples as a collective group, using the Tagalog term "Tao" to collectively refer to all of the indigenous peoples of the islands. My treatment of indigenous "Tao" life and culture, although admittedly limited and simplified, is deemed enough to emphasize the point that highly complex, developed, intelligent, and diverse indigenous cultural groups were thriving in the island archipelago long before the first Westerner ever got there. This is important knowledge to better understand what and how much was lost due to Western colonialism, and thus, important knowledge to understand (as discussed in Part II) and address (as discussed in Part III) colonial mentality or internalized oppression. Similarly, although my discussions of Filipino colonial and postcolonial (and neocolonial) experiences in this section of the book are also limited, they are deemed enough to emphasize the point that there are negative aspects of such experiences (i.e., oppression) and that such experiences have contributed to the development of colonial mentality or internalized oppression among many Filipinos and Filipino Americans.

However, although my presentation, coverage, and discussion of Filipino history is limited to only the parts that are necessary to contextualize and understand colonial mentality or internalized oppression, Filipino indigenous and colonial history is nevertheless rarely presented in the manner in which I present them here. Unlike common treatments and discussions of Filipino indigenous and colonial history that are Western-centric, perhaps my presentation and discussion of Filipino history in Part I can be considered to be Filipino-centric – at least for now, because I deem it necessary to present history in a way that may be empowering to Filipinos and Filipino Americans. I begin with the Filipinos' – or the Tao's – cultures and ways of life before Spanish contact.

*   *   *

CHAPTER 1

THE TAO: PRE-COLONIAL HISTORY

ᜉ᜔3l ᜴ᜀᜀᜀᜃ ᜃᜐ

This chapter provides an overview of various aspects of indigenous Filipino life, ranging from the tools and ways of everyday living, art, literature, and education to concepts and systems of spirituality and government. This history and indigenous culture has to be told, as it is essential for everyone, those with Filipino heritage and those without, to know that the *Tao* (The People; pronounced as "Ta-o") who inhabited the islands we now know as the Philippines had practiced and established impressive systems of living and beliefs even before Europeans arrived on the islands. This is important knowledge so that Filipinos and Filipino Americans today can have something they can be proud of that is truly and authentically theirs; for them to know that their ancestors and therefore them as modern Tao were and are capable of surviving without European or outsider help; for them to know that they do not have to be dependent on foreigners; for them to not feel like they owe everything to European colonizers; and for them to appreciate what was taken from them, what they have lost, what they might be missing, and thus, what they might be searching for and what they might want to have again.

Clothing, Ornaments, and Accessories

The culturally diverse groups of indigenous Tao who inhabited the islands we now know as the Philippines had a very vibrant culture and lived in complex societies. Their clothing was often symbolic of their rank in society and of what their capabilities are. For instance, among several indigenous tribes, red clothing is reserved only for chiefs and a red headgear (putong) expresses that the wearer had killed a man in battle. Added embroidery and design on a red putong represents that the wearer had killed several men during war (Agoncillo, 1974). Their tops were often sleeveless or short-sleeved vests, and their bottoms were usually bahags for men and tapis for women (bahags and tapis are cloth wrapped around the waist). Such clothing kept them cool in such a hot and humid environment, and I doubt such clothing was designed to keep their skins from getting too dark. Similarly, the ornaments and other bodily accessories they wore were symbolic of their social status and were made of materials found in their lands. There was an abundance of gold at that time (Halili, 2004), and due to this gift from the land, many wore gold bracelets, armbands, rings, earrings, and pendants. Many also used gold teeth fillings for aesthetic reasons.

Also for symbolic and aesthetic reasons, both men and women of various tribes carried tattoos on their bodies. Among women, having facial and arm tattoos meant you were more beautiful. Among men, tattoos represented their accomplishments in war, with more tattoos meaning more war experiences and more warriors killed. It is likely that these highly tattooed men were who early Spanish explorers and missionaries were referring to when they described seeing *pintados* (painted people) upon their arrival on the islands (Agoncillo, 1974).

The clothing, ornaments, and accessories that the indigenous Tao wore were inspired by their experiences and important events in their daily lives. Such clothing, ornaments, and accessories were made of materials obtained from the land they were living in; materials that naturally developed from their environment. More importantly, they were made by the indigenous Tao – locally.

Homes and Daily Living

The indigenous Tao lived in houses also inspired by, and made of materials from, their land and daily living. For many who lived in the flatter lands, their houses were built of bamboo, wood, and nipa palm leaves, which were perfect materials for living in a tropical island environment. This is what many individuals today might call the bahay kubo. For others who lived in mountainous areas such as the northern islands, their houses were built on top of trees. For others who made their living closer to the ocean or rivers, their houses were made on their boats or by the shore (Halili, 2004; Legarda, 2001). Depending on where they lived, the indigenous Tao practiced various forms of subsistence activities. Agriculture is common, and their knowledge and expertise in growing crops is evidenced by the highly advanced irrigation systems they developed, including the world famous rice terraces that, if placed end to end, would stretch halfway around the world (about 12,000 miles) (Agoncillo, 1974).

Due to their proximity to the ocean and countless rivers, fishing was also a common form of subsistence, and various methods were used such as nets, bow and arrow, spears, wicker baskets, and hooks. Other Tao were involved in poultry, raising animals, lumbering, weaving, and shipbuilding (Halili, 2004). In fact, early Spanish explorers complimented the indigenous Tao for their expertise in building highly efficient and effective ocean vessels for various purposes such as travel, fishing, war, or trading (Agoncillo, 1974). Indeed, the indigenous Tao were also involved in trading, both with nearby tribes (domestic trading) and those coming from what we now consider to be other countries outside the Philippines (international trading) (Halili, 2004; Legarda, 2001). It is evident that there were plenty of thinking, planning, and adaptation that went on during early times that shaped the culture, living preferences, and conditions of the indigenous Tao. Such an ability to survive and live adaptively and efficiently according to their environment is evidence that they were highly intelligent and resilient peoples.

Art, Literature, Music, and Dances

To celebrate, document, depict, and display their culture and daily lives, the indigenous Tao had various forms of art, literature, music, and dances. In addition to the ornaments, accessories, and tattoos that they wore on their bodies that evidence their artistic abilities, their tools, weapons, and potteries were also adorned with artistic designs. Much of the designs depict plants, animals, and humans, suggesting that their artistic inspiration came from their natural and indigenous environment. There were also various forms or written and oral literature that depicted and celebrated important events and activities such as boating (talindaw), wedding (ihiman), love (kumintang or kundiman), war (kumintang), victory (tagumpay), cradling an infant (hele), fun riddles (bugtong), history (Ifugao Hudhod), and battles of heroic individuals (Indarapatra at Sulayman) (Agoncillo, 1974; Halili, 2004).

Many of these literatures were presented with music, and the wind and stringed musical instruments they used were made of wood or bamboo such as the gangsa, kudyapi, and bansic. Relatedly, dance often accompanied the music and the lyrics, and the dances were again often inspired by natural and daily-occurring events and activities by both humans and animals. For instance, the popular Filipino traditional dance of Tinikling was inspired by a tikling bird tiptoeing over traps set-up by rice farmers. Furthermore, another popular Filipino dance, the Singkil, depicted how a young warrior defended and rescued a beautiful princess from harm (fairy- or nymph-caused earthquake). There were other forms of art, such as a well-developed system of indigenous Tao mythology (diwata, anito, tala, dwende, enkanatada, enkanto, etc.) and accompanying stories (Makiling, Sinukuan), as well as martial arts (eskrima, kali, or arnis) (Agoncillo, 1974). All of these were inspired by their natural environments, with mythical creatures being the guardians of mountains, trees, the skies, and oceans who need respect and occasional offerings, and the weapons for self-defense usually being composed of sticks and other easily accessible materials. However, many of them are rarely practiced or told today, if even known and remembered, due to colonialism and its effects.

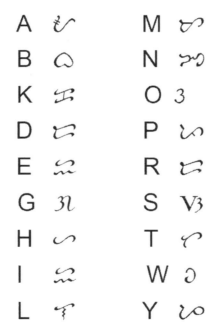

Figure 1. Baybayin

Language and Education

In order to be able to develop so much literature and art, the indigenous Tao must have had a system of writing. This writing system or alphabet is referred to as *baybayin* (Figure 1) (Agoncillo, 1974; Halili, 2004). Although there are variations among the very diverse groups of indigenous peoples in terms of language, many of the indigenous Tao languages did not include the "F" sound (as can be seen in Figure 1). Thus, it is understandable why even many modern day Filipinos and Filipino Americans may confuse their "Ps" and "Fs" when they speak – the "F" sound is simply not indigenous, perhaps even unnatural, to them. In utilizing their indigenous languages and writings, the Tao used tree sap as ink and pointed sticks as writing utensils to write on leaves, trees, bamboo tubes, and tree barks – again, using what was naturally available to them and living off of the land. Along with spiritual beliefs related to the mythology system, music, stories, and daily living skills, reading and writing in baybayin were taught to children by their parents. This was their educational system and ways of passing along the culture to the next generations. In fact, early Spanish explorers and missionaries were amazed when they found out that the majority of the indigenous Tao were literate and proficient in their native alphabet (Agoncillo, 1974). This is evidence that a complex, well-developed, well-functioning, and well-cultured (and arguably well-educated) society was in existence for many generations in the islands prior to European arrival.

Religion and Spiritual Beliefs

What is probably the most influential and longest lasting effect of Spanish colonialism among the indigenous Tao is the Catholic Religion (discussed in more detail in Chapter 2). Indeed, it was the Spanish explorers and missionaries who taught the indigenous Tao the beliefs and practices of the Catholic Church, which has led to the fact that the majority of modern day Filipinos and Filipino

Americans are Catholic. However, this does not mean that the Tao were godless and had no system of spirituality, or that they did not have and practice what people today may consider an organized religion. This indigenous system of spiritual beliefs was also inspired by their daily living and their natural environment, as they worshipped a god of animal raising and agriculture (Idiyanale), god of rainbow (Balangaw), goddess of harvest (Lalahon or Lakampati), god of crops and animals (Lakapati), god of the sea (Maguayen), goddess of the moon and of women (Mayari), god of fire (Agni), god of wind and rain (Anitun Tabu), god of sun and war (Apolake), and god of love, pregnancy, and childbirth (Dian Masalanta). All of these Gods were governed by a supreme god who the Indigenous Tao believed created the universe and humanity – Bathala (or Bathalang Maykapal). There is even indication that they had concepts of evil or wrongdoing, as well as a concept of an undesirable afterlife for those who lived a life of sin, with a belief in a god of death (Sidapa) and a god of hell (Siginarugan) (Agoncillo, 1974).

The indigenous Tao also regularly offered the gods and these natural entities gifts and had ceremonies to honor, thank, or appease them (Halili, 2004) – suggesting that their beliefs are organized and complex enough to have hierarchies among the gods, to have traditions and rituals, to have concepts of good and evil, and have ideas about heaven and hell. Indeed, such a well-developed spiritual belief system suggests that the indigenous Tao had a deep understanding of and connection with nature. They worshipped and respected the natural entities in their environment such as the rivers and the seas, the land and the skies, and the animals and the plants. The indigenous Tao strived to live harmoniously with their natural environment for their survival is dependent on these natural entities and the gifts they provide. For instance, it was forbidden to cut down old trees because they were considered as sacred and divine (Agoncillo, 1974). Such a highly organized, complex, and respectful system of spirituality is evidence that the indigenous Tao had established an adaptive and extremely perceptive society.

Government and the Law

The indigenous Tao also had a well-established system of government prior to Spanish arrival on the islands. The basic unit of government was called *balangay* or *baranggay* (tribe or village), which is composed of approximately 60 families. Each balangay is headed by a *Datu* or *Rajah* (Chief) (Agoncillo, 1974; Constantino, 1975; Halili, 2004), who led in consultation with a council of balangay elders – suggesting that the indigenous Tao highly regarded and valued the wisdom of their elders, and suggesting that the Tao did not simply place all the governing power in the hands of their Datu (Constantino, 1975). The chief held the responsibility of governing the people and ensuring their welfare and survival. The chief, along with the council of elders, developed laws and settled disputes among the balangay people. In addition to regular contact between balangays through trade, chiefs from multiple balangays often came together to combine the resources of their groups in order to achieve a common cause, such as win a war against other indigenous tribes or survive tough times. When this happened, the chiefs each dropped their blood in a cup and they all took a drink from it, making the chiefs and their balangays blood brothers or sisters (a blood compact or *sanduguan*) and creating a deep connection between them (Agoncillo, 1974).

In the indigenous Tao's form of government, women may also become chiefs in the absence of a male heir. In general, women were treated as equal to men (Halili, 2004), with women being allowed to own property, engage in trade and industry, and often holding high positions in society such as a *babaylan*, who were regarded as the healers, shamans, wisdom-keepers, philosophers, and spiritual leaders of a balangay. Women were deeply respected and valued by the indigenous Tao, and it is even customary for men to walk behind women in order to show this respect (Agoncillo, 1974). These examples suggest that the indigenous Tao were advanced enough to create a well-functioning system of government to efficiently run their society and preserve their culture and ways of life. Furthermore, they even practiced the concept of gender equality long before the women's rights movement in the United States during the 1960s. In fact, the indigenous Tao regarded men and women so equally that they did not even have words such as "he," "she," "him, "her", "his," or "her" to differentiate between men and women. This is probably why many Filipinos and Filipino Americans today still confuse such terms when they speak English. Also, traces of such an equal regard for gender can be seen in the fact that modern Filipino culture continue to hold women in high regard, often expecting the women in the family to pursue higher education and become leaders in education, industry, and even the government, as exemplified by the fact that the Philippines have already elected two women as president in its relatively (as compared to its former colonial rulers Spain and the United States, for instance) brief history of being a democratic country.

Chapter Summary

Similar to how Christopher Columbus did not "discover" the Americas, famed explorer Ferdinand Magellan also did not discover the islands we now know as the Philippines (discussed in more detail in Chapter 2). Contrary to this Western-centric presentation of Philippine history, the indigenous Tao have been living in the islands for many generations before the first Europeans even set foot on the islands. Indeed, there is plenty of evidence to suggest that the indigenous Tao lived in a well-developed, highly complex, and culture-rich (also very diverse and multicultural) society prior to Spanish occupation. They had their own form of music, art, literature, written and spoken language, religion, and government. The indigenous Tao also had a variety of ways of surviving and thriving in their natural environment, making use of the natural resources that were abundant in the lands, the mountains, the rivers, and the oceans. Their economy was not based on or dependent upon foreign goods or resources. They took pride in what they created and the materials that were naturally available to them. They did not depend on foreigners to survive, nor did they regard anything "Made in the USA" or "imported" as being more valuable or better than what they created. The existence of such a society is evidence that the indigenous Tao were resilient, independent, proud, creative, resourceful, intelligent, and respectful peoples. These are characteristics that modern Filipinos and Filipino Americans should be proud of, and they need to have knowledge of such a history.

*   *   *

The discussed history and such a presentation of the Tao's indigenous culture and ways of life, however, are unknown to many modern day Filipinos and Filipino Americans because it is either erased by colonialism, distorted by dominant historical narratives, and, consequently, not readily or easily available for those who are searching for it. Such a lack of an accurate and positive knowledge of indigenous Filipino history and culture makes it difficult for one to be proud of their Filipino heritage. Such a lack of positive regard toward an important and highly salient piece of one's self can lead to many undesired outcomes such as identity confusion and even self-hate, which are highly distressing and may develop into serious psychological concerns. I will further discuss these psychological and mental health consequences in Part II, but for now, the rest of Part I will focus on how the majority of the rich and highly admirable culture of the indigenous Tao were demonized, distorted, inferiorized, and eventually erased and forgotten. I begin with the advent of Spanish colonialism.

Chapter 2

The Catholic Convent: Spanish Colonialism

ᜃᜂ ᜊᜇᜒᜌᜇᜒ 3ᜇ ᜆᜒ ᜐᜓᜎᜓᜎᜓ

Despite the rich and significant amount of cultural beliefs, attitudes, and behaviors, as well as the well-established and complex social systems and institutions that existed prior to European occupation, as discussed in the previous chapter, Filipino history is often summarized by many Filipinos and Filipino Americans in one phrase – "300 hundred years in the convent and 50 years in Hollywood." This is evidence suggesting that many individuals with Filipino heritage may not have a very good understanding of their historical and cultural roots; that they may lack a strong, authentic, and positive Filipino knowledge base that may contribute to developing pride toward their heritage. This limited and inaccurate representation of Filipino history sends the message that nothing existed prior to the arrival of Europeans; that Filipinos owe everything they know, and even their survival, to their European or Western colonizers. This popular summary of Filipino history also touches on the persistent legacies of both colonial periods on modern day Filipinos and Filipino Americans. It expresses the continued Catholic influence on most Filipinos and Filipino Americans, and suggests that Filipinos and Filipino Americans view American colonialism as a liberating, pleasurable, and enlightening experience. Certainly, this simplified but popular single sentence summation of Filipino history reveals that Filipino culture, and how culture influences Filipinos' and Filipino Americans' thoughts, behaviors, attitudes, and emotions, cannot be completely understood outside the context of Spanish and American colonialism. Furthermore, the simple fact that modern day Filipinos and Filipino Americans are mostly Christian (primarily Catholic), have high English proficiency, and are highly familiar with American culture instead of worshipping Bathala or being highly proficient in Baybayin tells us that something historically significant must have happened for the indigenous Tao to have changed so much. Such historically significant events and periods are the indigenous Tao's colonial experiences. Thus, I now provide a brief discussion of Filipinos' colonial experiences, beginning with Spanish colonization.

Tackling Some Historical Myths

In 1521, Portuguese explorer Ferdinand Magellan landed and claimed a large set of island archipelago in the Pacific Ocean for Spain (Agoncillo, 1974; Constantino, 1975; Halili, 2004). This signaled the beginning of the Spanish occupation of the Tao, exploitation of the Tao and their lands, and transformation of the Tao's indigenous culture and ways of life. Remembering the existence of the Tao and their highly developed culture and society is important to emphasize here, because it reifies the fact that Ferdinand Magellan did not "discover" the Philippines. After Ferdinand Magellan, other Spanish voyages followed the path he took to get to the island archipelago, and in 1542, Spanish explorer Ruy Lopez de Villalobos named the islands "Las Islas Filipinas" (The Philippine Islands) in honor of Spain's King Charles I's son

Filip, who would later become king of Spain himself (King Phillip II) (Agoncillo, 1974; Constantino, 1975; Halili, 2004). All early Spanish voyages to the Philippines were met by resistance from the indigenous Tao, and it was not until 1571 when a later Spanish exploration led by Miguel Lopez de Legazpi established the walled Spanish city of Manila (Intramuros) that Spain finally subdued the Tao's struggles and secured Spanish rule over the islands (Agoncillo, 1974).

It is crucial to point out that it took Spain approximately 50 years to quell the indigenous Tao's opposition to Spanish rule and cultural transformation. This particular point is important, because it shows that the indigenous Tao fought the occupiers, resisted the Spanish impositions, and tried to protect their ways of life and did not simply welcome the Spanish colonizers with open arms wanting to be "civilized." Such strong resistance by the indigenous Tao is evidence that they were proud of their culture and ways of life, and that they did not automatically regard the Western people, the Western belief system, and the Western culture as better than what they had. The *balangay* or *baranggay* warriors (Tribal warriors), who were led by their respective *Datus* or *Rajahs* (Kings or Chiefs), fought fiercely to protect the culture and ways of life that the Tao were so proud of (Constantino, 1975). In fact, the person who is considered to be the first to circumnavigate the world, Ferdinand Magellan, lost his life in the Philippines against the warriors of one of the greatest indigenous *Datus* in Filipino history – Lapu-Lapu (Agoncillo, 1974). Thus, Ferdinand Magellan was not able to return to Spain and did not circumnavigate the world. Some of his men (led by Juan Sebastian de Elcano) and one ship (Victoria) from his voyage did, but Ferdinand Magellan did not.

The Spanish colonizers also did not establish the capital city of Manila. Manila, or *Maynila* (or *Maynilad*) as the indigenous Tao called it, was a prosperous Muslim kingdom in the island of Luzon. Maynila was strategically located by the Pasig River and the bay opening up to the ocean (Manila Bay), allowing indigenous tribes such as the *Tagalog* (or *Taga-Ilog* which literally means "of the river") and the *Kapampangan* (which literally means "of the river bank") to trade with each other as well as with other neighboring Asian cultures such as the Chinese, Indians, and Indonesians (Halili, 2004; Legarda, 2001). This early form of commerce made Maynila and the indigenous tribes who inhabited the lands and waters around it very wealthy. Datus (or *Rajahs*) such as Sulayman, Lakandula, and Matanda were some of the leaders who governed the indigenous tribes around Maynila prior to and during Spanish occupation. The fact that multiple indigenous tribes were, for the most part, peacefully living with and mutually benefitting from each other in Maynila before Spanish occupation, is evidence that the indigenous Tao had developed an effective and mutually beneficial system of living and thriving. However, upon the discovery of the vast wealth in Maynila and the economic potential of its location, the Spanish explorers focused their attention on obtaining control over the area (Agoncillo, 1974). Again, the indigenous Tao fought and resisted Spanish occupation. Through the help of advanced weaponry and the strategy of dividing and conquering, however, the Spanish defeated the Tao and eventually took over Maynila.

Spanish Oppression of the Tao

All Spanish voyages to the archipelago that followed Ferdinand Magellan's initial exploration consistently reported to the Spanish king that vast amounts of spices, gold, and other valuable resources may be found in the islands, especially in Maynila. By 1574, The Philippines' namesake – King Philip II of Spain – designated Maynila as "*Insigne y Siempre Leal Ciudad de España*" (Distinguished and ever loyal city of Spain) and the capital of the new colony, where governmental policies for all of the islands would begin (Agoncillo, 1974). Increasing numbers of Spanish officials, missionaries, and soldiers from Spain and from Mexico (another Spanish colony at that time) were assigned to live in and govern the new colony (Agoncillo, 1974; Halili, 2004). Indeed, there were many similarities between the Philippine and Mexican colonies in terms of how they were governed by Spain. For instance, there was the union of church and state in such colonies, and not surprisingly, the strong push for the propagation of Catholicism among the indigenous peoples (Agoncillo, 1974). Indeed, as part of Spain's civilization efforts, the Tao's indigenous culture and spiritual beliefs were replaced by Spanish culture and the Catholic religion. As a matter of fact, the Catholic religion was the primary tool by which the Spanish colonizers were able to convince the indigenous Tao that the Spanish ways of life were superior to and more civilized than the Tao's indigenous ways and temper their resistance (Constantino, 1975; Rimonte, 1997). Another significant governmental similarity between the Philippine colony, the Mexican colony, and other Spanish colonies in South America during that time is that the governments in such colonies were highly centralized and the Governor-General (the Spanish King's appointed representative in the colony) had control over the armed forces, the executive branch, the judiciary branch, the local provincial officials, and even the church (Agoncillo, 1974).

Because of the immense power of the Governor-General, it was easy for corruption to arise. This corruption trickled down to the Governor-General's appointed judicial, executive, military, provincial, and church officials. These Spanish officials, who were called *Filipinos* along with other Spanish people living in the colony at the time, also abused their power to the detriment of the colony and the lives of the indigenous Tao (Constantino, 1975). During Spanish rule, the indigenous Tao experienced severe exploitation, abuse, rape, slavery, brutality, corruption, injustice, and tyranny as their "dignity and honor…were (continuously) taken for granted" by the Spanish (Agoncillo, 1974, p.124; Rimonte, 1997). The Filipino National Hero Jose Rizal, along with other indigenous Tao leaders, argued against the oppression of the Tao or the *Indios* – as the Spanish referred to the indigenous Tao – and attempted to work toward the equal treatment of all who lived in the colony – the

Filipinos and the Tao (or Indios). In fact, Jose Rizal promoted the idea that everyone in the colony, including the Tao or Indios, be called Filipinos to erase the division between the privileged and the oppressed and promote equality for all. Among his many writings that documented the oppressed lives of the Tao under Spanish rule are the popular and powerful novels *Noli Me Tangere* and *El Filibusterismo*. However, these peaceful attempts at reform were not welcomed by those in control and in 1896 Jose Rizal was executed by Spain in *Bagong Bayan* or *Bagumbayan* (or New City, now called Rizal Park) because of his criticisms of Spanish rule.

Figure 2. A Portrait of Filipino Hero Jose Rizal (public domain image)

The Golden Legend and Colonial Debt

One of Jose Rizal's many writings included the following passage:

> "…little by little they lost their old traditions, the mementos of their past; they gave up their writing, their songs, their poems, their laws in order to learn by rote other doctrines which they did not understand, another morality, another aesthetics different from those inspired by their climate and their manner of thinking…degrading themselves in their own eyes; they became ashamed of what was their own; they began to admire and praise whatever was foreign and incomprehensible; their spirit was dismayed and it surrendered to…this disgust of themselves" (as cited by Rimonte, 1997, p. 58).

Based on Jose Rizal's description of the indigenous Tao's living conditions under Spain and its resulting psychological effects, the centuries in which the Tao were under Spanish rule can be marked as the time when the Tao began to develop colonial mentality, a condition in which the oppressed perceives oneself as inferior to the oppressor, or as Jose Rizal described it, when the Tao began to degrade themselves, to be ashamed of their culture, and to be disgusted of their characteristics. Colonial mentality has immense implications in the thinking, behaviors, emotions, and attitudes of modern day Filipinos and Filipino Americans, and is a phenomenon that is explored in more detail later (beginning in Part II). In addition to and related with colonial mentality, the Tao also developed a sense of *colonial debt* – a condition that is characterized by a deferential attitude toward Spanish culture and Spanish people and the tendency to accept maltreatments by the Spanish rulers as the natural cost for progress or civilization (Rimonte, 1997). This feeling of indebtedness toward their Spanish colonizers that developed during Spanish rule may still be widely held among modern day Filipinos and Filipino Americans as maintained by the *Golden Legend*. The Golden Legend is a popular historical belief that pre-Hispanic Filipinos were uncivilized savages who were nobly civilized by Spain through the gifts of Spanish culture and Catholicism. During Spanish rule, Rimonte (1997) asserted that the Catholic Church and its friars were instrumental in endorsing the Golden Legend by promoting the idea that those who do not "Hispanicize" have "strayed from the prescribed Catholic path of righteousness" (p. 59). The Golden Legend has been maintained throughout the years in more contemporary presentations of Filipino history, as even noted Filipino historian Teodoro Agoncillo (1974) was known to praise the "beautiful Spanish language" (p. 85) and the Catholic religion, which he regarded as "the most poetic of all religions" (p. 89).

Chapter Summary

The Spanish occupation of the islands we now know as the Philippines was driven by the Spanish Kingdom's desire for more power and wealth, as well as to propagate the Catholic religion. Such motivations were typical among the Western nations such as Spain, Portugal, France, and others during that time. This typical set of motivators for expansion and colonization are usually referred to as the Three G's: God, Gold, and Glory. The now world-famous explorer Ferdinand Magellan led the first of many Spanish voyages motivated by the Three G's to land in the Philippines. Because we now know that many other peoples with diverse languages and cultural worldviews had been living, developing, and thriving in the Philippines long before Ferdinand Magellan got there (as discussed in Chapter 1), we now also know that the Western-centric myth that Ferdinand Magellan "discovered" the Philippines is not true. It is perhaps more accurate to say that Ferdinand Magellan and the resulting Spanish colonization significantly changed the lives of the indigenous Tao who lived in the islands now known as the Philippines.

Despite more advanced weaponry, it took the Spanish occupiers approximately half a century to defeat the indigenous Tao, evidencing the Tao's impressive combat skills and supporting the notion that the Tao fiercely fought for the protection of their culture and ways of life. Furthermore, although there were many similarities between the colonial experience of indigenous Tao and those of other Spanish colonies in Latin America (as mentioned above), one major difference is the continued survival of hundreds of indigenous Tao languages to this day despite centuries of Spanish colonialism and oppression, unlike many formerly Spanish colonies in Latin America that are now predominantly Spanish speaking. This is another evidence of the strong resistance among the indigenous Tao against Spain in order to keep their indigenous cultures and ways of life, and also speaking to the Tao's resilience as peoples. Despite the strong resistance from the indigenous Tao, however, Spain was eventually able to take control over the island archipelago including the major city of Maynila. Spain established a corrupt colony that oppressed the indigenous Tao, exploited the rich natural resources and the people, changed their indigenous ways of life, and propagated the Catholic religion. By this time, many of the indigenous ways of life, forms of government, spiritual beliefs, languages, arts, writing systems, and other aspects of indigenous culture (described in Chapter 1) were demonized as being those of the uncivilized and were replaced by the supposedly more civilized and better ways of the Spanish. Such an oppressive process is exactly what the influential postcolonial scholar Edward Said (1979) described in his seminal book *Orientalism*, where he presented the ways in which various European colonizers have portrayed peoples of the "Orient" as primitive, uncivilized, or inferior. The Spanish period in the lives of the Tao may be marked as the beginning of the development of colonial mentality, a condition explored later beginning in Chapter 5.

*   *   *

After being subjected to more than 300 years of ethnic and cultural subjugation, and partly sparked by the unjustified execution of Jose Rizal, a series of Filipino revolutions seriously disrupted Spain's control over the Philippines toward the end of the 19th century (Agoncillo, 1974; Constantino, 1975). Such revolutions were led by recognized Filipino heroes such as Andres Bonifacio, Emilio Aguinaldo, Marcelo H. Del Pilar, and Apolinario Mabini, among many others. Although such revolutions were encouraged by the United States (because the United States were involved in a war against Spain at that time), the Filipino revolution against Spain was already successful before American forces even landed in the Philippines. Indeed, the Filipino revolutionaries were already able to gain control of the entire island of Luzon, where Maynila is located, and declared their independence. They also established the first Asian government (the First Philippine Republic) based on a democratically developed constitution (the Malolos Constitution), and elected their first president in General Emilio Aguinaldo. However, the Filipinos' independence was short-lived as Spain sold the Philippines along with Puerto Rico, Cuba, and Guam to the United States for $20 million during the Treaty of Paris in 1898, which signaled the end of the Spanish-American War and setting the stage for the beginning of yet another long period of colonization for the Filipinos (Constantino, 1975; Ignacio, de la Cruz, Emmanuel, & Toribio, 2004). The next chapter will discuss the American occupation and colonization of the Philippines.

CHAPTER 3

HOLLYWOOD: UNITED STATES COLONIALISM

ᜬ᜴ ᜏᜃᜒᜎ ᜳᜓ ᜩ ᜢᜩᜒᜆᜒᜎ

Americans talk about and remember the Vietnam War. Americans also remember the Korean War. Americans honor the soldiers – American, Vietnamese, Korean – who fought in such wars. What is probably one of the most controversial topics when remembering such wars, at least for Americans, is the question of whether it was a good decision for the United States to have gotten involved in such wars. More recently, people talk about and remember the Gulf War. People also talk about and are still debating the Iraq-Afghanistan War that began in 2003. People honor the soldiers – American, Kuwaiti, Iraqi, and Afghan – who fought and are still fighting this war. What is definitely the most controversial issue about the war in the Gulf, Iraq, and Afghanistan is the question of whether it was a good decision for the United States to have gotten involved in such wars. Indeed, American efforts of occupation, colonialism, imperialism, or even just war involvements around the world has been historically met with anti-occupation, anti-colonialist, anti-imperialist, and anti-war sentiments, primarily due to the negative consequences (financial and life) of such involvements. Long before all of these wars, however, was the Philippine-American War that began in 1899, a result of the United States' first attempt at colonialism and empire-building outside the continental United States (Ignacio, de la Cruz, Emmanuel, & Toribio, 2004). Perhaps if we remember and understand the consequences of the Philippine-American War and the Pacification Campaign that followed, then maybe we would have learned from the mistakes of the past and not repeat them again. Perhaps we would have been able to avoid the loss, pain, and suffering that accompanies war. Perhaps Americans would have a deeper understanding, knowledge, and appreciation of Filipinos and Filipino Americans and their experiences. Perhaps more attention would be given to the issues facing Filipinos and Filipino Americans today. Perhaps Filipinos and Filipino Americans today would have a more accurate perception of America. Perhaps Filipinos and Filipino Americans today would have a more accurate and empowering view of themselves.

It is unfortunate, but the reality is that few remember the Philippine-American War. Furthermore, few remember America's involvement in, occupation of, and colonization of the Philippines. Even further, few remember the negative and painful experiences of Filipinos under American rule. Filipinos did not just "party in Hollywood," there were also many years of discrimination, oppression, suffering, and loss – physically, emotionally, psychologically, and culturally. Such losses, pain, and suffering are probably the reasons why the Philippine-American War has come to be known as the "Forgotten War," and why the period of American colonization of the Philippines has come to be often regarded as a fallen victim of "historical amnesia" (Ignacio, de la Cruz, Emmanuel, & Toribio, 2004). It is important for Filipinos and

Filipino Americans to have a more complete, accurate, and critical understanding of such a historical period, however, because it may assist in identifying the source of their colonial mentality (as discussed in Part II of the book) and facilitate their journeys of decolonization (as discussed in Part III of the book). To this end, this chapter will discuss America's occupation, colonization, and oppression of the Filipinos, setting the context with which to understand the concept of colonial mentality. A more detailed account of such a painful and forgotten part of Filipino and American history, including the political and economic factors that played a role in it, is presented in *The Forbidden Book: The Philippine-American War in Political Cartoons* (Ignacio, de la Cruz, Emmanuel, and Toribio, 2004). Let us begin with a brief summary of America's annexation of the Philippines and a discussion of how the United States inferiorized the Filipino ethnicity and culture.

Inferiorizing the Filipino Ethnicity and Culture

Before the Treaty of Paris in 1898 was formalized by American and Spanish peace commissioners, Filipino representatives in Paris attempted to argue that because Spain had already been ousted from the Philippines and because Filipinos already had an independent government before the treaty was signed, Spain had no right to transfer ownership of the archipelago to the United States (Agoncillo, 1974). Filipino representatives in the United States used the same argument before the treaty was approved and, thus, finalized, by the United States Senate. However, both efforts to keep Filipino sovereignty failed and the United States proceeded to take control of the islands. From 1899-1902, Filipinos desperately attempted to keep their independence from the United States in what is known as the Philippine-American War, a war that cost the United States $600 million and approximately 10,000 soldiers (Brillantes, 2008). Among Filipinos, about 16,000 soldiers and 200,000 civilians were killed in three years (Brillantes, 2008). Consequently, led by Mark Twain's Anti-Imperialist League, many Americans began questioning America's presence in the Philippines (Ignacio, de la Cruz, Emmanuel, & Toribio, 2004). As a response to such anti-Imperialist criticisms, President William McKinley used the idea of *Benevolent Assimilation* (Blount, 1913; Ignacio, de la Cruz, Emmanuel, & Toribio, 2004; Rusling, 1903) to defend his motivation and intentions for colonizing the Philippines. For example, in a speech delivered to a delegation of Methodist church leaders in 1903, McKinley explained:

> "I walked the floor of the White House night after night until midnight; and I am not ashamed to tell you, gentlemen, that I went down on my knees and prayed Almighty God for light and guidance more than one night. And one night late it came to me this way: (1) That we could not give them back to Spain – that would be cowardly and dishonorable; (2) that we could not turn them over to France and Germany – our commercial rivals in the Orient – that would be bad business and discreditable; (3) that we could not leave them to themselves – they were unfit for self-government – and they would soon have anarchy and misrule over there worse than Spain's was; and (4) that there was nothing left for us to do but to take them all, and to educate the Filipinos, and uplift and civilize and Christianize them, and by God's grace do the very best we could by them, as our fellow-men for whom Christ also died. And then I went to bed...and the next morning I sent for the chief engineer of the War Department, and I told him to put the Philippines on the map of the United States (pointing to a large map on the wall of his office), and there they are, and there they will stay while I am President!" (Rusling, 1987, p. 23).

The United States Senate debates surrounding the acquisition and occupation of the Philippines were also very heated, with Republican Senator Albert Beveridge (1900) of Indiana providing the following rationale for why the United States needed to colonize the Philippines and its peoples:

> "…we have one of the three great ocean possessions of the globe, located at the most commanding commercial, naval, and military points in the Eastern seas, within hail of India, shoulder to shoulder with China, richer in its own resources than any equal body of land on the entire globe, and peopled by a race which civilization demands shall be improved. Shall we abandon it? We must remember that we are not dealing with Americans or Europeans. We are dealing with Orientals. We are dealing with Orientals who are Malays. They mistake kindness for weakness, forbearance for fear. It could not be otherwise unless you could erase hundreds of years of savagery, other hundreds of years of Orientalism, and still other hundreds of years of Spanish character and custom. . . They are not capable of self-government. How could they be? They are not of a self-governing race…Savage blood, Oriental blood, Malay blood, Spanish example - are these the elements of self-government?...We must never forget that in dealing with the Filipinos we deal with children." (pp. 704-712).

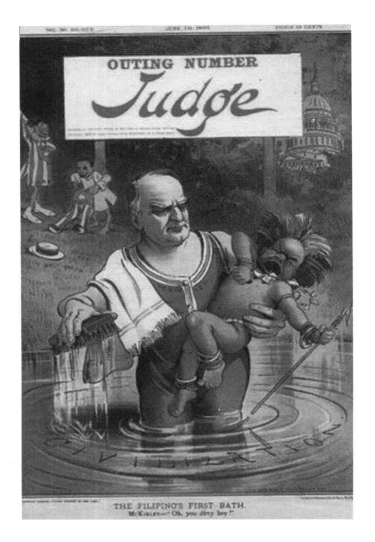

Figure 3. A political cartoon depicting Filipinos as child-like savages needing to be civilized and educated, led by President William McKinley. (Hamilton, Grant, 1899. *Judge,* Judge Company: New York, NY) (public domain image)

It is clear from the quotations above that the motivators behind the United States' forced entry and occupation of the Philippines are similar to those of Spain's approximately 400 years prior: The Three G's (God, Gold, and Glory). It is also clear from the quotations above that many in the United States, including their highest leaders such as its senators and even its president, saw Filipinos in an inferior manner (also, see Figure 3 for a political cartoon published in 1899 featuring President McKinley giving a savage, child-like Filipino his first bath using the waters of civilization and the brush of education).

Despite the fact that Filipinos had already declared their independence, democratically developed a national constitution, and had democratically elected their leaders, they were still perceived as Peoples who were not intelligent enough, sophisticated enough, and civilized enough to govern themselves (Ignacio, de la Cruz, Emmanuel, & Toribio, 2004). Nevermind the fact that the majority of Filipinos by this time were already Christians, that the Philippines already had an established university (University of Santo Thomas, founded in 1611) long before the first American university (Harvard, founded in 1636) was founded, and that many of their leaders were highly educated (Ignacio, de la Cruz, Emmanuel, & Toribio, 2004), the United States still felt that it was their duty to "Christianize," educate, and civilize the Tao. They were regarded as children or savages, needing to be trained and taught, similar to how African Americans and Native Americans or American Indians were treated by the United States (Espiritu, 2003; Ignacio, de la Cruz, Emmanuel, & Toribio, 2004). Indeed, in her discussion of the oppression of Filipinos under United States rule, Yen Le Espiritu (2003) wrote:

> "Theodore Roosevelt...repeatedly linked Native Americans to Filipinos, employing words like 'wild and ignorant,' 'savages,' 'Apaches,' and 'Sioux' to refer to the Filipino people. In the same way, white American soldiers in the Philippines used many of the same epithets to describe Filipinos as they used to describe African Americans, including 'niggers,'

'black devils,' and 'gugus'...If we positioned Filipino/American history within the traditional immigration paradigm, we would miss the ethnic and racial intersections between Filipinos and Native Americans and African Americans as groups similarly affected by the forces of Manifest Destiny. These common contexts of struggle were not lost on African American soldiers in the Philippines. Connecting their fight against domestic racism to the Filipino struggle against U.S. imperialism, some African American soldiers – such as Corporal David Fagen – switched allegiance and joined the native armed struggle for independence." (pp. 52-53)

Espiritu's (2003) analyses reveal the similarities between the experiences of oppression between America's First Peoples, African Americans, and Filipinos – similarities that are lost in popular presentations of American history and even Filipino and Filipino American history, which often simplistically portray Filipinos as one of the largest voluntary immigrant groups in the United States. The true history reveals to us that it was not the Filipinos who initiated contact with and tried to begin a relationship with the United States; it was the other way around through the avenue of colonialism, imperialism, and oppression. The true history also reveals to us that, similar to America's First Peoples and African Americans, Filipinos and their ethnic and cultural characteristics were systematically degraded and inferiorized, primarily to rationalize the United States' occupation and colonization of the Philippines. Indeed, whenever questions and criticisms arose regarding America's occupation of the Philippines, United States leaders were quick to point to the ideas of *Manifest Destiny* and *Benevolent Assimilation* as their primary motivators and rationale (Ignacio, de la Cruz, Emmanuel, & Toribio, 2004). Unfortunately, very few bothered to pay serious attention to the flip side of both of these ideas – that for Americans to see themselves as being responsible for civilizing the rest of the world, they also had to buy the assumption that everyone else are inferior, wild, savage, and uncivilized. In fact, to convince Americans of their superiority over the Filipinos, demonstrate the savagery and uncivilized nature of Filipinos, and rationalize America's civilization and benevolent intention in the Philippines, the United States brought over 1,100 Filipinos to the St. Louis World's Fair in 1902 and sequestered them in what was called "The Philippine Reservation." This 47-acre reservation, complete with "authentic" dwellings and "natural" living environments of the "savage Filipinos," presented the American public a range of Filipino civilization levels, with the Negritos and other indigenous tribes being portrayed as the most savage and the Philippine Scouts (United States-trained Filipino soldiers) being the most civilized (Espiritu, 2003; Ignacio, de la Cruz, Emmanuel, & Toribio, 2004). The Philippine Reservation was the most popular site during the St. Louis World's Fair, as Americans curiously watched the captured Filipinos as if they were animals being displayed in a zoo.

Another American Genocide

As discussed above, the portrayal of Filipinos as uncivilized savages who needed to be tamed, trained, and taught is similar to how the United States perceived their earlier colonial victims, the Native Americans or American Indians (as depicted in the editorial cartoon in Figure 4). Some scholars have even made convincing arguments paralleling the United States' perception and treatments of Filipinos with those of America's First Peoples (Williams, 1980). One infamous connection between the experiences of Filipinos under the United States and of those by Native Americans or American Indians is United States Army General Jacob H. Smith, who was a veteran of the Civil War and many other battles against the First Peoples of America. Gen. Smith was assigned to lead the war against the Filipinos during the Philippine-American War, where he proudly publicized that he was willing to repeat strategies that worked against the Indians with Filipinos. Among the many war crimes Gen. Smith committed is the infamous "Kill Everyone Over Ten" order he gave his troops in the Philippines (Ignacio, de la Cruz, Emmanuel, & Toribio, 2004).

Furthermore, although the Philippine-American War was declared to have been won by the United States in 1902, Filipinos continued to fight and resist American presence in the islands (Constantino, 1975; Ignacio, de la Cruz, Emmanuel, & Toribio, 2004). Thus, the United States military continued to battle Filipinos in what is known as *The Pacification Campaign* that lasted until 1913. The Pacification Campaign included the infamous Moro Crater Massacre in 1906, where hundreds of Filipino civilians, women, and children were executed by American soldiers. It is estimated that about one and a half million Filipinos died as a result of American occupation of the islands between 1898-1913, leading some scholars to conclude that Filipinos experienced genocide in the hands of Americans (San Juan, Jr., 2005). These examples of the Filipino experiences against American soldiers are painfully similar to the many massacres that Native Americans and American Indians experienced just a few years prior. Among America's First Peoples, the devastating physical, emotional, and psychological pain as well as the vast amounts of cultural loss that accompanied the European colonization of their ancestral lands have caused immense individual, collective, and inter-generational trauma among these indigenous groups. Such trauma has been identified as being the root cause of the many social and psychological ills facing America's First Peoples today (Braveheart, 1998; Duran, 2006; Duran & Duran, 1995; Gone, 2009; McBride, 2002; discussed in more detail in Chapters 5 and 9). Deservedly, the trauma and intergenerational effects of colonialism among America's First Peoples have been receiving attention and are being addressed, at least to some extent. Unfortunately, the same cannot be said about the Filipino experience.

As American imperialist efforts proceeded, and as part of the Pacification Campaign, the United States established a nationwide public school system in which most of the educators were *Thomasites* – over 500 American teachers who came to the Philippines in 1901 through the St. Thomas transport (Ignacio, de la Cruz, Emmanuel, & Toribio, 2004). In 1902, the number of Thomasites sent to the Philippines more than doubled as the United States became convinced that "education, instead of outright military suppression, was the more effective means to pacify the Filipinos" (Espiritu, 2003, p. 26) and "win the confidence, respect, and affection of the inhabitants of the Philippines" (Blount, 1913, p. 649). The establishment of American-controlled and American-taught public schools throughout the Philippines is similar to what the United States did with America's First Peoples when Native American or American Indian boarding schools were established throughout the United States to "civilize" America's indigenous groups. As part of the United States' "benevolent" and "noble" effort to "educate…uplift…civilize and Christianize" the Filipinos (Rusling, 1987, p. 23) and uphold the United State's tutelary regime (Go, 2003), the Americanized educational system taught Filipinos the English language, inculcated Filipinos with American culture and values, and replaced Filipino worldview with American political ideals (Constantino, 1982; Pido, 1997). Thus, the Thomasites' information about the United States may have begun to distort the Filipinos' view of American culture.

The United States also selected promising Filipinos to go to the United States as scholars and study in some of the most prestigious American universities. These *Pensionados* learned the American form of government as well as the American culture, and many returned to the Philippines, became leaders, and governed the Philippines after the American model, which was the intention behind the "scholarship program." The Pensionados, knowingly or not, may have supplemented the teachings of the Thomasites and, through the way they led and interacted with the Tao, contributed to propagating the message that anything American is better than anything Filipino. Consequently, a majority of Filipinos may have developed a grandiose picture of the American life that contributed to their large-scale migration into the western United States where they experienced blatant racism (discussed in more detail in Chapter 4). Simultaneous to the development of their superior perceptions of American culture, Filipinos may have begun to devalue Filipino culture (e.g., Espiritu, 2003; Strobel, 2001), similar to how Filipinos are argued to have developed the belief that the Spanish and their ways of life were naturally superior and that the indigenous Filipino culture was that of uncivilized savages (Rimonte, 1997).

Figure 4. Political cartoon depicting the Filipino experience of colonialism as similar to that of America's First Peoples. "Speaking from experience," (American Indian to Filipino) "be good or you will be dead." (Gillam, Victor, 1899. *Judge,* Arkell Publishing: New York, NY.) (public domain image)

Chapter Summary

This chapter provided a discussion of a part of American history that many do not remember. This history contains painful, traumatic, shameful, and embarrassing events. It is possible that this may be the reason why many do not remember it – it is too difficult to talk about and thus, remember. However, it is important for all of us to know that American culture and the United States are not perfect, so that we do not develop an inaccurately grandiose perception of America. Similar to the discussion in Chapter 2, it is important for us to know that the Filipinos fought bravely and heroically against American occupation to protect the independence they gained from Spain, independence that they worked so hard for and that many of them lost their lives for. It is important for us to remember that Filipinos fought valiantly against the United States to protect their ways of life and their rights for self-determination and self-government. Similar to what took place under Spanish rule (Chapter 2), it is important for Filipinos and Filipino Americans to know that they experienced maltreatments, miseducation, inferiorization, and even deaths in the hands of the United States. Another crucial realization is the fact that it was the United States who initiated contact with Filipinos, colonizing the Philippines, portraying anything American as better than anything Filipino, and opening the doors for large numbers of Filipinos to want to immigrate to America. The history of Filipinos in and with the United States, therefore, is more complex than the common "voluntary immigrant" narrative, and reveals to us that the Filipino experience is similar to those of African Americans and America's First Peoples. It is important for Filipinos and Filipino Americans to have a complete picture of such a history so that they can develop a more accurate perception of American culture and the United States; to develop a more accurate perception of themselves and their Filipino heritage. It is important for Filipinos and Filipino Americans to know and understand the catalysts for their colonized thoughts, attitudes, emotions, and behaviors – their colonized psychology.

*   *   *

Because of the United States' presence and colonization of the Philippines, the doors were opened for large numbers of Filipinos to work, study, and live in the United States. Simultaneously, the doors were opened for many Americans to work, study, and live in the Philippines. Thus, cultural mixes, cultural integration, and cultural conflicts took place in both United States and Philippine soils. Differing ideas as to how the world works, how the world should be, what is better, what is worse, what is desirable, and what is undesirable all collided. Naturally, the attitudes, thoughts, ideas, and desires of those in power eventually won, and the ones who are not in power are left trying to live up to the standards of the powerful. The ones who were powerful, in both the United States and even the Philippines, were the Americans. In the following chapter, I discuss how Western-centric or American-centric standards and ideals that have their roots in colonialism but have lasted throughout the decades, and to which Filipinos and Filipino Americans are subjected, operate to continually subjugate and oppress the Filipino ethnicity and culture. Such neocolonial and contemporary experiences of oppression continue to send inferiorizing messages about the Filipino culture and ethnicity, and one way in which the legacies of colonialism have lasted for many generations. Although many of such forms of oppression take place outside of what some might consider as formal colonial contexts, they are forms of oppression nonetheless and their deleterious effects on Filipino and Filipino American cognition, emotion, attitude, and behavior are the same.

CHAPTER 4

NEOCOLONIALISM AND CONTEMPORARY OPPRESSION

ᜎᜅᜒᜀᜂᜐᜒ ᜎᜅᜒᜊᜒᜍᜒᜈ

Filipinos were one of the first Asians on United States soil, with documentation of shipwrecked Filipinos landing in California as early as the mid-1500s (Gomez Borah, 1995) and of Spanish-speaking Filipino slaves settling in the bayous of Louisiana as early as the mid-1700s (Cordova, 1983; Espina 1988). The Filipinos who landed in California were crewmembers of a Spanish ship that was part of the famous Manila-Acapulco Galleon Trade while the Philippines were still under Spanish rule. Similarly, the Filipinos who settled in Louisiana were slaves in Spanish Galleon ships during the Manila-Acapulco Galleon Trade as well. Shortly after leaving Acapulco, Mexico, the Filipino slaves jumped ship to escape the maltreatments and brutality of their Spanish masters. The Filipinos swam to the closest shore they could find, and unknowingly landed and settled in what is now known as the bayous of St. Malo in Louisiana. Indeed, even before the United States defeated Spain in the Spanish-American War, before the United States even began to colonize the Philippines, and even before the United States were "the

United States," there were already Filipinos on American soil. Furthermore, it is also clear that early Filipino presence in the lands now known as the United States (California and Louisiana) was influenced by colonialism and oppression (by Spain), and that Filipino presence in America was not as simple as Filipinos wanting to leave the Philippines for better opportunities in the United States (as discussed in Chapter 3).

Although there were Filipinos in the United States between the 1500s and the 1800s, however, it was not until toward the end of the 19th century when large numbers of Filipinos began to work, study, and live in the United States. This is due to the fact that the Philippines was a United States territory between 1898-1946 and Filipinos were regarded as United States Nationals until 1938, making Filipino Americans the only Asian American ethnic group to have a history of being directly colonized by the United States of America. Because of their status as United States Nationals, which allowed them to easily enter and work in the United States, the American colonial period sparked the beginning of large-scale migration to the United States of Filipino laborers, mostly men. Filipinos in America during this period were mostly plantation and cannery workers in the western states of California, Hawaii, Oregon, Washington, and Alaska. However, because they were not citizens and because the United States viewed Filipinos as uncivilized savages (as discussed in Chapter 3), American laws did not protect Filipinos and their rights and they became the subject of brutal discrimination, maltreatments, and injustices (Cordova, 1983; Bulosan, 2002).

Oppression of Early Filipinos in the United States

The lives of Filipinos in the United States during the first half of the 1900s were dark, difficult, and dangerous. Blatantly racist signs such as "Positively No Filipinos Allowed" and "No Dogs or Filipinos Allowed" (also, see Figure 5) were common sights in storefronts in order to keep Filipinos from using hotels, restaurants, swimming pools, apartments, barber shops, and other public facilities (Cordova, 1983). Filipinos were exploited by their employers, were derogatorily regarded as "little brown monkeys," and were hunted, beaten, and murdered by civilians and police officers (Bulosan, 2002; Cordova, 1983; Espiritu, 2003). Carlos Bulosan, whose many writings such as *America is in the Heart* (1974) are regarded as "the first and best account...of ...what it was like to be a Filipino in California and its sister states...between...1930 to 1941" (McWilliams, 2002, p. vii), stated that he felt "like a criminal running away from a crime (he) did not commit. And this crime is that (he is) a Filipino in America" (as quoted by McWilliams, 2002, p. vii). Bulosan further explained that a Filipino in America during the first half of the 20th century "is the loneliest thing on earth...He is enchained, damnably, to his race, his heritage" (as quoted by McWilliams, 2002, p. xiii).

Just like Carlos Bulosan, other early Filipino immigrant workers were separated from their families and thus, terribly missed home (i.e., the Philippines). Because the majority of early Filipino immigrants to the United States were men, many of them went to dance halls after their day's work, or during their days off from work, to socialize with other Filipinos, play poker, watch cockfights, dance, and temporarily get a feeling of home. Indeed, as documented in the film "Dollar a Day, Ten Cents a Dance" (Center for Asian American Media), many of the Filipino laborers spent much of their hard earned money in such dance halls paying to dance with women - white women. Thus, the mainstream American population began to view them as hypersexualized beings who were out to steal white women. Such a negative and deviant perception of Filipinos were connected to the fear of inter-racial relationships taking place between Filipinos and White women and giving way to mixed-race children, furthering mainstream America's anxiety of the white race being tainted by savage Filipino blood. As a result, similar to the experiences of African Americans at that time, the Filipino *manongs* (the term used to refer to early Filipino immigrants) were subjected to brutal acts of racism in various states wherein they worked and lived. They were hunted, beaten, dragged by horse, hung, and murdered. As Yen Le Espiritu (2003) described (and also as evidenced by the sign depicted by Figure 5):

> "The most explosive and publicized incident took place in 1930 near Watsonville, California, where four hundred white vigilantes attacked a Filipino dance club, beating dozens of Filipinos and killing one. In the days that followed, hundreds of white men roamed the streets of Watsonville, beating or shooting Filipinos on sight. A Filipino laborer described the violent scene: 'The mob came into the pool halls and with clubs bludgeoned all of us and followed us until we were out of the city. The residences where Filipinos were quartered were ransacked and burned to the ground. Automobiles that contained Filipinos were fired upon, and many of the boys were wounded.'" (pp. 65-66)

As revealed by the quotation above and by the accounts of Carlos Bulosan, the life of Filipinos in America while the Philippines was under United States colonial rule was not at all how the Thomasites described it. The roads were not made of gold, the opportunities for a better life were not really there, and not everyone in the United States were as welcoming as what one might expect given such a "civilized" country, society, and culture. In fact, there was no equal opportunity, no equal access, no equal representation, and no equality between Filipinos and European Americans at all. Similar to how African Americans were regarded and treated by mainstream America, Filipinos in the United States between the 1900s up to the Civil Rights Movement in the 60s were maltreated, brutalized, and inferiorized simply because their Filipino characteristics were associated by the dominant society with undesirability, deviance, inferiority, and negativity.

Figure 5. A recreation of a sign commonly seen in storefronts depicting discrimination against Filipinos in the United States, circa 1930-1941.

Contemporary Oppression of Filipinos in Neocolonial Philippines

Although the Philippines was "given" its independence in 1946, American influence continues to persist in contemporary Philippines as evidenced by the maintenance of United States military bases in the Philippines until 1992, the continued presence of American soldiers in the Philippines to "train" Filipino soldiers in suppressing terrorism and insurgency, and the continued use of English as the primary language in Philippine education, law, government, business, and science. Indeed, as Karnow (1989) suggests, "...in no place is the (American) imperial legacy more alive than in Manila, where America's presence is almost as dynamic now as it was during the days of U.S. rule" (p.16). Today, the Filipino immigration rate into the United States (60,000 per year) is behind only to that of Mexicans and Chinese, attesting to this group's rapid population growth and making Filipinos one of the largest immigrant groups in the United States (Hoeffel, Rastogi, Kim, & Shahid, 2012). According to the 2010 United States Census, Filipinos are the second largest Asian ethnic group in the United States today (3.4 million total) and the largest Asian subgroup in the most populated state of California (Hoeffel, Rastogi, Kim, & Shahid, 2012). Filipinos are also the largest Asian group in the states of Alaska, Arizona, Hawaii, Idaho, Montana, Nevada, New Mexico, Washington, Wyoming and South Dakota (Hoeffel, Rastogi, Kim, & Shahid, 2012).

For contemporary Filipinos and Filipino American immigrants and their children, the psychological legacy of colonialism and more recent experiences of oppression may continue to exist through inter-generational family socialization, continuous endorsement of the American version of the Golden Legend (i.e., perceiving Americans as freedom fighters, liberators who saved Filipinos from Spain, the masters of democracy, and enlightening heroes), continued oppression in the United States, and continued Americanization of the Philippines that further endorses the notion of American superiority over the Filipino ethnicity and culture (David & Okazaki, 2006a; Espiritu, 2003). To this day, the large annual influx of Filipinos into the United States is argued to be an effect of colonialism and continued Americanization of the Philippines (David & Nadal, under review). Indeed, as political scientist Rodriguez (1997) stated:

"Colonialism has fostered a perception that…the standard of living…in the United States is the mark of a highly sophisticated society (and culture)… adults dream of going to the United States as if longing to be reunited with a long-lost parent… children dream of becoming Americans in the hope that they will finally be able to live in Disney's Kingdom…For many Filipinos, coming to America means the fulfillment of a lifelong dream…" (p. 317-318).

Thus, based on the quotation above and as discussed in Chapter 3, the Filipino and Filipino American experience cannot simply be understood in the traditional voluntary immigration paradigm, wherein individuals choose to leave their home countries for better opportunities in America and that "their presence in the U.S. (is not) forced upon them by the U.S. government or by white Americans" (Ogbu & Simons, 1998, p. 164). Although it is clear that the majority of Filipinos in the United States today are immigrants and that the Philippines is the source of one of the largest immigrant groups in the United States today, we need to remember that it was United States colonialism that initially opened the doors for large scale Filipino migration and it is the contemporary American neocolonial and oppressive context – a legacy of colonialism – that continues to harbor a desire among many Filipinos today to immigrate to the United States.

Indeed, contemporary Philippine society is filled with messages that perpetuate American or Western ideals and standards that have colonial roots. For instance, the continued use of English as the primary language for school instruction, formal government businesses, and other important communications (e.g., courts, business, science, etc.) sends the message that English is the language of the educated and the civilized and, thus, better than indigenous Filipino languages. The continued presence of American soldiers in the Philippines to train Filipino soldiers sends the message that Filipinos lag behind the United States in terms of military skill, cannot adequately protect their country, and thus, are still dependent on the United States for protection. The Philippines' economy being developed (largely due to American colonialism) in a way that it is based on and dependent upon outside resources to survive, whether it is exporting raw materials to bring them back as products or exporting people to send money back to the Philippines, sends the message that the Filipinos cannot sustain themselves and survive through their own natural resources – which is surprising given that the indigenous Tao thrived in these islands for centuries because of its rich and abundant natural resources (as discussed in Chapter 1). The continued regard for lighter skinned people and those with bridged noses as more attractive than the Filipino brown skin and flat nose sends the message that natural Filipino physical characteristics are not as desirable as European physical traits. Indeed, the abundance of skin whitening creams, skin bleaching products, and skin-lightening clinics (as shown in Figure 6) throughout the Philippines is evidence that the masses have fully bought into this Western-centric standard or ideal for what is beautiful and desirable. The continued discrimination against, and low regard of, non-Christians, non-English proficient, non-Manilans, and non-Westernized Filipinos sends the message that the more Western or American you look, think, and behave, the better off and more accepted you will be. The continued regard of existing indigenous Tao in various parts of the Philippines as uncivilized peoples sends the message that the less Filipino you look, think, behave, and live, the better off you are. These messages that are still being propagated and still highly ubiquitous in contemporary Philippines have their roots in colonial times. Thus, in contemporary Philippine life, the Filipino ethnicity and culture are still being inferiorized and the Western or American culture is still being highly idolized. Indeed, in contemporary Filipino life, colonialism and thus, oppression, is still happening (David & Nadal, under review).

Figure 6. Signs for Skin-Whitening clinics, which is a common form of business in modern day Philippines. (Photo credits: Keisha Guangko and E. J. R. David)

Contemporary Oppression of Filipinos in the United States

In terms of their contemporary experiences in the United States, a recent study examining Chinese and Filipino Americans' experiences of racism showed that 98% experienced racism in the past year and 99% reported witnessing other Asian Americans being subjected to racism (vicarious racism). Within this sample, Filipino Americans reported a higher frequency of vicarious racism and direct daily racism than Chinese Americans (Alvarez, Juang, & Liang, 2006). A more recent study found that 99% of Filipino Americans directly experience a racist event on a yearly basis, and that such experiences leads to psychological distress, low self-esteem, anxiety, and depression (Alvarez & Juang, 2010).

Filipino Americans also commonly report experiencing a more subtle and more modern form of racism called racial microaggressions (Nadal, Escobar, Prado, David, & Haynes, 2012). *Racial microaggressions* are common acts by an individual or group that send subtle messages of racism to target groups and individuals. Furthermore, racial microaggressions are often unconscious and unintentional, but may be just as psychologically damaging as blatant forms of racism or discrimination (Sue, 2010). For Filipino Americans, some specific forms of racial microaggressions that they experience include being treated like a second-class citizen (e.g., being given substandard service or attention compared to others), pathologizing their cultural behaviors and beliefs (e.g., being berated, teased, or punished for displaying cultural behaviors and values that are different from mainstream Americans), assuming that Filipinos are deviant in some way (e.g., such as when others assume that a Filipino is a criminal, gang member, or is up to no good), and assuming that Filipinos are of inferior status or intellect (e.g., such as when Filipino-trained professionals are treated as not being as good as others). Filipinos who experience such racial microaggressions report that they feel intense negative emotions such as anger, fear, belittlement, rage, frustration, and alienation because of such events (Nadal, Escobar, Prado, David, & Haynes, 2012). These experiences of modern racism send the message to Filipino Americans that they are not as good as members of the dominant group simply because they are Filipino. They send the message that because of their Filipino brown skin and other Filipino physical traits, that others will associate them with deviance, criminality, and inferiority. They send the message that Filipino cultural values and behaviors are not as "normal" or acceptable as mainstream American cultural values and behaviors. Similar to what Filipinos experienced during colonial times under Spain and the United States, their contemporary experiences in America send the message that their Filipino physical and cultural characteristics, as well as their values and behaviors, are not good enough.

Despite the fact that such ethnic and cultural oppression is happening within the United States and outside of what some may consider to be formal colonial contexts, scholars have argued that the current racial dynamics within the United States that is characterized by racial inequality and cultural imposition by the dominant group on the minority groups is similar to formal colonial processes. Indeed, some scholars have termed the conditions within the United States to be that of *internal colonialism* – because the systems and institutions in the country that are controlled by members of the dominant group operate in the same manner as what happens in a colonial society: the systems and institutions function to maintain the superiority and uphold the ideals and standards of the dominant groups, and continually subjugate the minority groups who are never regarded to be good enough to meet the standards and ideals set forth by the dominant group (David, 2009; David & Okazaki, 2006a; Lott, 1976). Thus, in the contemporary lives of Filipinos in America, the oppression and inferiorization of the Filipino ethnicity and culture is still a major component of their daily experiences.

Chapter Summary

It is clear from the discussion above that Filipinos in the Philippines continue to be bombarded with messages that having Filipino physical characteristics (e.g., brown skin, flat nose) and displaying Filipino cultural values and behaviors (e.g., speaking a Filipino language) are not desirable, or at least, not as desirable as possessing Western physical characteristics (e.g., lighter skin, being of mixed blood or mestizo/a) or displaying adherence to Western culture (e.g., speaking English well, having been in the United States to live or for vacation). Such messages are so strong and omnipresent in postcolonial Philippine society that it largely contributes to many Filipinos developing a life-long desire or goal to immigrate to the United States. Thus, the continuous large-scale migration of Filipinos into the United States for the past five decades is largely due to such Filipino inferiorizing and American idealizing messages that have their roots in colonialism. Within the United States itself, the ethnic and cultural oppression of the Filipino body and culture continues, as Filipinos in America are faced with both blatant and subtle forms of racism and discrimination on a daily basis. Such experiences further send the message that Filipino physical and cultural characteristics are inferior to those of Americans or those who are Western. Thus, Filipinos and Filipino Americans have experienced centuries of direct, vicarious, explicit, and subtle forms of ethnic and cultural subjugation in the Philippines and in the United States (David & Nadal, under review; Lott, 1976), forms of ethnic and cultural subjugation that began during colonial times and have lasted throughout the generations through the context of neocolonialism and internal colonialism. Given that Filipinos and Filipino Americans have faced centuries of both historical and contemporary forms of oppression, it is possible that oppression has influenced their psychological experiences – how they think, feel, and act – toward themselves, other Filipinos, and non-Filipinos.

*   *   *

Part I has provided us with some historical and contemporary understanding of Filipinos and Filipino Americans. We now know that the indigenous Tao lived in well-established, highly developed, and richly-cultured societies. Thus, we also know that they were resilient, creative, perceptive, and intelligent peoples. Because of Spanish and American colonialism, however, we learned that the indigenous Tao lost much of their indigenous ways of living and believing. In other words, we now realize that the indigenous Tao suffered under Spanish and American colonialism and, consequently, have lost so much. Through the oppressive practices of colonial and neocolonial institutions and systems, we have come to understand how the Tao's indigenous culture and physical characteristics were demonized and inferiorized. Furthermore, we also now understand how Western or American ideals and standards were portrayed as better, superior, more desirable, and more attractive than the indigenous ways, and thus, came to replace the beliefs, cultures, and behaviors of the indigenous Tao. It is now clear that Filipinos and Filipino Americans have experienced ethnic and cultural subjugation both in the Philippines and the United States. Finally, it is also clear that Filipinos and Filipino Americans have been experiencing oppression for approximately 500 years. The psychological consequences of oppression among this group are discussed in detail in Part II.

PART II:

THE AFTERMATH

In the field of psychology, particularly ethnic minority psychology, the psychological consequences of oppression have received some scientific attention. *Internalized oppression* – a condition in which an oppressed individual or group come to believe that they are inferior to those in power or who are part of the dominant group – has been identified by various psychological scholars as a salient and possibly the most insidious consequence of oppression. Historically in ethnic minority psychology, the concept of internalized oppression and its psychological implications have mostly been investigated as experienced by African Americans. For instance, Thomas (1971) theorized that internalized racism or internalized oppression among African Americans leads to identity confusion and to the development of an inferiorized identity which he called "negromachy." The seminal Black Identity Development Model (Nigrescence Models) proposed by Cross, Parham, and Helms (1991) also argued that internalized racial oppression may lead African Americans to highly value the dominant culture and simultaneously devalue their own, leading many African Americans to hold anti-Black sentiments or have black self-hate. In terms of its mental health implications, it has been empirically demonstrated that racial oppression is negatively related to African Americans' physical and mental health (Carter, 2007; Landrine & Klonoff, 1996; Klonoff, Landrine, & Ullman, 1999; Speight, 2007).

More recently, internalized oppression has also been argued to be common among members of sexual minority populations. For example, in his minority stress model for Lesbian, Gay, and Bisexual (LGB) individuals, Meyer (2003) argued that experiences of discrimination based on sexual orientation and the need to conceal one's sexual orientation – an important and salient part of one's self or identity – negatively influences LGB individuals' mental health. What is probably the worst consequence of discrimination against sexual orientation is *internalized homophobia* – a specific form of internalized oppression in which LGB individuals eventually re-direct negative homophobic societal attitudes toward themselves. It is another form of self-hate due to experiences oppression. Empirically, it has been shown that internalized homophobia is related to negative mental health outcomes (Hatzenbuehler, 2009; Williamson, 2000).

Based on the psychological literature among African Americans and LGB individuals that are reviewed above, oppression has immense psychological and mental health implications. As discussed in Part I, Filipinos and Filipino Americans have extensive experiences of oppression, with the Filipino ethnicity and culture being historically and contemporarily attached to inferiority. Thus, similar to African Americans, LGB individuals, and other historically and contemporarily oppressed groups, the psychological experiences and mental health of Filipinos and Filipino Americans may also be impacted by oppression. To this end, Part II will focus on colonial mentality or internalized oppression – the consequence of historical colonialism (which is a specific form of oppression) and contemporary oppression – as experienced, expressed, and manifested by Filipinos and Filipino Americans. Part II will also discuss in detail how colonial mentality or internalized oppression plays a major role in the psychological experiences and mental health of modern day Filipino -/ Americans.

*   *   *

CHAPTER 5

COLONIAL MENTALITY: PSYCHOLOGICAL IMPACT OF COLONIALISM

ꤢꤟꤢ ꤚꤢ ꤞꤢꤘꤣ ꤦꤢꤩ ꤘꤣ ꤘꤢꤟꤢꤛꤢꤘꤢ

Psychologists Prilleltensky and Gonick (1996) defined *oppression* as the unequal power relationships in which dominating persons or groups exert their power by restricting access to resources and instilling fear and a sense of inferiority among the dominated persons or groups. In other words, oppression refers to a process and condition wherein a group denies the rights, dignity, and worth of another group. Such a denial of one's rights, dignity, and worth – as related to the person as well as to one's social group – may lead to a condition known as internalized oppression, which in turn may lead toward several psychological, behavioral, and social concerns. In this chapter, I delineate how colonialism is a specific form of oppression, and I begin to discuss how the experience of oppression has negatively influenced various ethnic and cultural groups, with a focus on Filipinos and Filipino Americans. More specifically, this chapter will introduce the concept of colonial mentality, framing it within the broader literature on internalized oppression as experienced by various groups. Also, this chapter will provide qualitative descriptors of the different manifestations of colonial mentality as specifically experienced by Filipinos and Filipino Americans. I will begin by presenting the classic framework for colonialism and its psychological consequences.

Internalized Colonialism: A Consequence of Classical and Internal Colonialism

The colonial model initially described by Frantz Fanon (1965) provides a theoretical framework for understanding the psychological effects of oppression on the oppressed. According to Fanon, the classical colonial model is composed of four phases, with the first phase being the forced entry of a foreign group into a geographic territory with the intention of exploiting the new territory's natural resources, including its inhabitants. In the experiences of the indigenous Taos, this phase is clearly seen in the fact that Spain and the United States forcefully entered the island archipelago we now know as the Philippines despite strong resistance from the indigenous inhabitants. Spain and the United States also colonized the Philippines with the intention of gaining control over the islands' natural resources and its people (e.g., as slaves, source of cheap labor). The second phase of colonialism is characterized by the colonizer imposing its culture on the colonized, disintegrating the indigenous culture of the colonized, and recreating the culture of the colonized as defined by the colonizer. Such a cultural transformation of the colonized people's indigenous culture is intended to more clearly differentiate between the colonizer's superior or more civilized ways of life and the colonized people's inferior or savage ways. The second phase of colonialism is also clearly seen in the experiences of Filipinos under Spanish and American rule, during which the Filipino ethnicity and culture were demonized, inferiorized, or attached with undesirability while European standards, ideals, beliefs, and ways of life were portrayed as superior or more civilized. Once the colonial society has clearly contrasted the colonizer and the colonized *other*, the third phase of colonialism begins as the colonized are portrayed as wild, savage, and uncivilized peoples whom the colonizer have to nobly monitor, tame, and civilize. Thus, the third phase essentially conveys that tyranny and domination, and hence oppression, is necessary. As discussed in Part I, Filipinos experienced brutality, injustice, and maltreatments under Spain and the United States, with the provided rationale behind such oppression being the desire of the colonizers to educate, uplift, Christianize, teach, train, or civilize the Filipinos. The implementation of the first three phases eventually leads to the fourth phase of colonialism, which involves the establishment of a society where the political, social, and economic institutions are designed to benefit and maintain the superiority of the colonizer while simultaneously and persistently subjugating the colonized. The fourth phase of colonialism can be clearly seen in the establishment of institutions (e.g., the Catholic Church, highly powerful leaders and corrupt governmental systems, foreign-dependent economy, and public school systems) in colonial and neocolonial Philippines. Thus, based on the discussed characteristics of classical colonialism, colonialism is another specific form of oppression. Furthermore, it is clear that the indigenous Tao experienced classical colonialism and its oppressive umbrella under Spain and the United States.

Based on the description of what typically happens in a colonial society as discussed above, we now understand that "there is enormous social, psychological, and infrastructural work in producing the colonized person" (Okazaki, David, & Abelmann, 2008, p. 96). Thus, let us now turn our attention to how such an oppressive context may influence those groups and individuals who are experiencing such oppression – the colonized persons or groups. Similar to Jose Rizal's description of how Filipinos were affected by Spanish colonialism (as discussed in Chapter 2), more modern scholars of the consequences of colonialism (e.g., Fanon, 1965; Freire, 1970; Memmi, 1965) in various parts of the world also argue that internalized oppression, or more specifically, *internalized colonialism,* is the major psychological effect of colonialism. Based on his work in French colonized Algeria, psychiatrist Fanon (1965) argued that the sustained denigration and inhumane treatments that the colonized are subjected to under colonialism often lead to self-doubt, identity confusion, and feelings of inferiority among the colonized. Based on his work in French colonized Tunisia and Algeria, Albert Memmi (1965) added that the creation of a colonizer-defined cultural identity for the colonized often leads the colonized to eventually believe such an inferior identity. Noted postcolonial educator Paolo Freire (1970) further contended that because of the inferior connotations the colonial society has attached to their cultural and ethnic identities, the colonized might develop an intense desire to rid oneself of such identities and try to emulate the colonizer as much as possible. Thus, the colonized may begin to talk, act, and dress like the colonizer because the colonizer's ways are seen as superior. Simultaneously, the colonized may also begin to shed oneself of anything from his/her heritage culture and ethnicity because such a heritage is seen as inferior. Furthermore, the colonized may eventually feel a sense of gratitude and indebtedness (i.e., colonial debt) toward the colonizer for civilizing and enlightening the colonized (Rimonte, 1997).

Thus, based on the observations and conclusions of prominent postcolonial scholars, the effects of colonialism or oppression on colonized or oppressed individuals can take at least three forms: (1) buying into or accepting their alleged inferiority and buying into or accepting the colonizers' or oppressors' alleged superiority; (2) developing a desire to separate oneself from the perceived inferiority of one's heritage group and emulate the colonizers or oppressors as much as possible; and (3) regarding colonialism and oppression as necessary for growth, progress, or civilization. Additionally, noted community psychologist Jennifer Kofkin Rudkin (2003) also stated that colonialism "leads to self-debasement, alienation, loss of cultural identity, dependency, and internally-directed hostility" (p. 290), similar to the descriptions of the effects of colonialism (i.e., internalized oppression) provided by Jose Rizal and prominent postcolonial scholars, and suggesting that the psychological consequences of colonialism have been identified as an important factor by various scientific and scholarly fields. Before diving into a detailed discussion of how Filipinos and Filipino Americans may have been affected by colonialism and oppression, let us first examine how common, salient, and damaging internalized oppression is among other historically and contemporarily oppressed groups.

Internalized Oppression Among Other Oppressed Groups

Within the United States, noted community psychologist Edison Trickett (1991) described the current racial climate as one that is consistent with the idea of oppression, as he stated that "the opportunities (in the country) are not randomly (or equally) distributed across race...and social structures are not equally supportive for minorities..." (pp. 213-214). Thus, the historical and contemporary oppression that various minority groups in the United States have experienced may be seen as one of *internal colonialism*. Although there is no recent forceful entry by a foreign group, which is the first phase of classical colonialism, internal colonialism is analogous to classical colonialism in that the established society is characterized by racial inequalities, cultural imposition of the dominant group on the minority groups, cultural disintegration of the oppressed groups' indigenous culture, and cultural recreation of the oppressed groups' ethnic and cultural identities as defined by the dominant group.

Harrell's (1999) theoretical discussion of the psychological consequences of oppression among African Americans is an excellent example of how applicable the classical colonial model is in describing the experiences of oppressed American minority groups. In his analyses, Harrell (1999) used Fanon's (1965) term to describe an oppressive society – *Manichean*. A Manichean society is one that is essentially based on incompatible opposites such as good versus evil, light versus dark, white versus black (or brown), or more generally, the superior colonizer versus the inferior colonized other. In a Manichean society, anything that is of the dominated group, including language, physical traits, and cultural values and traditions, is ascribed with inferior, undesirable, or negative characteristics. Concurrently, anything that is of the dominant group is attached with superiority and desirability. Furthermore, a Manichean society also involves the destruction and reinterpretation of the history and culture of the oppressed through the eyes of the dominant group. Consequently, a Manichean society creates conditions that lead African Americans to develop self-hatred and encourage them to behave in self-destructive ways. Consistent with Fanon's and Harrell's theories, Tatum (1994) also proposed that colonialism, or more specifically, internal colonialism, is another possible explanation for the high rates of crime and delinquency among African Americans. She argued that crime and delinquency may be seen as the self-destructive behavioral responses to a society wherein opportunities for social mobility are limited because of one's race, which is commonly referred to as racial discrimination. More recently, stress associated with cultural adaptation (i.e., acculturative stress, which includes racism and racial discrimination; Berry, 2003) has been found to be associated with depression among African Americans (Walker, Wingate, Obasi, & Joiner, 2008). Furthermore, Walker and colleagues (2008) also found acculturative stress and ethnic identity – the extent to which members of an ethnic group positively value their heritage – to be moderating the link between depression and suicide among African Americans, in that depressed African Americans who do not positively regard their heritage are more likely to think about suicide.

Another oppressed minority group within the United States are Native Americans or American Indians. Among America's First Peoples, their experiences may be described as involving both classical and internal colonialism. The colonization that Native Americans or American Indians experienced and the colonizer's efforts to destroy and recreate the indigenous culture of America's First Peoples, as exemplified by the boarding school era, attempted genocide, and geographic displacement (i.e., relegating America's First Peoples to reservations), is argued to have led many Native Americans or American Indians to lose their cultural identity and spirituality (McBride, 2002). The internalization of such historical and contemporary forms of oppression is also argued to contribute to cultural isolation, vocational stresses, and problematic behaviors such as substance abuse and domestic violence among Native Americans or American Indians (McBride, 2002). Duran and Duran (1995) and Brave Heart (1998) also argued that internalized oppression is promoted and passed on intergenerationally by continued oppression, lack of opportunities to critically and accurately understand history, forced Americanization, and socialization – contemporary forms of oppression that may be seen as internal colonialism. Furthermore, using the colonial model and the theories of postcolonial scholars Fanon (1965), Freire (1970), and Memmi (1965), among others, Duran and Duran (1995), Brave Heart (1998), and McBride (2002) also argued that colonialism and contemporary forms of oppression that continue to send inferiorizing messages about Native American or American Indian identity (e.g., the drunk native stereotype) may contribute to the high rates of suicide, alcoholism, and domestic violence among America's First Peoples.

The salience of internalized oppression and its intergenerational transmission have also been described among Alaska Native Peoples (Napoleon, 1996). The oppression that Alaska Native Peoples experienced historically and contemporarily are argued to have resulted into historical trauma and passed on through intergenerational trauma, which contribute to the high rates of depression, suicide, domestic violence, and substance use among Alaska Native Peoples today (Napoleon, 1996). Similarly, the salience of internalized oppression and the intergenerational transmission of such a psychological consequence of oppression has also been observed among Jewish holocaust survivors and their children (e.g., Major, 1996; Sorscher & Cohen, 1997) and Japanese American internment camp survivors during World War II and their children (e.g., Nagata & Cheng, 2003; Nagata, Trierweiler, & Talbot, 1999).

Internalized oppression has also been identified as a salient phenomenon among Hispanic or Latino/a Americans (e.g., Cubans, Dominicans, Mexicans, Puerto Ricans, etc.). Hall (1994) argued that colonization – both historically and contemporarily – and its accompanying "domination model of assimilation" (pp. 309-310) lead many Hispanic or Latino/a Americans to believe that light skin is the most advantageous, attractive, and desirable skin color. The internalization of such a skin-color ideal that is perpetuated in American society consequently results in a perceived necessity among members of this group to become as white as possible in order for social mobility or acceptance. Similar to the effects of historical and contemporary oppression among Filipinos and Filipino Americans, this desire to shed one's natural, but societally undesired, physical traits has been argued to lead many Hispanic or Latino/a Americans to use "beauty" creams and other products such as bleach in order to whiten their skin, a phenomenon known as the *bleaching syndrome* (Hall, 1994). Indeed, according to Hall, many Hispanic or Latino/a Americans "will value and internalize all aspects of the mainstream culture – including the idealizations of light skin color – at the expense of their (heritage) culture" (p. 310). Empirically, using a Mexican American sample, Codina and Montalvo (1994) found that darker skin color and loss of Spanish culture (i.e., language) were associated with higher levels of depression, suggesting that historical and contemporary oppression negatively affects Hispanic or Latino/a Americans' mental health.

A specific Hispanic or Latino/a American ethnic group that has received some psychological research attention in terms of their experiences of internalized colonialism is the Puerto Rican population. Strikingly comparable to the colonial experiences of Filipinos, Puerto Ricans were also colonized by Spain in 1493 and were sold to the United States during the same Treaty of Paris in 1898. Puerto Rico remains an American territory and Puerto Ricans continue to be regarded as United States Nationals to this day. The effects of centuries of Spanish and American colonialism on the psychological experiences of modern day Puerto Ricans are remarkably similar to descriptions of the psychological consequences of Spanish and American colonialism among Filipinos and Filipino Americans (David & Okazaki's (2006a; 2006b). For instance, Varas-Diaz and Serrano-Garcia (2003) found that it is common for Puerto Ricans to (1) experience identity confusion, (2) feel ashamed of their ethnic and cultural identity, (3) feel inferior about being Puerto Rican, and (4) not have national pride. The quote below touches on this point.

> "One feels bad about being Puerto Rican when they highlight the bad things about one's country. They could say good things. Instead, they speak of the country's bad things, the people's bad attitudes. When they highlight the bad things, I feel ashamed of being Puerto Rican" (quoted by Varas-Diaz and Serrano-Garcia, 2003, p. 109).

Furthermore, Varas-Diaz and Serrano-Garcia (2003) also reported that Puerto Ricans despise the stereotypical and mythical perceptions often imposed on them by mainland Americans, including other Puerto Ricans who live in the mainland United States who may be more Americanized or assimilated into the American culture, a form of within-group discrimination between highly- and less-Americanized individuals that is also commonly found among Filipinos and Filipino Americans (described in detail in the following section). Finally, Varas-Diaz and Serrano-Garcia (2003) also found that negative emotions such as shame, anger, desperation, and disillusion were associated with what the researchers called "the Puerto Rican experience" (p. 112). A similar psychological phenomenon related to loss of cultural identity has also been observed among the indigenous Chamorro group in the currently United States colonized island of Guam (Perez, 2005), which interestingly, was also obtained by the United States from Spain during the Treaty of Paris in 1898 along with the Philippines and Puerto Rico.

Indeed, based on the existing psychological literature on the experiences of various historically and contemporarily oppressed groups, internalized oppression is a salient phenomenon that consistently has negative psychological and mental health consequences. Furthermore, it is clear that internalized oppression may be passed on to later generations through socialization and continued experiences of oppression. Let us now turn our attention to internalized oppression – or colonial mentality – as experienced by Filipinos and Filipino Americans. It should be noted at this point that although the term "internalized oppression" is what is often used in the scientific and scholarly literature, I will use this term interchangeably with "colonial mentality" throughout the rest of book. This is primarily because colonial mentality is the term often used in the Filipino and Filipino American community and thus, the term many Filipinos and Filipino Americans may be more familiar with (David & Okazaki, 2006a).

Colonial Mentality Among Filipino Americans

In her description of how centuries of colonialism (and, thus, oppression) may have affected the psychological experiences of

Filipinos and Filipino Americans, noted psychologist Maria Root (1997b) stated:

> "Four hundred years of combined colonization... widened the Filipino gene pool with the possibilities of lighter skin, hair, and eyes...Spain introduced colorism; preferential treatment was clearly associated with lighter skin color. Centuries of this education primed the Filipino for vulnerability to internalize American rules of race. Colorism and then racism inculcated the notions 'White is beautiful,' 'White is intelligent,' and 'White is powerful' in the psyches of many brown-hued Filipinos, thus inferiorizing the Filipino" (p. 81).

It has been argued that, among Filipinos and Filipino Americans, ideas of superiority, pleasantness, or desirability have been associated with, not just physical characteristics (Whiteness), but also anything American or Western – a condition of internalized colonialism popularly referred to as *Colonial Mentality* (David & Okazaki, 2006a; 2006b; Root, 1997b; Strobel, 2001). My mentor (Sumie Okazaki) and I (David & Okazaki, 2006b) conceptualized Colonial Mentality (CM) as being "...characterized by a perception of ethnic or cultural inferiority that is...a specific consequence of centuries of colonization under Spain and the U.S." and that it "...involves an automatic and uncritical rejection of anything Filipino and an automatic and uncritical preference for anything American" (p. 241). It is important to note, however, that although many Filipinos and Filipino Americans are argued to have internalized the historical and contemporary oppression they have faced, not all Filipinos and Filipino Americans may hold CM. This may be especially true for many of the Muslim Filipinos in the southern Philippine island group of Mindanao who has been resisting colonization and westernization ever since the beginning of Spanish occupation. The same can be said about the numerous existing indigenous tribes in modern day Philippines such as the Igorot, Ifugao, Negrito, Bagobo, Kalinga, and Tboli tribes, among many others, who continue to survive and thrive by living their lives in accordance to the indigenous ways. Furthermore, internalizing one's experiences of oppression is only one way in which one can respond to oppression. Another common way to react to oppression is to develop *cultural mistrust*, which is the theoretical opposite of colonial mentality because cultural mistrust refers to a general distrust of dominant peoples and the institutions they control due to past negative experiences with such people and institutions (cultural mistrust is discussed in further detail in Chapter 9). Therefore, it is important to remember that CM is conceptualized as an individual-differences variable whose existence and strength within Filipinos and Filipino Americans may greatly vary (David & Okazaki, 2006a).

Although the existence and strength of CM may vary among Filipinos and Filipino Americans, scholars and community leaders have nonetheless speculated that CM is prevalent among members of this ethnic group. Fred Cordova (1973), a distinguished Filipino American historian, argued that colonialism and the accompanying cultural imposition, cultural disintegration, and cultural recreation have contributed to the ever-present Filipino *ethnic/cultural identity crisis* – confusion as to what constitutes an authentic Filipino culture and identity. Because Filipino culture and history is often presented in a mythical, distorted, and inferiorizing manner (as tackled in Part I), such an identity crisis is believed to lead Filipino Americans toward the conclusion that there is no authentic Filipino culture and identity that one can be proud of, and thus, may lead to the perception of inferiority toward anything Filipino (David & Okazaki, 2006a; David, 2010a). Lott (1976) also discussed the common presence of such a condition among contemporary Filipino Americans, which she attributed to the continued subjugation or oppression of this group within the United States (i.e., internal colonialism) and the likelihood that immigrant Filipinos may have brought with them such a condition from the persistently Americanized postcolonial Philippines. An analysis of Filipino American student essays and community newsletters suggest that CM is indeed a common phenomenon within this ethnic group (Revilla, 1997). Bergano and Bergano-Kinney (1997) also estimated that at least half the Filipino American population has some form of CM or internalized oppression.

In terms of its impact on the Filipino American population, editorials in Filipino American community publications cite CM as a major reason for the lack of societal presence, political clout, and social unity of the Filipino American community, and the lack of cultural pride, historical knowledge, and cultural appreciation among Filipino and Filipino American individuals (e.g., Gaston, 2003). Furthermore, CM has also been found to negatively influence the psychological experiences and mental health of Filipinos and Filipino Americans, with CM being associated to lower levels of self-esteem and more depression symptoms (e.g., David, 2008; David & Okazaki, 2006b) (the psychological and mental health consequences of colonial mentality are described in more detail in Chapters 7, 8, and 9). Thus, based on scholarly and community discourse, CM seems to be a common and problematic phenomenon among Filipinos and Filipino Americans.

Capturing and Measuring Colonial Mentality

In our effort to assess, quantify, and more systematically study the psychological construct of CM and its impact on Filipinos and Filipino Americans, my mentor and I (David & Okazaki, 2006b) used methods called *exploratory and confirmatory factor analyses* that are commonly utilized in the field of psychology to develop psychometrically-sound tests or measures to help us create the Colonial Mentality Scale (CMS) (examples of CMS items are provided in Figure 7).

The CMS					
I find persons with lighter skin-tones to be more attractive than persons with dark skin-tones.					
Strongly Disagree	Disagree	Somewhat Disagree	Somewhat Agree	Agree	Strongly Agree
1	2	3	4	5	6
There are situations where I feel inferior because of my ethnic/cultural background.					
Strongly Disagree	Disagree	Somewhat Disagree	Somewhat Agree	Agree	Strongly Agree
1	2	3	4	5	6
I generally think that a person that is part white and part Filipino is more attractive than a full-blooded Filipino.					
Strongly Disagree	Disagree	Somewhat Disagree	Somewhat Agree	Agree	Strongly Agree
1	2	3	4	5	6
I generally do not like newly-arrived Filipino immigrants.					
Strongly Disagree	Disagree	Somewhat Disagree	Somewhat Agree	Agree	Strongly Agree
1	2	3	4	5	6
Filipinos should be thankful to Spain and the United States for transforming the Filipino ways of life into a White/European American ways of life.					
Strongly Disagree	Disagree	Somewhat Disagree	Somewhat Agree	Agree	Strongly Agree
1	2	3	4	5	6

Figure 7. Example items from the Colonial Mentality Scale

The CMS is composed of 36 items that are believed to be common manifestations of CM among Filipinos and Filipino Americans. People taking the CMS are asked to rate their level of agreement to each of these statements, and higher CMS scores suggest stronger presence of CM. Using data obtained from over 600 Filipino Americans from all over the United States, we found that CM may be manifested or expressed covertly (e.g., feelings of shame, embarrassment, and inferiority) and overtly (e.g., desiring to look and behave more White, discriminating against less Americanized Filipinos). Below is an example of covert CM manifestations such as feeling shame, embarrassment, and inferiority because of one's Filipino heritage as expressed by a young Filipina American (as quoted by Revilla, 1997) (parenthetical comments are added):

> "Throughout my days at elementary school I had an acute fear that someone would discover that I was Filipino…There were…derisive nicknames created by students (e.g., 'FOBs' or 'bukbok'), and a large number of stereotypes expounded and attributed to Filipinos. They were labeled as being stupid, backwards, and capable of only the most menial jobs available…In my own experiences, I knew that these generalizations were false, but still I feared association with them. These images and stereotypes persisted in the consciousness of the student body for so long that I began to look at being Filipino as a curse. It embarrassed me that I should be a part of a race so disregarded and dehumanized by society" (p. 101).

Also, psychologist Root (1997b) had argued that many Filipinos might have equated being American or White to being beautiful and intelligent. For example, it is common for Filipinos or Filipino Americans to refrain from basking under the sun to avoid getting too dark, pinch their noses to make them "less flat" and look more White, believe that "marrying-up" means marrying a White person, and to generally perceive that Filipinos with White ancestry are more attractive than full-blooded Filipinos (e.g., Gaston, 2003; Revilla, 1997; Root, 1997b). Such descriptions are consistent with what my mentor and I (David & Okazaki, 2006b) considered as overt CM manifestations. Below are examples of how Filipinos and Filipino Americans may desire to look and behave more White or Western, or to regard European physical characteristics such as having a lighter skin tone and bridged nose as more attractive and desirable:

> "...white skin is considered better. I cannot tell you how many products are advertised and sold (in the Philippines) to 'whiten' our skin. Marrying a white man for Filipinas is a step up...socially and economically. Mixed children by white men...are thought of as more valuable, precious, and better prepared for modern society. This mentality isn't new. Many of the elders...believe 'White is right.' All white boyfriends, husbands, and mixed children are shown off...as trophies." (Expressed by a Filipina American, as quoted by Bergano & Bergano-Kinney, 1997, p. 202).

> "My ambition as a kid was to be like an American. We'd been taught in school that the Americans were our saviors, that they brought us democracy. When I saw cowboy-and-Indian movies, I always rooted for the cowboys. I preferred American-style clothes. Americans were rich, handsome and superior. Jesus Christ and the Virgin Mary looked like Americans, with their white skins and long noses. I degraded Filipinos because they were ugly, with flat noses and brown skins. But I was also ugly. I wasn't a good student, and could not speak English well." (Expressed by a young man from the Philippines, as quoted by Karnow, 1989, p. 17).

Another display of overt CM among Filipinos and Filipino Americans is the common use of English proficiency as an indicator or measure of status and intelligence (Karnow, 1989). Those who cannot speak English or those who speak it with a Filipino accent are reported to be given subjugating labels such as "FOB" (fresh-off-the-boat), "backward," or "bukbok," among others. Based on her longitudinal interviews with eight Filipino Americans, Strobel (1997) stated that, "A newly arrived immigrant who speaks a variety of Filipino English can be discriminated against by other Filipinos who speak fluent 'standard' English because the former's language is often associated with inferiority, lack of intelligence, and 'otherness.' This arrogant perception is based on the assumption that 'standard' English is a universal norm and…marker of intelligence" (p.74). Such a colonial attitude toward the English language, and thus CM manifestation, is also common among Filipinos in the Philippines. An example of this is expressed by a Filipino in the Philippines who is advocating for the use of local languages for school instruction:

> "As I go around the country (The Philippines) to advocate for mother tongue based multilingual education, I am aghast to see the extent of colonial mentality among our people. Parents reject the use of the mother tongue in school believing that we are depriving their children of English. It does not matter that their grade one children end up not understanding what they read and would resort to memorization and rote learning, as long that they are able to parrot 'good morning' and 'how are you.' When our Asian neighbors like Japan and South Korea are at the top in international Science and Math tests, we rank at the bottom because we insist in using English, a second language, to teach difficult and abstract concepts. " (in personal communication with author)

In addition, my mentor and I (David and Okazaki, 2006a) also argued that such forms of colonial and discriminative attitudes among Filipinos and Filipino Americans can also extend beyond language to other aspects of culture such as mannerisms, values, clothing, and interests, in that those who display characteristics that are associated with being Filipino are teased, berated, ignored, discriminated against, or are called by the derogatory terms mentioned above (e.g., "FOB," "bukbok," etc.). We termed this overt form of CM as Within-Group Discrimination (David and Okazaki, 2006b), and an example is expressed by a 26-year old Filipina American below:

> "My idea…of Filipino culture and identity is split into two forms: the FOB…and the Filipino American. I didn't associate with FOBs. They were backward, had accents, and just acted weird…Then there was me, the non-"FOB," who spoke perfect English, born and raised here, had only white friends…I was "white" in every way except for the color of my skin, my nose, and eyes…I hate to admit but I have been an accomplice to the cruel acts that have been perpetrated against Filipinos." (as quoted by Strobel, 1997, p.67).

Furthermore, related to the notion of the Golden Legend that the indigenous Tao did not have anything of value prior to Spanish and American colonialism (as discussed in Part I), which promotes the concept of Colonial Debt, CM may also be expressed in beliefs and behaviors that portray Spanish and American colonialism as solely positive and necessary. In other words, many Filipinos and Filipino Americans today may express CM by simplistically regarding Spanish and American colonialism as civilizing and liberating, and thus, necessary experiences, which gives way to potentially minimizing the historical and contemporary injustices and maltreatments that Filipinos and Filipino Americans faced and are still facing. For example, when writing about his experiences and observations of other Filipino Americans, Dario Villa (1995) illustrates how colonial debt (as insisted by the "Golden Legend") may be displayed by many Filipino Americans:

> "I know many Filipinos (in America who) would deny that they have been discriminated against. Too many are so thankful to be (in America) that they shut their eyes to avoid seeing the injustices, political and economic injustices. This type of attitude stifles our community." (p. 179).

Connie Tirona (1995), narrating one of her experiences with discrimination at a hospital in San Diego in which she stood up for herself, provides another support for the existence of colonial debt:

> "So after that incident, they started sensitivity courses there at the hospital. So you have to complain. If you sit back and don't say anything, they tend to walk all over you. And I think for the most part, Filipinos have a colonial mentality. They tend to not do anything." (p. 79).

The descriptions of CM manifestations that are presented above reveal that CM may be expressed in a variety of ways, and suggests that a person may endorse overt CM but not covert CM, endorse covert CM but not overt CM, endorse both types, or endorse neither. Furthermore, using the CMS, we found that approximately 30% of our sample (David & Okazaki, 2006b) endorsed at least one type of CM manifestation, suggesting that many, 3 out of 10 Filipino Americans, hold CM.

In addition to describing how CM may manifest itself among Filipinos and Filipino Americans, some of the quotations presented above also touch on the mechanisms in which CM may be passed on from one generation to the next. More specifically, continued experiences of contemporary oppression such as the ascription of negative and undesirable stereotypes may lead Filipinos and Filipino Americans to feel ashamed, embarrassed, or inferior for being Filipino, or may lead them toward wanting to become more White or Westernized in their appearances and behaviors. Furthermore, such experiences of oppression may even lead Filipinos and Filipino Americans to discriminate against others with Filipino heritage who are perceived to possess Filipino characteristics that have been associated with inferiority, undesirability, or backwardness. In addition to oppressive messages about their heritage that Filipinos and Filipino Americans receive from the general society, CM may also be passed on intergenerationally through familial socialization (e.g., learning from their parents that lighter skin is more attractive, seeing their relatives make fun of someone for speaking English with a Filipino accent, hearing family members talk negatively about the Philippines and Filipinos in the Philippines, etc.) that sends such Filipino inferiorizing messages as well. Below is an example of how Filipino and Filipino American parents may pass on CM to their children:

> "A lot of Filipinos prefer light skin. They think it's beautiful. Even my mom would say so. She hates it when I get dark from being outside too much. I remember that she would say that I looked 'ugly' because I was so dark…and it seems that many other moms feel that way too from hearing stories from other Filipino kids." (Expressed by a 21-year old Filipina American during the Filipino American Decolonization Experience, discussed in Chapter 11)

Following is another example of how CM may be passed on from one generation to the next. In addition, the quotation below also touches on how CM elicits intense negative emotions such as anger, distress, confusion, and self-hate that may lead to serious mental health concerns.

> "My father is Filipino-American. He was born in San Francisco, CA in...(the 1930s). I feel deeply saddened to say it, but my father was a victim of the 'colonial mentality.' My mother is (of European ancestry)...I truly believe my father married my mother simply to improve his status in the U.S. and to produce the ideal 'mestiza' child, namely me. I grew up with my father worshipping my 'half white' status. Of course, as a teenager, I felt superior because of my mestiza look and bloodline. I grew up 'ignoring' and sometimes 'hating' my Filipino side, just as my father has done. My father died (some years) ago and my eyes opened up to the truth. My mother treated my father as a 'house negro.' He would do anything for her, even though she cheated on him and basically treated him like an errand boy. She would often brag to me how she could get him to do anything she wanted him to do...I guess the point I'm trying to say here is I was deeply affected by my father's 'colonial mentality.' I, too, was caught up in the colonial mentality. At the moment, I'm in an identity crisis, a war within myself. I feel 'white guilt.' I feel ashamed for being 'half white.' I feel horrible that my father hated himself so much for being Filipino. I feel like I'm half oppressed and half oppressor. It sucks to say the least." (Expressed by a 37-year old Filipina American, in personal communication with author)

The experiences expressed by the person above is, unfortunately, very common among the Filipino and Filipino American population.

Many, approximately 22% or 1 out of 5 (Nadal, 2009) Filipinos and Filipino Americans, primarily due to colonialism, are of mixed race ancestry (e.g., meztizos/as). Among Filipino Americans, even those who are not of mixed race may experience such conflicts between their Filipino and American identities, both of which are important to them and are salient parts of their selves or identities. As shown in the quotation, regarding any part of our self or of our identity as negative or undesirable can lead to intense psychological distress and mental health concerns. Thus, this is one way in which CM may negatively influence the mental health of Filipinos and Filipino Americans (the mental health consequences of CM are described in more detail in Chapter 9).

Chapter Summary

Various oppressed groups within the United States (e.g., African Americans, Latino/a or Hispanic Americans, American Indians or Native Americans, etc.) and around the world (e.g., the different countries in Africa) consistently report that internalized oppression is common among many of their members (e.g., David, 2009; David & Okazaki, 2006a; Duran & Duran, 1995; Harrell, 1999; Napoleon, 1996). Furthermore, internalized oppression seems to have negative psychological effects among those who experience it. Moreover, research suggests that internalized oppression may be passed on intergenerationally through familial socialization and continued experiences of oppression (e.g., internal colonialism, neocolonialism, or contemporary forms of oppression such as microaggressions). Similarly, the literature on Filipinos and Filipino Americans also suggest that colonial mentality (CM) – a specific form of internalized oppression that has its roots in colonialism and has been transmitted through the generations by more contemporary forms of oppression such as neocolonialism and internal colonialism – is a salient psychological construct among members of this group. Based on the literature on CM among Filipinos and Filipino Americans (David & Okazaki, 2006a; 2006b), members of this group may express CM in a variety of ways including: (1) feelings of shame, embarrassment, and inferiority for being Filipino and for Filipino cultural behaviors, values, traditions, foods, and others; (2) regarding Filipino physical characteristics such as having brown skin and flat noses as less attractive than European physical characteristics such as having light skin and bridged noses; (3) discriminating against other individuals with Filipino heritage who cannot speak English well or who are perceived to be less Westernized or Americanized in terms of their mannerisms, values, and behaviors; and (4) simplistically regarding historical colonialism and contemporary oppression as the natural cost for progress or civilization, to the point that one may minimize experiences of injustice and not stand up against them. The different types of CM manifestations among Filipinos and Filipino Americans are summarized in Table 1.

As can be extracted from the descriptions and examples of the various CM manifestations provided in this chapter, historical colonialism and contemporary oppression has influenced how Filipinos and Filipino Americans perceive and feel about themselves (e.g., possessing inferior characteristics), perceive and feel about other individuals with Filipino heritage (e.g., as backwards or less attractive), and perceive and feel about their past colonizers or others with similar characteristics (e.g., Europeans or Westernized individuals as more attractive and superior). Cognitions (thoughts) and attitudes usually determine, or at least partly influence, our behaviors (Beck, 1995). Thus, the colonial perceptions and attitudes of Filipinos and Filipino Americans can easily lead to colonial behaviors toward themselves (e.g., using skin-whitening products), toward other individuals with Filipino heritage (e.g., discriminating against or not associating with less-Westernized or less-Americanized Filipinos), and their past colonizers or those with similar characteristics (e.g., not standing up against discrimination and injustice). It is clear from the empirical and theoretical literature that was reviewed in this chapter that colonialism and contemporary oppression have influenced the psychological experiences of Filipinos and Filipino Americans.

Table 1. Types and Descriptions of Colonial Mentality Manifestations

Category	Description	Examples
Covert Manifestations		
Internalized Inferiority	Tendency to feel inferior about one's Filipino ethnicity and culture	Regarding anything that is "Made in the USA" as automatically better than anything made in the Philippines
Cultural Shame and Embarrassment	Tendency to feel ashamed and embarrassed toward the Filipino culture	Denying one's Filipino heritage; claiming to be of mixed heritage
Overt Manifestations		
Physical Characteristics	Tendency to perceive Filipino physical traits as inferior to White physical traits	Using skin-whitening products; staying from the sun; fear of getting too dark
Within-Group Discrimination	Tendency to discriminate against less-Americanized or less-Westernized Filipinos	Teasing or berating FOBs or those with thick Filipino accents; not associating with newly-arrived immigrants
Colonial Debt	Tendency to feel fortunate for having being colonized and to feel indebted toward their past colonizers	Believing that the indigenous Tao had nothing before Western colonialism; not standing up against discrimination

*   *   *

As discussed in this chapter, in our desire to generate more scientific and societal attention to the construct of CM as experienced by Filipinos and Filipino Americans, my mentor and I (David & Okazaki, 2006b) developed a measurement tool that can easily be used to capture and quantify CM (i.e., the Colonial Mentality Scale, or CMS), with the hope that the availability of such a tool will increase systematic research focused on the psychological and mental health consequences of colonialism and oppression. Although there is psychometric evidence supporting the reliability and validity of this measurement tool, and that this self-report tool can be used as one indicator of the presence and strength of CM among Filipino and Filipino American individuals, it is not perfect. Just like other psychological constructs (e.g., depression, intelligence, self-esteem, etc.), CM or internalized oppression is a complex and abstract phenomenon that is very difficult, if not impossible, to perfectly capture and measure. Furthermore, given the sensitive and self-threatening nature of the CM construct, it is likely that some individuals may find it difficult to admit and/or disclose the presence of CM-consistent thoughts, attitudes, and behaviors within themselves. Thus, because the CMS is limited in this way, we need other tools that can serve as another indicator or measure of CM and complement the CMS in order to more accurately and completely capture the complex psychological construct of CM, and allow us to further understand its psychological and mental health implications. The next chapter will discuss the automaticity of CM and how it may exist and operate among Filipinos and Filipino Americans without their awareness, intention, or control.

CHAPTER 6

AUTOMATICITY OF COLONIAL MENTALITY

ᜎᜒᜊᜒᜇᜓᜊᜓᜍᜒᜑ ᜅ ᜃᜎᜒᜎ ᜅ
ᜎᜒᜈᜒᜈᜒᜏᜒ

Although the Colonial Mentality Scale (CMS) allows for an easy and systematic assessment of colonial mentality (CM), it is not without limitations. For instance, some Filipinos and Filipino Americans may not endorse the covert manifestations of CM for a variety of reasons (e.g., they discriminate against less Americanized Filipinos but do not necessarily feel ashamed of the Filipino culture; they are unaware of presence of covert CM; they are denying that they feel ashamed, embarrassed, or inferior for being Filipino; etc.). Indeed, because it is difficult to admit that one may be ashamed or embarrassed of one's Filipino heritage or of the Filipino culture, it is easy to hide such feelings and refrain from endorsing them through the CMS. The possibility that one may feel inferior because of one's Filipino heritage may also be difficult to admit, or if true, difficult to disclose. Thus, simply asking if such is the case – which is what the CMS does – may be limited because Filipinos and Filipino

Americans may easily deny it. Furthermore, I know many Filipinos and Filipino Americans who outwardly express their pride for being Filipino, but at the same time also see them make fun of FOBs, regard English proficiency as a marker of intelligence, and perceive the effects of Spanish and American colonialism as absolutely positive. Even though the CMS attempts to tap into both the overt and covert aspects of CM, it is still only a direct, explicit, and introspection-dependent self-report questionnaire that may be more oriented toward capturing the overt manifestations of CM. Several of our findings (David & Okazaki, 2006b) are suggestive of such a limitation. For example, we found that fewer individuals admitted to holding covert CM than overt CM, and only about 30% of the sample endorsed at least one type of CM manifestation, which is a lower frequency estimate of CM than what some scholars have suggested (e.g., Bergano & Bergano-Kinney, 1997; Pido, 1997; Revilla, 1997). Thus, the CMS is not a perfect measure of CM.

Furthermore, CM is conceptualized as involving "an *automatic* and uncritical rejection of anything Filipino and an *automatic* and uncritical preference for anything American" (David & Okazaki, 2006b, p. 241). Thus, in theory, there are two critical characteristics of CM: (1) it involves associating Filipino-related objects with inferiority, unpleasantness, or undesirability and American-related objects with superiority, pleasantness, or desirability; and (2) *it may operate automatically without intention or control*. Given that some aspect of CM is theorized to operate automatically, introspection-dependent self-report tools to measure CM such as the CMS may be insufficient to assess its implicit or automatic aspect. That is, CM may exist and operate among Filipinos and Filipino Americans without them even knowing it, even if they do not intentionally try to behave in CM-consistent ways, or even if they deny it. Therefore, a more subtle, implicit, or indirect method of measuring CM may provide a more accurate estimate of CM frequency and how it influences the psychological experiences and mental health of modern day Filipinos and Filipino Americans. Fortunately, there is an emerging body of research in implicit social cognition that may provide us with conceptual frameworks and methodological paradigms to go "beyond questionnaires" (Okazaki, 2002) in order to better capture and understand the automatic and possibly less consciously accessible aspect of CM. To this end, this chapter will summarize studies and experiments that suggest that the Filipino and Filipino American mind may have been shaped by historical and contemporary experiences of oppression in a way that is consistent with internalized oppression or CM, and that CM may operate automatically within Filipinos and Filipino Americans without their awareness, intention, or control. A more complete and detailed description of such experiments may be found in previously published papers (David, 2010b; David & Okazaki, 2010). Let us begin with a basic explanation of social cognition paradigms.

Social Cognition Paradigms

In the field of psychology, scholars agree that there are two types of cognitions or thoughts – conscious and unconscious (Greenwald & Banaji, 1995). This widely accepted notion has its roots from implicit memory research, which has empirically demonstrated that past experiences (i.e., learning or exposure) unconsciously or implicitly influence later performance (e.g., recall). The acknowledgment that unconscious memory (or learning) exists has been documented as early as the late 1800s (Ebbinghaus, 1885/1964; Freud & Breuer, 1895/1960) and has been more recently supplemented by studies investigating implicit memory among amnesics (Baddeley & Warrington, 1970; Milner, Corkin, & Teuber, 1968) and implicit retention among participants with no memory problems (e.g., Jacoby, 1988). Perhaps some of the best examples to serve as evidence for the notion that implicit learning exists is the fact that many of us, after several years of practice, may no longer specifically and explicitly remember how we learned to ride a bike, drive a car, or type on a computer keyboard. For many of us, these skills are now automatic – we do not even have to consciously, purposefully, and deliberately think about all of the complex steps we need to follow in order to perform these tasks properly. These skills are now imprinted within us, whether we remember or not remember all of the events in our lives that contributed to us developing and refining such complex behaviors and the cognitions behind them. In a way, we are now able to do these complex tasks automatically and perhaps unconsciously, without much effort.

The existence and influence of implicit memory or learning are further supported by more contemporary psychological research. Typically, participants are exposed to, or *primed* with, a word such as "DOG" in the beginning of a study and then later asked to complete several tests, including word fragment completion (e.g., D _ G and C _ T), word stem completion (e.g., D _ _ and C _ _), word identification (presenting the word "DOG" and "CAT" rapidly on a computer screen and asking participants to report what they saw), anagram solution (e.g., GDO and TCA), and picture fragment identification (e.g., showing an incomplete picture of a dog and a cat), among others (Roediger, 1990; Roediger, et al., 1992). Priming is said to occur when individuals perform better or remember better the studied (or previously exposed) words (i.e., "DOG") than non-studied words (i.e., "CAT") in these tests. Also, notice that most of the dependent tasks that are typically given to individuals after they are exposed to the primes (as presented above) may be completed in multiple ways, such as "DIG" for word fragment completion, "DOT" in word stem completion, and "GOD" for anagram solution. Priming is also said to occur if participants who were primed with (or exposed to) the word "DOG" in the beginning of the study consequently respond with the word "DOG" instead of the other possible responses in the subsequent dependent task. In other words, their previous and most recent exposure to certain stimuli primed them, or prepared them, to respond in a particular way. Finally, implicit memory research have also shown that prior exposure (e.g., learning) to an object or stimulus may later influence a person's ability to remember or identify the object or stimulus even if the person cannot explicitly remember being exposed to (or learning about) the stimulus; hence the term *implicit learning*. People can learn without them even knowing that they did.

The priming paradigm described above has since been extended to test the *spreading activation theory* of cognition, which states that the human mind is composed of a complex network of nodes (representing concepts) and links (representing associations or relations between concepts) and that exposure to a particular stimulus (e.g., the word "MOTHER" or seeing one's mother) will activate the corresponding node (i.e., the "mother" node) in one's cognitive network which, in turn, activates other linked nodes (e.g., "loving," "caring," etc. if a person's experience with his/her mother is that she is loving, caring, etc.) that a person may have developed through learning and experience (e.g., Anderson & Pirolli, 1984; Collins & Loftus, 1975; Fazio, et al., 1986). In other words, the activation of one node (concept) spreads to activate other nodes that represent other thoughts that we have associated with the originally activated node through our learning or experiences. One way to explain this is by using Charles Manson as an example. For those of us who have heard of Charles Manson and what he did, if we see his picture or hear his name (stimulus), it will activate neurons in our brains that correspond to thoughts such as "evil," "bad person," "murderer," and perhaps other negative thoughts that we have associated with Charles Manson because of what we have been taught about him (our learning experiences). However, for those of us who may have never heard of Charles Manson before and have no idea what he did, if we see his picture or hear his name, it will not activate anything in our minds because we have not learned to associate "Charles Manson" with anything – positive nor negative. This is the basic idea behind the spreading activation theory.

Taking this theory another step, research has also shown that exposure to a particular stimulus and the resulting chain or spread of activation may also function outside of a person's awareness or control. That is, the activation of the other associated nodes representing other thoughts may take place even without our conscious awareness that such activations are happening. Using the popular semantic priming paradigm (e.g., Neely, 1977), where participants are presented or primed with a word and then asked to perform a consequent task after the prime, numerous studies have found evidence supporting the notion that judgments or actions may be influenced by unperceived stimuli (the prime) that automatically activates the cognitive network which, in turn, guides consequent judgment or action (e.g., Balota, 1983; Bornstein, 1992; Fazio, et al., 1986; Fazio, et al., 1995; Greenwald, Klinger, & Liu, 1989; Perdue, et al., 1990). The priming paradigm has also been used to demonstrate that mere exposure to highly emotionally-valenced objects or words (e.g., "DEATH") automatically activates and increases the accessibility of the corresponding affective or attitudinal evaluation (e.g., UNPLEASANT), suggesting that evaluations of or attitudes toward objects are automatically activated and may operate outside of one's awareness, intention, or control (e.g., Draine & Greenwald, 1998; Greenwald, Draine, & Abrams, 1996). Thus, in this area of research, priming no longer simply refers to implicit learning as in implicit memory research, but also *implicit activation* of particular attitudes, emotions, judgments, and behaviors (Greenwald, Klinger, & Schuh, 1995).

Cultural Priming

More recently in the field of psychology, the priming technique has been applied to the study of culture, demonstrating that cultural influences on psychological processes may be investigated using indirect methodologies or procedures that do not depend on accurate introspection and self-report. For example, the cultural priming technique has been used to study cultural cognition (e.g., Benet-Martinez, & Haritatos, 2005; Benet-Martinez, Leu, Lee, & Morris, 2002; Hong, Chiu, & Kong, 1997; Hong, Morris, Chiu, & Benet-Martinez, 2000), cultural differences in self-construals (e.g.,

Gardner, Gabriel, & Lee, 1999; Trafimow, Silverman, Fan, & Law, 1997; Trafimow, Triandis, & Goto, 1991), and in activating the salience of one's racial, ethnic, or gender identity (e.g., Ambady, Shih, Kim, & Pittinsky, 2001; Devos, 2006; Steele, 1997; Steele & Aronson, 1995). Of particular relevance to the study of CM or internalized oppression is the study by Hong, Chiu, and Kung (1997). Hong and her colleagues primed Hong Kong biculturals, who are believed to have internalized two separate cultural knowledge systems (Western and Chinese) because of Hong Kong's long colonial history under British rule, with pictures of either Western cultural icons or Chinese cultural icons to activate either their Western cultural knowledge system or their Chinese cultural knowledge system, respectively. Next, all participants were asked to interpret an ambiguous stimulus (i.e., a picture of a school of fish, wherein one fish was swimming separately and ahead of the other fish). They found that those primed with Western cultural pictures interpreted the ambiguous stimulus in a more individualistic manner (e.g., the lone fish is the leader), whereas those primed with Chinese cultural pictures interpreted the fish picture in a more collectivistic manner (e.g., the group of fish is chasing the lone fish). Such results suggest that Hong Kong biculturals have internalized two sets of cultures and that their Chinese cultural knowledge system involves the concept of collectivism whereas their Western cultural knowledge system involves the concept of individualism. Hong and her colleagues concluded that activating a particular cultural knowledge system may influence later behavior or judgment so that it is consistent with the activated cultural system.

Based on their findings, Hong and colleagues (2000) formally proposed the *Dynamic Constructivist Approach* to the study of culture and cognition. They argued that many bicultural individuals possess two internalized cultures that take turns in guiding their thoughts, feelings, and behaviors. Furthermore, they stated that "…internalized culture (is) a network of discrete, specific constructs that guide cognition only when they come to the fore in an individual's mind" (p. 709) and that "...activation of (a particular) cultural knowledge (system or network) may have important influences on (consequent) emotions and motives as well as judgments and decisions..." (p. 718). For many ethnic and cultural minority groups, their experiences of their heritage ethnicity or culture may involve constant denigration and oppression, which they might internalize. For Filipinos and Filipino Americans, it is possible that their Filipino cultural knowledge system involves ideas of inferiority, undesirability, or unpleasantness, whereas their American cultural knowledge system involves ideas of superiority, desirability, or pleasantness. Indeed, the existence of such a cultural knowledge construction will be indicative of the extent to which oppression has been internalized and CM exists among these individuals. Thus, can the priming techniques described above be used to activate and observe such a CM-consistent cultural knowledge system among Filipino Americans? If so, can we activate it implicitly or indirectly and test whether CM may be activated automatically?

Due to centuries of classical and internal colonialism (as discussed in Part I), many Filipinos' Filipino cultural knowledge system may indeed now be developed in such a way that it includes ideas of inferiority, shame, and unpleasantness, whereas their American cultural knowledge system may include ideas of superiority, desirability, and pleasantness. Such a possibility is consistent with learning theories in the field of psychology. Thus, when the Filipino cultural system is activated, the activation may influence or guide an individual to make an unpleasant, negative, or undesirable interpretation of an ambiguous stimulus. Similarly, it is possible that when the American cultural system is activated, such activation may influence or guide an individual to make a pleasant, positive, or desirable interpretation of the same ambiguous stimulus. Such possibilities are consistent with the spreading activation theory in the field of psychology. Thus, based on the literature on learning and cognition, priming, spreading activation, the dynamic constructivist approach to culture and cognition (as discussed earlier in this chapter), internalized oppression as experienced by various groups (as discussed in Chapter 5), and CM among Filipinos and Filipino Americans (as described in Chapter 5), it is possible that a CM-consistent cultural knowledge system construction – one that indicates inferior perceptions of the Filipino culture and superior perceptions of the American culture – can be observed using social cognition methods. To capture such a CM-consistent cultural knowledge system, my mentor and I (David & Okazaki, 2010) initially conducted two simple priming experiments that I describe next.

Activating Colonial Mentality

Using data from 172 self-identified Filipino Americans from all over the United States, my mentor and I (David & Okazaki, 2010) tested for the first time if CM or a CM-consistent cultural knowledge system may be activated using social cognition methods. We randomly assigned the participants into two conditions: the Filipino condition and the American condition. The Filipino condition contained 81 participants and the American condition contained 91 participants. A series of statistical tests suggested that participants between the two conditions did not vary significantly in several demographic characteristics such as sex, age, marital status, educational level, income, generational status, and membership in Filipino American organizations, suggesting that random assignment was successful in equalizing the two groups and controlling for possible confounding variables.

We borrowed the word fragment completion (WFC) task often used in implicit memory research (e.g., Rajaram & Roediger, 1993; Roediger, et al., 1992) and used it as a way to activate either the American cultural knowledge system or the Filipino cultural knowledge system. Activating one of the cultural systems will make related constructs in the particular system more accessible and, as mentioned above, "the more accessible a construct, the more likely it

is to come to the fore in the individual's mind and guide interpretation (of an ensuing ambiguous stimulus)" (Hong, et al., 2000, pp. 710-711). There were two separate WFC tasks used in this experiment, one containing Filipino cultural terms and the other containing American cultural terms. We generated 10 common terms that are easily and clearly identifiable as belonging to either the Filipino culture (five terms) or the American culture (five terms) in order to activate either the Filipino or the American cultural knowledge system. We also generated one word fragment that may be completed in two different and oppositely-valenced manner –
_ _ _ ERIOR. This word fragment, which serves as the dependent variable, may be completed either as "Superior" or "Inferior" (or other possibilities such as "Interior," "Exterior," "Ulterior," etc.) and was presented as the last word fragment in both the Filipino and American WFC lists. Participants randomly assigned to the Filipino condition completed the Filipino WFC task, whereas participants who were randomly assigned to the American condition completed the American WFC task (Table 2).

Table 2. Word Fragment Completion Tasks Used to Activate Colonial Mentality

Word Completion Tasks	
American Culture Priming Condition	Filipino Culture Priming Condition
AMER_CA_S	FILI_I_OS
UNI_ED S_ATES	PHIL_P_INES
ENGL_S_	TAGA_O_
W_SHIN_TON	M_NI_A
WHIT_	BRO_N
_ _ _ ERIOR	_ _ _ ERIOR

Under "normal" circumstances, or if the priming conditions did not have an effect, the number of participants who answer "Inferior" in the last word (i.e., _ _ _ ERIOR) of the Filipino condition should not be significantly higher than the number of participants who answer "Inferior" in the American condition; and the number of "Superior" responses in the Filipino condition should not be lower than "Superior" responses in the American condition. That is, because participants were randomly assigned to the conditions, there should be no such differences in the distribution of responses between the two conditions if CM does not exist or if a CM-consistent cultural knowledge system was not activated within some Filipinos and Filipino Americans. However, because of Filipinos' and Filipino Americans' extensive experiences of oppression that we believe may have led to the development of CM, we predicted that such "normal" circumstances will not apply to our sample. Therefore, we hypothesized that the number of participants in the American condition who will fill-in the last word so that it is "Superior" will be significantly higher than participants in the Filipino condition who answers "Superior." On the other hand, it was also predicted that the number of participants in the Filipino condition who will fill-in the same word fragment so that it is "Inferior" will be significantly higher than the number of participants in the American condition who answers "Inferior."

Our results showed that about 27% of Filipino Americans primed to think of the Filipino culture interpreted the ambiguous stimulus (i.e., _ _ _ ERIOR) as "Inferior," whereas only 11% of Filipino Americans primed to think of the American culture interpreted the ambiguous stimulus as "Inferior." Instead, about 72% of Filipino Americans primed to think of the American culture interpreted the ambiguous stimulus as "Superior" compared to only about 57% of Filipino Americans primed to think of the Filipino culture who interpreted the ambiguous stimulus as "Superior." More

Filipino Americans in the Filipino condition responded with "Inferior" (frequency=22) than what should be expected (15) under "normal" conditions, and fewer responded with "Superior" (frequency=46) than what should be expected (53) under "normal" conditions, suggesting that inferior perceptions were activated when they were thinking of the Filipino culture. The opposite pattern was observed in the American condition, where more Filipino Americans responded with "Superior" (frequency=66) than what should be expected (59) under "normal" conditions, and fewer responded with "Inferior" (frequency=10) than what should be expected (17) under "normal" conditions, suggesting that superior perceptions were activated when they were thinking of the American culture. Such a frequency distribution is significantly different from what is expected in the population and provides support to the hypotheses that a CM-consistent cultural knowledge system exists among many Filipino Americans. It should be noted, however, that about 57% of Filipino Americans who were primed to think of the Filipino culture still answered with "Superior" in the word fragment, indicating that these participants may not have CM. Again, this reinforces the notion that although CM may be common, it is an individual-differences variable in that not all Filipinos and Filipino Americans possess it.

To test the replicability of the results of the previous study, or to make sure that the initial results were not a fluke, the same experiment (David & Okazaki, 2010) was conducted with a sample of 78 Filipino American college students attending a regional conference for Filipino Americans. Thus, these participants can be reasonably assumed to be highly proud of their Filipino heritage and are interested in the history and culture of their heritage. Similar to the previous study, participants were randomly assigned to be either in the Filipino (37 participants) or the American (41 participants) condition. Random assignment seemed to be effective as the participants did not differ significantly across various demographic variables. Similar to the results obtained from the first experiment, about 54% of Filipino Americans primed to think of the Filipino culture interpreted the ambiguous stimulus as "Inferior," whereas only about 19% of Filipino Americans primed to think of the American culture interpreted the ambiguous stimulus as "Inferior." On the other hand, about 76% of Filipino Americans primed with American culture interpreted the ambiguous stimulus as "Superior" compared to only about 46% of Filipino Americans primed with Filipino culture who interpreted the ambiguous stimulus as "Superior." More participants in the Filipino condition responded with "Inferior" (frequency=20) than what should be expected (13) under "normal" conditions, and fewer responded with "Superior" (frequency=17) than what should be expected (23) under "normal" conditions, suggesting that inferior perceptions were activated when they were thinking of the Filipino culture. The opposite pattern was observed in the American condition, where more participants responded with "Superior" (frequency=31) than what should be expected (25) under "normal" conditions, and fewer responded with "Inferior" (frequency=8) than what should be expected (15) under "normal" conditions, suggesting that superior perceptions were activated when they were thinking of the American culture. Such a frequency distribution is significantly different from what is expected in the population, and supports the hypothesis that, for some Filipino Americans, activating the Filipino cultural system may influence them to make inferior interpretations and activating the American cultural system may guide them to make superior interpretations. It should be noted again, however, that about 46% of Filipino Americans primed to think of the Filipino culture still responded with "Superior," suggesting that they do not have CM and that CM is an individual-differences variable.

The consistent findings of the two experiments summarized above suggest that many Filipinos' and Filipino Americans' cultural knowledge systems are constructed in a way that reflects CM. This is evidence that the perceptions of many Filipinos and Filipino Americans of the Filipino and American cultures may have been shaped by past and contemporary experiences of oppression. Furthermore, such results suggest that CM, or a CM-consistent cultural knowledge system, may be activated using priming techniques, indicating that CM or internalized oppression can be systematically investigated using rigorous scientific methods. However, despite the observed reliability and robustness of the results, both studies are not without limitations. First, both experiments did not allow for completely assessing CM because the participants were primed with either the American culture or the Filipino culture, but not both. Given that CM theory suggests that individuals may simultaneously hold both a superior regard of the American culture and an inferior regard of the Filipino culture (David & Okazaki, 2006a), the two experiments' use of the WFC method limited their ability to completely capture the CM phenomenon. Second, the two experiments did not use a control group to which the two conditions may be compared in order to further strengthen the argument that superior, pleasant, or positive thoughts were indeed activated by the American cultural primes and inferior, unpleasant, or negative thoughts were indeed activated by the Filipino cultural primes. Finally, because the primes used were clearly and easily recognizable as either Filipino- or American-related terms, it is possible that some participants may have become aware of the purpose of the task and, thus, may have intentionally altered their interpretation of the ambiguous stimulus. In other words, the word fragment completion task may not be as implicit as intended and explicit cognitive strategies (e.g., denial, intentional manipulations of responses, etc.) may have contaminated the responses. Therefore, the two experiments may not have satisfactorily addressed the question of whether colonialism and oppression has indeed been internalized enough by some Filipinos and Filipino Americans so that negative or unpleasant thoughts may now be automatically activated by mere exposure to Filipino-related stimuli, and positive or pleasant thoughts may now be automatically activated by mere exposure to American-related stimuli (David &

Okazaki, 2010). These limitations were addressed in the experiment that I summarize next.

Automatic Activation of Colonial Mentality

To overcome the methodological limitations of the previously described experiments, my mentor and I (David & Okazaki, 2010) used the *lexical decision priming technique* that is also commonly used in cognition research. This technique asks participants to categorize target stimuli into two groups (i.e., WORD or NON-WORD), by pressing "A" on the computer keyboard if the target stimuli they see on the computer screen is a word (e.g., "BEAUTIFUL," "UGLY," etc.), or pressing "5" if the target stimuli they see on the computer screen is not a word (e.g., "BEFALUTUI," "LUGY," etc.). The target stimuli are either pleasant (e.g., BEAUTIFUL) or unpleasant (e.g., UGLY) words, or scrambled target words (e.g., BEFALUTUI or LUGY) for the non-words. Before being presented with the target stimulus that is to be categorized either as a WORD or a NON-WORD, participants are briefly presented with a prime stimulus (i.e., "American" or "Filipino" or "YYYYYY"). If a person has closely associated a prime (e.g., the word "Filipino") with a particular category (e.g., Unpleasant), the person's reaction time when presented with a compatible prime-target task (e.g., "Filipino" followed by an Unpleasant word or "American" followed by a Pleasant word) will be faster than when the person is presented with an incompatible prime-target task (e.g., "Filipino" followed by a Pleasant word, or "American" followed by an Unpleasant word, or "YYYYYY" followed by a Pleasant word, or "YYYYYY" followed by an Unpleasant word). Thus, responses will be faster if the target stimulus belongs to the same category or cognitive network that the prime stimulus activated.

The inclusion of neutral primes (e.g., "YYYYYY") in this study in addition to "Filipino" and "American" primes is crucial to understanding whether Filipinos and Filipino Americans have indeed incorporated ideas of inferiority, unpleasantness, and negativity within their Filipino cultural knowledge system, and if they have incorporated ideas of superiority, pleasantness, and positivity with their American cultural knowledge system. Similar to how many of us do not have a negative or positive reaction to objects or concepts that we have never encountered or have had little exposure to before, it is believed that the neutral primes in this study are also such – that is, they are neutral in the sense that they do not activate ideas of pleasantness (or positivity) or unpleasantness (or negativity). In other words, as discussed above about spreading activation theory, if we have never learned or no one taught us to associate an object or a concept with a particular valence (e.g., pleasant or unpleasant), then our reactions to such objects or concepts will be neutral. The participants' reaction times and errors when responding to Filipino and American primes, objects and concepts to which they have arguably learned to associate with unpleasantness and pleasantness, respectively, due to historical colonialism and contemporary oppression, were compared to their reactions times and errors when responding to neutral primes. With this method, we (David & Okazaki, 2010) were able to test whether a CM-consistent cultural knowledge system can be activated and if it indeed exists within Filipinos and Filipino Americans.

Methods such as the lexical decision priming task assume that although an individual may not become aware of the purpose of the prime, the mere exposure to the prime alone activates links and nodes that the individual may have learned to closely associate with the prime stimulus. The lexical decision task also asks participants to categorize the target stimulus as either a Word or a Non-word, instead of categorizing them as either Pleasant or Unpleasant. Thus, the pleasantness valences of the prime words or the target words are not explicitly apparent or asked. Furthermore, because the task does not seem to involve ideas of pleasantness or unpleasantness regarding the prime and target words, participants are less likely to know the specific purposes and hypotheses of the task, which in turn, makes it less susceptible to socially desirable responding such as denial or lying. Thus, it was believed that a lexical decision priming procedure will allow for a better test of whether a CM-consistent cultural knowledge system may be automatically activated by mere exposure to either Filipino- or American-related stimuli and for an assessment of both the American preference and the Filipino rejection components of CM as both may simultaneously exist within Filipinos and Filipino Americans.

Based on a sample of 26 Filipino Americans, participants' reaction times were faster when responding to pleasant target terms (e.g., the word "Beautiful") after being exposed to American primes (e.g., the word "American" or "United States") than after being exposed to a neutral stimulus (e.g., "YYYYY"). Their reaction times when responding to unpleasant targets (e.g., the word "Ugly") after being exposed to American primes were not substantially slower than baseline (e.g., "YYYYY" followed by "Ugly"). This suggests that they have not associated American with negativity, similar to how they do not associate "YYYYY" with negativity. The opposite pattern was observed when participants were exposed to Filipino primes (e.g., the word "Filipino" or "Philippines") in that their reaction times were faster when responding to unpleasant target terms (e.g., "Ugly") compared to their reaction times to unpleasant targets after being exposed to a neutral stimulus (e.g., "YYYYY"). Their reaction times to pleasant targets (e.g., Beautiful") after being exposed to Filipino primes were not noticeably different from baseline (e.g., "YYYYY" followed by "Beautiful").These results suggest that Filipinos and Filipino Americans have associated Filipino with negativity but not with positivity. Statistical analyses (repeated measures analyses of variance) suggest that the sample had reliably faster reaction times during Filipino prime+Unpleasant target trials than when unpleasant target terms followed American or Neutral primes, and that the sample had reliably faster reaction times during American prime+Pleasant target trials than when pleasant target terms followed Filipino or Neutral primes (David & Okazaki, 2010). Overall, these findings provide support to the notion that mere exposure to American-related stimuli automatically activates pleasant thoughts whereas mere exposure to Filipino-related stimuli automatically activates unpleasant thoughts, consistent with CM theory. Furthermore, such findings provide initial evidence to the notion that CM involves an automatic association of pleasantness, superiority, and desirability with American culture and an automatic association of unpleasantness, inferiority, and undesirability with Filipino culture.

All of the experiments summarized in this chapter thus far suggest that Filipino culture-related stimuli activate unpleasant, negative, undesirable, or inferior perceptions, and that American culture-related stimuli activate pleasant, positive, desirable, and superior perceptions within Filipinos and Filipino Americans. Such results suggest that unpleasant or inferior constructs are contained in, or closely linked with, the Filipino cultural knowledge system and that pleasant or superior constructs are contained in, or closely linked with, the American cultural knowledge system. The results are consistent with the spreading activation theory and provide evidence to the notion that the centuries of oppression experienced by Filipinos and Filipino Americans has been internalized deeply enough by some so that negative thoughts are automatically activated by mere exposure to Filipino-related stimuli and positive thoughts are automatically activated by mere exposure to American-related stimuli. Such results also suggest that there might be automatic links or associations between Filipino and unpleasant concepts and between American and pleasant concepts among Filipinos and Filipino Americans. However, given the small sample of the lexical decision priming experiment described above, the reliability of such findings remains unclear. Thus, my mentor and I (David & Okazaki, 2010) conducted another experiment that attempted to further test CM theory's contention that Filipinos and Filipino Americans have automatically associated Filipino culture with inferiority, undesirability, and unpleasantness and American culture with superiority, desirability, and pleasantness. The next study I describe tested CM theory by using a method specifically developed to measure implicit and automatic associations – the Implicit Association Test (IAT).

Colonial Mentality as Implicit and Automatic Associations

In addition to supplementing the findings from the previously summarized experiments that (1) CM may indeed be assessed using indirect methodologies, and that (2) CM may operate automatically without awareness, intention, or control, the next experiment also attempted to more directly test the theory that CM involves an "automatic and uncritical rejection of anything Filipino and an automatic and uncritical preference for anything American" (David & Okazaki, 2006b, p. 241) by investigating if Filipino Americans have developed strong associations between anything Filipino and unpleasantness, and between anything American and pleasantness, using the IAT paradigm. Greenwald, McGhee, and Schwartz (1998) developed the IAT to measure evaluative associations that underlie attitudes. Unlike questionnaires, the IAT does not depend on self-report and introspection and is less vulnerable to response biases. Instead, the IAT assesses learned, implicit, and automatic associations by asking individuals to categorize stimuli into their corresponding categories. For example, Block 1 asks individuals to press "A" on a keyboard if they see a FLOWER or press "5" if they see an INSECT. Block 2 asks individuals to press "A" if the word they see is PLEASANT or "5" if the word they see is UNPLEASANT. Block 3 asks participants to press "A" for either a FLOWER or PLEASANT word and press "5" for either an INSECT or UNPLEASANT word (Block 3). Block 4 asks individuals to switch the keys (i.e., "A" for INSECT or "5" for FLOWER) and Block 5 asks them to press "A" for either an INSECT or PLEASANT word and press "5" for either a FLOWER or UNPLEASANT word. In this example, one would expect people to find Block 3 easier (i.e., quicker reaction times, fewer errors) than Block 5 because of strong and automatic associations that people have of insects to unpleasant feelings and flowers to pleasant feelings.

Greenwald and Banaji (1995) stated that the "signature of implicit cognition is that traces of past experience affect some performance, even though earlier experience is not remembered…it is unavailable to self-report or introspection" (pp. 4-5). Filipinos and Filipino Americans may not report or realize that historical and contemporary oppression influence their attitudes and behaviors toward their heritage. This may explain the low CM endorsement on the CMS as this measure relies on self-report and introspection. Further, "implicit attitudes are manifest as actions or judgments that are under the control of automatically activated evaluation, without the performer's awareness…" (Greenwald et al., 1998, p. 1464). Thus, Filipinos and Filipino Americans may not accurately identify negative attitudes or thoughts toward their heritage (e.g., feelings of inferiority, shame, or embarrassment), possibly contributing to the low endorsement of covert CM when using the CMS. In a recent study, Hatzenbuehler and colleagues (2009) successfully used the IAT to capture internalized homophobia (another specific form of internalized oppression) among a sample of lesbian and gay participants. Thus, social cognition paradigms such as the IAT holds promise in examining automatic implicit attitudes that are not as readily, easily, and accurately expressed through self report. Therefore, my mentor and I (David & Okazaki, 2010) developed an IAT specifically for assessing CM or internalized oppression among Filipinos and Filipino Americans.

The Colonial Mentality IAT (CMIAT) was composed of five blocks, with the first block involving PLEASANT (e.g., "Beautiful") or UNPLEASANT (e.g., "Ugly") discrimination and the second block being the FILIPINO (e.g., Brown) or AMERICAN (e.g., "White") discrimination. The third block asks participants to press

"A" for <u>either</u> a FILIPINO or PLEASANT word and press "5" for <u>either</u> an AMERICAN or UNPLEASANT word. Block 4 asks individuals to switch the keys (i.e., "A" for AMERICAN or "5" for FILIPINO) and Block 5 asks them to press "A" for <u>either</u> an AMERICAN or PLEASANT word and press "5" for <u>either</u> a FILIPINO or UNPLEASANT word. The order of presentation of Blocks 3 and 5 were randomly alternated between participants (as shown in Figure 8).

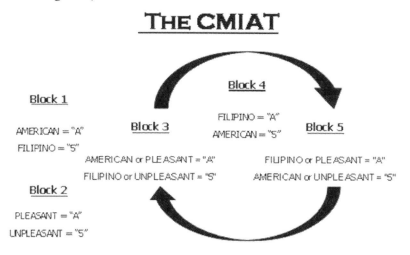

Figure 8. Pictorial representation of the tasks for the Colonial Mentality Implicit Association Test...

If Filipinos and Filipino Americans have automatically associated unpleasantness, undesirability, and inferiority with the Filipino culture and ethnicity, and have associated pleasantness, desirability, and superiority with the American culture because of centuries of colonialism and contemporary oppression, they will find Block 5 (compatible Block) easier (i.e., quicker reaction times, fewer errors) than Block 3 (incompatible Block). Based on data from 44 participants, 25 had faster reaction times and fewer errors during the compatible blocks (i.e., AMERICAN-PLEASANT and FILIPINO-UNPLEASANT) than during the incompatible blocks (i.e.,

AMERICAN-UNPLEASANT and FILIPINO-PLEASANT), suggesting that these individuals have associated pleasantness, desirability, or superiority with American culture and unpleasantness, undesirability, or inferiority with the Filipino culture. This finding suggests that about 57% of the sample has CM-consistent cognitions. Also, the average reaction time of the entire sample for the compatible block is significantly faster than their average reaction time for the incompatible block. That is, people were faster, had less errors, and found it easier to respond to stimuli when American was paired with PLEASANT and when Filipino was paired with UNPLEASANT, suggesting that, on average, Filipinos and Filipino Americans have strongly associated PLEASANT with American and UNPLEASANT with Filipino. Such a cognitive pattern is consistent with CM.

More recently, I replicated the same experiment with a sample of 102 participants (David, 2010b) and found that 56% had faster reaction times during the compatible block, suggesting that they have CM-consistent cognitions. Such results suggest that about 6 out of 10 Filipinos and Filipino Americans may have CM. Also, the entire sample, on average, found the compatible blocks easier (i.e., faster reaction times and fewer errors) than the incompatible blocks, suggesting that many Filipinos and Filipino Americans may possess a cultural knowledge system that is consistent with internalized oppression or CM. It should be noted, however, that about 4-5 out of 10 Filipinos and Filipino Americans have faster reaction times during the FILIPINO-PLEASANT and AMERICAN-UNPLEASANT trials than during the FILIPINO-UNPLEASANT and AMERICAN-PLEASANT trials, suggesting that these individuals have not internalized the oppression that they experienced, suggesting that they do not have CM, and reinforcing the notion that CM is an individual differences variable whose existence and strength among Filipinos and Filipino Americans may greatly vary.

Chapter Summary

Based on the findings of the previously published experiments (David, 2010b; David & Okazaki, 2010) described in this chapter, five main conclusions may be made concerning the cognitive operation of CM among Filipinos and Filipino Americans. First, historical colonialism and contemporary oppression has been deeply internalized by many Filipinos and Filipino Americans such that they now have a CM-consistent cultural knowledge system. Second, the findings suggest that CM among Filipinos and Filipino Americans may be activated using priming techniques typically used in the areas of social cognition and memory in the field of psychology. Third, CM among Filipinos and Filipino Americans may be automatically activated by mere exposure to either Filipino- or American-related stimuli. Fourth, historical colonialism and contemporary oppression among Filipinos and Filipino Americans has been deeply internalized such that Filipino-related stimuli are automatically associated with ideas of unpleasantness or inferiority and American-related stimuli are automatically associated with ideas of pleasantness or superiority (David & Okazaki, 2010). Lastly, CM or internalized oppression among Filipinos and Filipino Americans is an individual differences variable in that not all of them hold CM or have internalized the oppression they experience. Taken together, these conclusions are consistent with the argument that my mentor and I (David & Okazaki, 2006b) proposed: that the existence of strength of CM among Filipinos and Filipino Americans may greatly vary; that CM among Filipinos and Filipino Americans involves a covert component; that CM is characterized by an inferior perception of anything Filipino and superior perception of anything American; and that CM may operate automatically without awareness, intention, or control. In other words, Filipinos and Filipino Americans may have and display CM without them even knowing it, or even if it is not on purpose.

Also, the findings described in this chapter regarding the cognitive operation of CM highlights the potential influences on how Filipinos or Filipino Americans may behave in various contexts. For example, if a Filipino or Filipino American individual with CM is in a context wherein he/she is with several other Filipinos who speak English with strong Filipino accents or are speaking a Filipino dialect, his/her CM-consistent cognitions may be activated. Such cognitive activation, in turn, may lead the individual to behave in ways that are consistent with CM such as discriminating or distancing him/herself from the other Filipinos, especially if the activation of the CM-consistent cognition is not further scrutinized (i.e., cognitive elaboration) and the person is acting spontaneously. Indeed, a review by Gawronksi and colleagues (2007) of the literature on implicit social cognition suggest that activated associations predict spontaneous behaviors. Also, in a context wherein a Filipino person who may have CM is faced to make a decision between a Filipino product (or person) or an American product (or person), the Filipino person's CM-consistent cognitions may become activated and lead the person to choose or prefer the American product (or person). This latter example is especially salient in mere observations of modern day Philippines, where Western companies and products continue to promulgate and flourish over local ones as Filipinos continue to prefer and support anything Western over anything Filipino (as described in Part I, Chapter 4). The same example can provide explanation to the automatic preference of many Filipinos and Filipino Americans for American or Western brands, American or Western music, and American or Western people over their Filipino counterparts (as described in Chapter 5). Such effects of automatic cognitions on spontaneous behaviors also highlights the need for Filipinos and Filipino Americans to develop a deeper and more elaborate understanding of such automatic tendencies, in order to begin controlling and reversing them. The process of becoming aware of CM, controlling CM, and some strategies for facilitating the reversal of CM are discussed in more detail later in Part III.

Further, a note should be made regarding the conscious accessibility (i.e., awareness) of such automatic cognitions. Although the interpretation that such cognitions may be unconscious is consistent with the conventional conceptualization of cognitions or attitudes (e.g., Greenwald & Banaji, 1995), recent developments in the field of social cognition have challenged this assumption. Instead, recent empirical evidence (e.g., Gawronski, Hofmann, & Wilbur, 2006) suggests that automatic associations and cognitions are consciously accessible and, when activated, are used for explicit judgments and behaviors (Gawronski, LeBel, & Peters, 2007). That is, when associations between objects are automatically activated within us because we have learned to associate such objects together, we are aware of such activations. However, we then evaluate consciously, purposefully, or intentionally if we agree with such activated associations and if we will use such activations to guide our judgments or behaviors. Consequently, an alternative conceptualization proposed by Gawronski and his colleagues (e.g., Gawronski & Bodenhausen, 2006; Gawronski, LeBel, & Peters, 2007) argue for a model that does not depend on an unconscious assumption and one that instead distinguishes between *activation* and *validation* cognitive processes. These researchers argue that implicit measures of attitudes, such as the WFC, LDP, and IAT tasks, reflect the activation of learned associations in a person's memory. Validation, on the other hand, is reflected by self-report measures such as the CMS and is the process of assessing the subjective truth or falsity of the activated associations. They further explained that activation of associations in a particular person's cognitive system may take place independent of the result of the person's validation process; that is, regardless of whether the person considers such activation as accurate (true) or inaccurate (false).

Thus, using the activation-validation model, some Filipinos or Filipino Americans may disagree with the cognitive associations that are activated within them when they are faced with Filipino- or

American-related stimuli and, thus, do not endorse items on the CMS. However, as Gawronski and colleagues (2007) have argued, rejecting or deciding that a particular activation or association is not true does not necessarily erase the activation or mean that the activation did not take place. The mere fact that the activation took place suggests that there are learned associations between the activated node and the other nodes. Thus, although some Filipinos or Filipino Americans may not endorse CMS items as a result of their cognitive validation, a CM-consistent cultural knowledge system may still have been activated and still exist. The opposite pattern, though very unlikely, may also take place in that some Filipinos or Filipino Americans may endorse CM items as a result of their cognitive validation even when they do not hold a CM-consistent cultural knowledge system. Nonetheless, regardless of whether one subscribes to the conventional conceptualization of unconscious (or introspectively inaccessible) cognitions or to the alternative activation-validation model, the studies described in this chapter suggest that a CM-consistent cultural knowledge system exists and may be activated within Filipinos and Filipino Americans, and that CM may operate automatically without intention or control (David & Okazaki, 2010).

Lastly, the experiments described in this chapter provide evidence that internalized oppression or CM – among Filipinos, Filipino Americans, and other historically and contemporarily oppressed groups – can be investigated in a scientifically rigorous manner. It is hoped that such studies which may be perceived as more "acceptable," palatable, and convincing by the believers of conventional science will bring more attention and efforts toward better understanding and addressing internalized oppression or CM as experienced by Filipinos and Filipino Americans, as well as experienced by various other minority groups – attention they definitely deserve and undoubtedly need.

*   *   *

Based on empirical studies and experiments, it is clear that historical colonialism and contemporary oppression has resulted into internalized oppression or CM among many Filipinos and Filipino Americans. In turn, the described studies in this chapter also suggest that CM has significant effects on Filipino and Filipino American cognitions (thoughts), emotions (feelings or attitudes), and behaviors (actions). In the following chapters, I provide more specific discussions of how CM influences various aspects of Filipino and Filipino American psychology – including mental health. I will begin with how historical and contemporary oppression, and consequently CM, may be contributing to the loss of what many scholars (e.g., Enriquez, 1977) consider to be the essence of being Filipino – Kapwa. The loss of Kapwa, in turn, is analogous to loss of culture, loss of a worldview, loss of identity, loss of connection with other people, loss of shared identity, loss of humanity or personhood, and the loss of being Filipino.

CHAPTER 7

"WALANG KAPWA": THE LOSS OF INDIGENOUS CORE VALUES

ꯑꯇ꯭ ꯃꯗꯤ ꯃꯗꯇ꯭ ꯇ꯭ ꯂꯨꯃꯇꯔꯛ

Psychologists, anthropologists, sociologists, and other scholars and professionals usually categorize the Filipino culture as *collectivistic.* Collectivistic cultures can be characterized as those groups of people who emphasize the fundamental relatedness of individuals to each other, which are often typically expressed by a strong desire among such individuals to fit in, prioritize the group's goals over one's personal goals, and maintain harmonious relationships with other people (Markus & Kitayama, 1991; Triandis, 2001). In contrast, *individualistic* cultures, which are typical of many Western societies including the United States, tend to emphasize individuality that is often expressed by the desire to be unique, to stand-out, and to rise above the rest, as well as to pursue one's personal goals and become "your own person" (Markus & Kitayama, 1991; Triandis, 2001). The collectivistic tendencies of Filipinos can be seen through what many scholars consider to be typical Filipino values such as *Hiya* (shame), *Utang na Loob* (sense of inner debt or gratitude), and *Pakikisama* (companionship). Hiya may refer to the feelings of shame one might bring to oneself or to one's group (such as family), and so all necessary behaviors and regulation of behaviors are done in order to avoid Hiya. Utang na loob is a feeling of indebtedness or gratitude that one gets after another person (or group) has provided assistance or help in any way, similar to reciprocity. Pakikisama may refer to prioritizing the group's goals or going along with the group's decision even though it may not be consistent with one's personal goals or decision due to the desire to maintain harmony within the group. Indeed, it is clear that these commonly-held and widely-practiced values and their meanings cannot be understood without relating them to other people, suggesting that such values are reflective of the collectivistic tendencies of Filipinos.

However, the highly influential and revolutionary Filipino psychologist, Virgilio Enriquez (1994), argued that such values that are often considered to be typical Filipino values are only surface values. According to Enriquez, the core Filipino value that drives and connects together such surface level values is Kapwa. Kapwa may be seen as the essence of being Filipino and the most important concept and value in the Filipino worldview. To this end, this chapter will discuss Kapwa and its relationships with other Filipino values. The coverage of Filipino values in this chapter, however, are only limited to the common surface values of Hiya, Utang na loob, and Pakikisama, and the core values of Pakiramdam and Kapwa, as they relate to CM or internalized oppression. A more comprehensive discussion of the entire Filipino value system may be found in the books of Virgilio Enriquez (1994) and Katrin de Guia (2005). It is also important to emphasize at this point that by discussing Hiya, Utang na Loob, and Pakikisama, I am not suggesting that these surface values capture the essence of Kapwa or the Filipino worldview and value system. As Enriquez (1994) himself argued, these surface values are "readily apparent attributes appreciated and exhibited by many Filipinos. In addition, these three are recognized as a triad whose legs emanate from a single trunk, the actual core value of the Filipino personality. This core value has been identified as kapwa. Surface values therefore are not free-standing values which anyone can assume at will" (p. 62). Thus, the use of commonly-practiced and easily-observed surface values when describing Filipino culture is not necessarily irresponsible. It is only problematic and dangerous if such surface values are portrayed as capturing the essence of the Filipino culture or are discussed outside the context of Kapwa.

Also, now that we know how historical and contemporary oppression (as discussed in Part I) has led to internalized oppression or CM (as discussed in Chapters 5 and 6) among many Filipinos and Filipino Americans, this chapter will also discuss how the sense of Kapwa and other values among many Filipinos and Filipino Americans may have been damaged because of historical colonialism and contemporary oppression. Although there are a variety of possible reasons for cultural loss, this chapter's goal is to introduce CM – the consequence of historical colonialism and contemporary oppression – as one theoretically plausible factor that contributes to Filipinos' and Filipino Americans' loss of Kapwa and loss of adherence to other Filipino values. It is hoped that future empirical research may result from such discussions.

Kapwa: The Core Filipino Value

Let us now begin to explore in some detail the meaning of Kapwa. When thinking about the English equivalent of the word Kapwa, one of the most common words that come to mind is "others." However, the true meaning of Kapwa is actually the complete opposite of others, because such a term connotes a separation of one's self from other people. In contrast, Kapwa is more accurately translated as "both" or "fellow being" (Kapwa-Tao) (Enriquez, 1994), and refers to the unity or oneness of a person with other people. It is the recognition that one shares an identity, or a shared inner self, with others and that one is not and should not be separated from others. In Enriquez's own words:

> "A person starts having kapwa not so much because of a recognition of status given to him (or her) by others but more because of his (or her) awareness of shared identity. The ako (ego or self) and the iba sa akin (others) are one and the same in kapwa psychology: Hindi ako iba sa aking kapwa (I am no different from others). Once ako starts thinking of himself (or herself) as separate from kapwa, the Filipino self gets to be individuated in the Western sense and, in effect, denies the status of kapwa to the other. By the same token, the status of kapwa is also denied to the self." (p. 45).

According to Enriquez (1994), Kapwa is the core Filipino value that serves as the base or the "trunk" that drives and connects together the surface values of Hiya, Utang na loob, and Pakikisama. Thus, one cannot have, display, or behave in a manner that is consistent with the surface values of Hiya, Utang na loob, or Pakikisama without the core value of Kapwa. According to de Guia (2005),

> "Individuals who are guided by kapwa can be recognized by their genuine, people-centered orientation, their service to those around them and their commitment to their communities. Among their barkada (group of close friends), they are often frontliners, leaders and organizers. As foot soldiers, they are reliable, the ones who step forward to volunteer. They are quick to lend a hand and share their skills and knowledge freely by teaching children, working with the poor or facilitating

workshops on crafts. Their help usually comes with a big smile. Community building is second nature to the people of such a bearing, as kapwa inspires them to facilitate in meetings, organize events, participate in civic affairs and so on." (p. 28).

In addition to possessing Kapwa, the type of person described above is one who may also be considered as displaying the *bayanihan* spirit – another cultural value in the Filipino worldview. According to Enriquez (1994), bayanihan may be defined as "mutual aid; cooperative behavior; cooperation" (p. 161). It is the common practice among Filipinos to come to the aid of, assist, or help others – their neighbors, friends, larger community – without any expectation of getting anything in return. In English, this may be best translated as "altruism." Thus, a person who is as involved and admired as the one de Guia (2005) described above cannot be so if the person does not have a sense of connectedness to other people. In other words, one cannot possibly behave in accordance with the bayanihan spirit if one perceives himself or herself as separate from, if not better than, others. It is impossible for someone to work harmoniously and effectively with other people if they do not have Pakikisama, to be regarded as reliable if they do not have Hiya, and to assist or participate in community or social events, gatherings, or celebrations if they do not have Utang na loob. Thus, it is impossible for people to display, or behave consistently with the Bayanihan spirit, Hiya, Utang na loob, or Pakikisama, if they do not see themselves as one and the same as other people, if they do not recognize the importance of being connected with other people, if they do not possess Kapwa.

Pakiramdam is another concept and value that, in English, can be most accurately translated to "feeling" or "intuition." It refers to feeling the needs, desires, intentions, motivations, moods, emotions, or other internal characteristics and states of other people.

Pakiramdam has been defined as a shared inner perception that is driven by a heightened sense of awareness and sensitivity, an ability to be highly sympathetic or empathetic, making Filipinos with Pakiramdam exceptionally adept at accurately sensing subtle, non-verbal, and invisible cues from other people (de Guia, 2005). Pakiramdam connects the core value of Kapwa to the surface values. Pakiramdam serves as the processor or the pivot that allows a person to express Kapwa and behave according to Kapwa. In other words, if one does not have the ability to feel for others and their internal states and characteristics, then it will be impossible for that person to also have and display shame (Hiya), feel a sense of gratitude (Utang na loob), or put others' desires ahead of one's own (Pakikisama). The person may still have Kapwa, but it is impossible to appropriately express and display Kapwa through the surface values without Pakiramdam.

Using Enriquez's example, perhaps the best way to make sense of such a hierarchy in the Filipino value system is to use Filipinos' understanding of what makes a masamang tao (bad or evil person). The traits of a masamang tao, in contrast to the ones described by de Guia (2005) above, will include not having or not displaying the surface values of Hiya, Utang na loob, and Pakikisama. If a person refers to you as someone who is without shame (walang Hiya), without a sense of inner gratitude (walang utang na loob), or without the ability to go along with others' desires (walang Pakikisama), then you should feel bad, guilty, or sorry. Indeed, being accused of being someone with such ineptness is a bad thing in the Filipino culture and worldview. However, being a person who lacks one of the surface values is still not as bad as someone who is considered to have no Pakiramdam. In turn, not having Pakiramdam, which is an ability that may be learned, developed, and sharpened over time, is not as bad as not having Kapwa. Kapwa is the core value, and it takes more than simple training and teaching for someone to recognize that one is not, should not, and cannot be separated or differentiated from others. Enriquez (1994) explained it best when he stated:

> "One argument for the greater importance of kapwa in Filipino thought and behavior is the shock or disbelief that the Filipino registers when confronted with one who is supposedly walang kapwa. If one is walang pakisama, others might still say 'He (or she) would eventually learn' or 'Let him (or her) be; that's his (or her) prerogative.' If one is walang hiya, others say, 'His (or her) parents should teach him (or her) a thing or two.' If one is walang utang na loob others might advise, 'Avoid him (or her).' But if one is walang kapwa, people say 'He (or she) must have reached rock bottom. Napakasama na niya. He (or she) is the worst." (p. 63).

The circles in Figure 9 is a pictorial representation of the Filipino value structure, showing that not having Kapwa (e.g., "Wala siyang Kapwa-Tao) is the worst a person can be in the Filipino worldview because they have now lost their personhood or pagkatao, and illustrating the relationships between the core and surface level Filipino values. According to Enriquez (1994), Kapwa is the essence and the foundation of the Filipino value system, and that this core value determines the extent to which a person is a person – or a human (personhood or pagkatao). Therefore, Kapwa is the most important value and concept that anyone with Filipino heritage must understand, have, and display, as it is the core of what makes a Filipino a Filipino, and what makes a human a human (their personhood or pagka-tao) in the Filipino indigenous perspective or worldview. As Enriquez stated, "Without kapwa, one ceases to be a Filipino. One also ceases to be human" (p. 63).

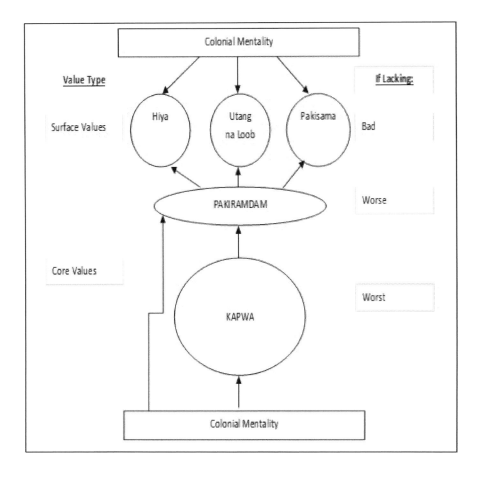

Figure 9. The Filipino Value System and Colonial Mentality

Colonial Mentality and Kapwa

Based on our understanding of CM among Filipinos and Filipino Americans thus far, CM generally refers to an automatic and uncritical preference for anything American or Western and an automatic and uncritical rejection of anything Filipino. Theoretically, it makes sense to make connections between CM and the extent to which Filipinos and Filipino Americans regard, subscribe, and adhere to Western or American culture, values, and behaviors, as well as how CM affects the extent to which Filipinos and Filipino Americans regard their heritage culture less than positively and begin to abandon their heritage values, expected behaviors, and traditions. In other words, individuals with CM may begin to regard Filipino culture, values, and behaviors less than positively and they may no longer adhere to or subscribe to Filipino cultural practices, beliefs, and traditions. Consequently, individuals holding CM may be more likely to become independent, pursue one's personal goals over the group's goals, and generally perceive one's self as separate from others. These characteristics are typical of Western societies. As Enriquez (1994) argued, once an individual comes to see himself or herself as individuated or separated from others, one ceases to have Kapwa. Thus, Filipinos and Filipino Americans who hold CM may be more likely to not have a sense of Kapwa, or at least, they may be in danger of losing Kapwa – the essence of being a person and the core of being Filipino.

The entirety of Figure 9 represents how CM or internalized oppression may theoretically affect Kapwa and the other Filipino values, but let us explore in some detail some specific examples of how this may happen. Filipinos and Filipino Americans who have come to accept the inferiority of their cultural beliefs, values, and practices, as well as those who may be ashamed or embarrassed of various aspects of their heritage culture (the covert manifestations of CM), may begin to perceive Kapwa as unnecessary, and perhaps even embarrassing. For instance, how would having Kapwa – which is a shared sense of self with others, especially with other Filipinos – supposed to be beneficial for someone who already perceives being Filipino and the Filipino culture as inferior, shameful, and embarrassing? In fact, it makes more sense for those who hold covert CM manifestations to separate themselves from other Filipinos, because such Filipinos may remind them of their own inferiority, or associating with other Filipinos only continues and maintains their membership to what they already perceive as an inferior ethnicity and culture. Thus, for those with covert CM manifestations, having a sense of Kapwa does not make sense, which may lead to the damaging, if not complete eradication, of Kapwa among such individuals. Indeed, for individuals who perceive being Filipino as undesirable, getting rid of the essence and the core of being Filipino – Kapwa – is the most logical strategy in order to escape from all the inferiorities and undesirabilities of the Filipino ethnicity and culture. This is one way in which CM – the consequence of historical colonialism and contemporary oppression – may influence Kapwa and the other Filipino values.

In order to separate themselves from the perceived inferiority and undesirability of their heritage ethnicity and culture, Filipinos and Filipino Americans may begin to exhibit overt CM manifestations such as discriminating against others who are perceived to be too Filipino or those who are perceived to be not American or Western enough. They may also begin to change the manner in which they talk, dress, behave, and look in ways that are more consistent with Western or American ideals. Thus, they may begin to adhere and subscribe to Western or American cultural values, beliefs, and practices, which are characteristic of individualistic cultures and are in stark contrast to the collectivistic, people-oriented cultural values, beliefs, and practices of the Filipino culture and worldview. The practice of overt CM manifestations further separates Filipinos and Filipino Americans from other people, especially others with Filipino heritage, further solidifying their adherence to individualistic viewpoints and making them less and less connected to others; making their sense of Kapwa smaller and smaller until it is completely gone. Perceiving one's self as more Americanized or Western (e.g., I speak better English than them; They have funny accents; They're all just a bunch of FOBs; I have lighter skin than they do; My nose is more bridged than yours; I was born in the United States; etc.), and using such characteristics as a way to differentiate or separate one's self from other Filipinos who are perceived to not have such Americanized or Westernized characteristics, is one way in which one begins to lose Kapwa. The common Filipino phenomenon called "I am Spanish-Chinese-Filipino" (*SCF syndrome*) (Nadal, 2009) often displayed by many Filipinos and Filipino Americans to dilute their Filipino-ness in some way, may be an example of a desire to distinguish or separate one's self from others as well. By discriminating against others or highlighting how one is distinguishable or different from others, it is implied that one is better than or at least different from other people, iba ako sa kanila (I am different from them), which is in direct opposition to what Kapwa is (Hindi ako iba sa aking kapwa; I am no different from my fellow beings).

Filipinos or Filipino Americans who have CM and are beginning to separate themselves from others, especially those who are perceived to be too Filipino or non-Americanized, may not attend Filipino cultural events, gatherings, celebrations or parties with their families. They may not cooperate, contribute, help-out, assist, or participate in family or community projects or efforts, and they may begin to personally perceive such events, celebrations, gatherings, projects, or efforts as embarrassing, shameful, unnecessary, or "too Filipino" despite the fact that their social group (e.g., family, friends, etc.) may perceive such things as important. Because of their absence, lack of cooperation, lack of contribution, and general disrespect for such things, such individuals may begin to bring shame to their families (nakakahiya) or other relatives. Their parents, other relatives, and friends may start perceiving them as someone who does not have any gratitude (walang utang na loob) and one who does not know how to go along with the group (walang pakisama). Thus, Filipinos and Filipino Americans who hold CM may begin to lack Hiya, Utang na loob, and Pakisama.

Family members, other relatives, or friends may begin to start sending messages to such individuals (those who are displaying lack of shame, gratitude, and cooperation) that express their disapproval and concern in very subtle, indirect, and unspoken ways (nagpaparinig) with the hopes that such individuals will begin to feel or notice that they are doing something wrong. In other words, they may still use their Pakiramdam to feel and recognize the concerns and disapproval of the people around them who are subtly and indirectly accusing them of lacking Hiya, Utang na loob, and Pakikisama. Such accusations and perceptions toward a person, if maintained over time as the person consistently fails to use his or her Pakiramdam to sense the concerns and disapproval of their social group (e.g., family, friends) and, as the person consequently continues to consistently display behaviors that are against the values of Hiya, Utang na loob, and Pakikisama, can turn into that person being perceived as someone without Kapwa. It should not be surprising, therefore, if Filipinos and Filipino Americans with CM who consistently separate themselves from others and who regularly do not participate in family, social, and community events and gatherings, are perceived as individuals who do not have Hiya, Utang na loob, Pakisama, Pakiramdam, and Kapwa, and are therefore avoided, looked down upon, or marginalized. Individuals with CM who are perceived to not have Hiya, Utang na loob, Pakikisama, Pakiramdam, and Kapwa may be referred to as "coconuts" (brown on the outside, but White in the inside) or "sell-outs."

A Different Conceptualization of Crab Mentality

Another common Filipino and Filipino American phenomenon that many individuals in this community often mention, if not complain about, is *crab mentality* – which is when other Filipinos try to "outdo, outshine, or surpass another (Filipino person)" (Nadal, 2010 p. 316), especially Filipinos or Filipino Americans who may have become successful in some way. Although the typical discussion about crab mentality within the Filipino and Filipino American community focuses on the group and how the rest of the group may just be acting out of jealousy, which is why they are trying to "bring others down" (hence the term – crab mentality), I believe there is another plausible way to conceptualize this phenomenon. It is possible that the person who is the "victim" or target of crab mentality is a person who is considered by the rest of the community as someone who no longer has Utang na loob or Pakikisama. Filipinos and Filipino Americans are not against success – in fact, they are generally very proud when they see other Filipinos and Filipino Americans become successful. Such a desire for, pride, and happiness toward others' success is probably why it is very common for many Filipinos and Filipino Americans to always claim that so and so of some celebrity or stature is of Filipino descent. Thus, it is possible that crab mentality takes place when community members begin to see someone who used to be one of them lose (if not deny) their connectedness to the Filipino culture. Someone who, because of some success, no longer help out, participate, contribute, or attend Filipino or Filipino American community gatherings, parties, events, or celebrations. Someone who may now have lost their bayanihan spirit. Someone who may now be perceived as one who thinks he or she is better than the rest of the community. Someone who may now be separating, or distinguishing one's self from the rest of the community. Someone who may now be perceived as one who does not have Utang na loob and Pakikisama. Someone who may now be perceived as one who may not have Kapwa. Thus, crab mentality should not just be interpreted as a result of jealousy by those who are less successful. Crab mentality should not just be interpreted as the Filipino and Filipino American community being jealous of others' success. Crab mentality should not just be conceived as the community's effort to "bring others down." Instead, it is also possible that perhaps the ones who are successful may now have lost or diluted their sense of Kapwa, which is why they have become marginalized or negatively regarded by the rest of the Filipino and Filipino American community. In this sense, CM or internalized oppression is related to the phenomenon of crab mentality because of the existence of CM – and the consequent loss of Kapwa – among some Filipino and Filipino American individuals.

The problem may not lie in the community, but among those who may be considered as "successful" and typically regarded as the "victims" or targets of crab mentality.

Chapter Summary

This chapter has introduced us to the concepts and values of Kapwa and Pakiramdam, which allowed us to more deeply understand the common Filipino surface values of Hiya, Utang na loob, and Pakikisama. We have now also been introduced to the phenomenon of bayanihan (helping others altruistically) and crab mentality (pulling others down). Kapwa refers to the indigenous worldview that all people are the same and equal regardless of sex, age, socioeconomic status, education levels, physical appearance, or whatever else. Kapwa is a shared inner self that makes a person fundamentally connected to and undifferentiated from others, which drives the collectivistic tendencies of the Filipino culture that are typically expressed by the surface values of Hiya, Utang na loob, and Pakikisama. With our understanding of the Filipino value system, we now understand that Kapwa is the core Filipino value and the most important concept in Filipino personhood and psychology, as it is considered in the Filipino worldview to be what makes a Filipino a Filipino, what makes a human a human.

Given that Kapwa is what makes a Filipino a Filipino, it is therefore important to explore the relationship between the effects of historical and contemporary oppression – CM or internalized oppression – and Kapwa. Thus, this chapter also discussed in some detail how CM among Filipinos and Filipino Americans may influence their sense of Kapwa, as well as how CM may affect other Filipino values such as Pakiramdam, Hiya, Utang na loob, Pakikisama, Bayanihan, and crab mentality. In general, CM may lead Filipinos and Filipino Americans to no longer adhere to or believe in the importance of Kapwa and the other Filipino values, or ignore or not foster their Pakiramdam, which may contribute to individuals with CM to become marginalized, avoided, or negatively regarded by other Filipinos and Filipino Americans. Thus, CM may lead many Filipinos and Filipino Americans to ignore, devalue, and eventually lose their sense of Kapwa, which in the Filipino worldview would make them no longer a person – no longer a Filipino.

*   *   *

Now that we have begun to understand how the consequence of historical and contemporary oppression – CM or internalized oppression – may influence Kapwa and other Filipino indigenous values, we have also begun to further illuminate how oppression has damaged the Filipino culture and ethnicity. Not only did colonialism and not only does modern-day oppression negatively affect how Filipinos and Filipino Americans regard their own cultural and ethnic characteristics, their core personhood or pagka-tao has also been damaged. To this end, the next chapter will further discuss how CM and its negative effects on Kapwa may influence the manner in which modern day Filipinos and Filipino Americans regard themselves, regard other people with Filipino descent, regard other ethnic and cultural groups, and regard the dominant White group. In other words, the next chapter will focus on how CM or internalized oppression may influence the manner in which Filipinos and Filipino Americans develop their sense of identity.

CHAPTER 8

COLONIAL MENTALITY AND THE FILIPINO -/ AMERICAN IDENTITY

ᜃᜋ᜔ᜊ ᜀᜆ᜔ ᜃᜎᜒᜈᜒᜀᜈ᜔ ᜀᜆ᜔ ᜉᜒᜎᜒᜉᜒᜈᜓ ᜀᜋᜒᜇᜒᜃᜈ᜔

Although the concept of Kapwa has received some attention in Filipino and Filipino American psychology, its coverage thus far has remained mainly in the theoretical realm. Indeed, empirical and data-based investigations of Filipino and Filipino American identity have yet to explore and incorporate Kapwa sufficiently. For instance, the research literature on Filipino American acculturation and enculturation includes important aspects of culture such as language, preferred food, holding typical collectivistic values (e.g., shame, deference to authority, expression of emotions, family solidarity, etc.), and the ethnic composition of one's social network (e.g., dela Cruz, Padilla, & Butts, 1998; dela Cruz, Padilla, & Agustin, 2010; del Prado & Church, 2010), but not the extent to which individuals with Filipino heritage still adhere to the notion of Kapwa. Indeed, even the most recent of these efforts (del Prado & Church, 2010) – although conducted in a scientifically and psychometrically rigorous manner – attempted to quantitatively capture common Filipino surface values such as Hiya, Utang na Loob (which the researchers called "reciprocal obligation"), and Pakikisama (which the researchers called "smooth interpersonal relationships") without any reference to Kapwa, which may lead to the erroneous and dangerous misinterpretation that these surface values are free-standing concepts that capture the essence of the Filipino culture and personhood (as discussed in Chapter 7). Thus, the set of values and behaviors that researchers often use as indicators of the extent to which a person with Filipino heritage is assimilated to the mainstream culture or enculturated to the Filipino culture still do not incorporate the core Filipino value of Kapwa. Furthermore, besides few exceptions (e.g., David & Okazaki, 2006b; David, 2008), psychological research on Filipino and Filipino American acculturation and identity typically do not incorporate CM or internalized oppression as potential influencing factors on the extent to which Filipinos and Filipino Americans adopt mainstream culture, practice their heritage cultural traditions, or identify positively as a member of their heritage ethnicity.

As discussed in Chapter 7, Kapwa may be considered to be the essence, or the core, of what makes a person Filipino and even what makes a person a person (pagka-Tao). Thus, Kapwa is and should be considered as the most central and important factor in Filipino and Filipino American psychology, especially when exploring factors such as identity, enculturation, and acculturation. Also in Chapter 7, I have explained how CM may be contributing to the loss of Kapwa among many Filipinos and Filipino Americans today. Thus, the non-inclusion of Kapwa, and the typical absence of CM as it affects Kapwa, in our current conceptualization and investigations of Filipino and Filipino American *enculturation* (the extent to which individuals adhere to their heritage cultural values and practices), *acculturation* (the process of adjusting to the influences of two or more cultures), and *ethnic identity* (the extent to which a person identifies with and positively regards his or her ethnic group) is a major limitation in this area of psychology, and increased research in this area is definitely needed. To this end, this chapter will discuss how CM and Kapwa may interact with each other to influence Filipino and Filipino American identity development. Although such a treatment of how CM and Kapwa may influence Filipino and Filipino American identity is still staying within the theoretical realm, I hope that such a discussion will nevertheless spark some empirical research in this area.

The Pilipino American Identity Development Model

Inspired by Atkinson, Morten, and Sue's (1998) and Kim's (1981) models for Asian American identity development, Nadal (2004) developed the Pilipino American Identity Development (PAID) Model to describe the process of ethnic identity formation among American-born, or second (or later) generation, Filipino Americans. Such models are also similar to the more general, highly popular, and widely-used Multigroup Ethnic Identity Model developed by Phinney (1992). The other ethnic identity models are composed of four stages, whereas the PAID model is composed of six non-linear and non-sequential stages, with two of the stages being argued as unique to the Filipino American experience (Nadal, 2004). In general, the PAID model describes how Filipino Americans may change the manner in which they perceive and regard themselves as Filipino, their perception of other Filipinos and Filipino Americans, as well as the manner in which they perceive and regard other ethnic and racial groups, depending on their experiences with their environment (e.g., family socialization, experiences with other minority groups, experiences with the dominant White group, etc.). In this chapter, I will discuss the PAID model and how CM and Kapwa may influence each of the six stages. Furthermore, for the purposes of this chapter, I will also apply the PAID model to Filipinos in the Philippines and Filipino Americans who were not born in the United States. Again, as mentioned in the Preface and as discussed in Chapters 3 and 4, it is an undeniable fact that Filipinos in the Philippines are also faced, challenged, and influenced by American cultural influences on a daily basis. Thus, this chapter will discuss how CM and Kapwa may negatively affect the ethnic identity development of Filipinos and Filipino Americans. Let us begin by briefly going over the six stages of the PAID model.

According to Nadal (2004), the first stage of PAID is the *Ethnic Awareness Stage,* which typically starts when the person is around 2-5 years-old. Given that children this young typically do not attend school yet, the only culture that they are exposed to is their parents' culture – the Filipino culture. Furthermore, the parents of Filipino Americans in this stage may teach their children the importance of the Filipino culture through food, values, dances, language, and others. Thus, according to Nadal (2004), Filipino Americans in this stage may be considered to be highly enculturated (connected to their heritage culture). Consequently, children at this stage of the PAID holds either a neutral or positive view of himself or herself, other Filipinos and Filipino Americans, other Asian Americans, other minority groups, and the dominant White group. In Stage 2, which is called the *Assimilation to Dominant Culture* stage, Filipino Americans may begin to receive messages about the superiority of the dominant culture and the inferiorities of their heritage culture, which may lead Filipino Americans in this stage to hold negative or self-deprecating attitudes toward their personal self, negative and group deprecating attitudes toward other Filipinos and Filipino Americans, negative and group deprecating attitudes toward other Asian Americans, and negative and discriminatory attitudes toward other minority groups, while positively regarding the dominant White group (Nadal, 2004). Stage 3, which is called the *Social Political Awakening* stage, is when Filipino Americans reverse their attitudes and beliefs from Stage 2 to more positively regard their personal selves, other Filipinos and Filipino Americans, other Asian Americans, and other minority groups, while holding a negative or suspicious attitude toward the dominant White group. Such a reversal may be sparked by direct or indirect experiences of discrimination or micoraggressions (as discussed in Chapter 4) from members of the dominant White group, or by the realization that Filipinos and Filipino Americans, as well as other minority groups, are historically and contemporarily oppressed.

Table 3. Nadal's Pilipino American Identity Development Model

	Attitudes Toward				
Stage	Self	Other Filipinos and Filipino Americans	Other Asian Americans	Other Minorities	Dominant White Group
Ethnic Awareness	P/Neutral	P/Neutral	Neutral	Neutral	P/Neutral
Assimilation to Dominant Culture	N/SD	N/GD	N/D	N/D	P/GA
Social Political Awakening	P/SE	P/GE	P/GA	P/A	N/D
Panethnic Asian American Consciousness	P	P/A	P/GA	P/A	N/D
Ethnocentric Realization	P/SE	P/GE	Neutral/GD	P/GE	N
Incorporation	SA	P/GA	A	P/A	Sel A

Note. P = Positive; N = Negative; SD = Self-Deprecating; SE = Self-Empowering; SA = Self-Appreciating; GD = Group-Deprecating; GE = Group Empowering; A = Accepting; GA = Group-Appreciating; D = Discriminatory; Sel A = Selective Appreciation.

According to Nadal (2004), the next stage in the PAID model (Stage 4), the *Panethnic Asian American Consciousness* stage, is unique to the Filipino American experience. In this stage, Filipino

Americans continue to hold the same attitudes about themselves, their heritage group, and different ethnic or cultural groups as in Stage 3, but with a stronger sense of solidarity with other Asian Americans. This more positive regard toward and stronger affiliation with other Asian Americans may be sparked by the realization that there is strength in numbers when sociopolitical change is desired. This may also be sparked by the recognition of the similarities between the experiences and cultures of Filipino Americans and those of other Asian Americans. In Stage 5, however, Filipino Americans enter the *Ethnocentric Realization* stage where they begin to also regard other Asian Americans with some suspicion or negativity because of the realization that Filipino Americans are often discriminated against or marginalized by other Asian Americans (Filipino American specific microaggressions, as discussed in Chapter 4). This stage may also be sparked by the recognition that there are key and important differences between the Filipino American experience and culture and those of other Asian Americans. As the name suggests, Filipino Americans may become ethnocentric at this stage, regarding anything Filipino as better than anything non-Filipino, including those that are of other Asian groups. According to Nadal (2004), this stage is also unique to Filipino Americans, similar to Stage 4. Finally, in Stage 6, Filipino Americans reach the *Incorporation* stage where their regard of other Asian Americans become almost neutral again (accepting) and their regard of the dominant White culture is that of "selective appreciation" (Nadal, 2004). Similar to the other ethnic identity development models (Atkinson, Morten, & Sue, 1998; Kim, 1981; Phinney, 1992), this last stage of the PAID model is regarded as the most ideal and beneficial stage of ethnic identity formation. Table 3 provides a summary of the PAID model and how a Filipino American may regard his or her personal self, other Filipinos and Filipino Americans, other Asian Americans, other minority groups, and the dominant White group in each of the six stages, as adapted from Nadal (2004).

Colonial Mentality, Kapwa, and Identity

As groundbreaking as Nadal's (2004) PAID model is, however, it does not go far enough to incorporate the effects of historical and contemporary oppression throughout all of the stages. Although it acknowledges that each stage may be influenced by the experiences of Filipino Americans with their environment, even going as far as to mentioning the possible influences of oppression, racism, and discrimination, the PAID model is limited in the sense that a Filipino American person's ethnic identity development may have already been affected by the extent to which such a person's parents, grandparents, relatives, and immediate social network may have CM or have lost or diluted their sense of Kapwa. In other words, Filipinos' and Filipino Americans' ethnic identity may have already been influenced many generations ago before they were even born. Nevertheless, such factors are probably beyond the scope of what the PAID model attempts to accomplish. Thus, the PAID model is still regarded as a significant contribution to the field. To this end, however, I believe that it is necessary to incorporate the influences of CM and Kapwa on the manner in which Filipinos and Filipino Americans develop their sense of ethnic identity. Thus, the following discussion is not so much a critique of the PAID model, but more so a use of the PAID model in discussing a CM model of ethnic identity development for Filipinos and Filipino Americans.

Filipino American children with parents, grandparents, or other relatives who have CM and may have lost or damaged their sense of Kapwa may influence their Filipino American children's ethnic identity development. More specifically, parents with CM may not teach their children their native language because they do not want their children to speak English with a strong Filipino accent. Parents and other relatives with CM may also display to their children their preference for lighter-skinned peoples and/or their discriminatory attitudes against darker-skinned peoples. Parents and other relatives with CM may also display to their children their discriminatory attitudes toward other Filipinos who are not very Americanized (FOBs), Filipinos who are in the Philippines, or anything about the Philippines in general (e.g., "it's too hot there," "it's too trafficky," "it's too dirty," "the pollution is so bad," etc.). Such attitudes about Filipinos and the Philippines may often come out during their visits to the Philippines as *balikbayans*, where they are treated differently – in a more special way – than other Filipinos. Furthermore, although Filipino American children around this age may not be attending school yet and may not have much exposure to others outside of their parents and family members, they may nevertheless also be exposed to such Filipino-inferiorizing messages through television, movies, and other forms of media, similar to what is observed among African American children (Miller, 1999; Stevenson, 1994). Thus, even this early in life, Filipino Americans may already be receiving messages from their parents, other relatives, and the outside world about the assumed superiority and desirability of anything American or Western, and inferiority and undesirability of anything Filipino. Receiving such messages consistently from important characters in one's life such as parents and other family members may lead to the development of CM, as familial expression of CM manifestations has been shown to be related to CM development (David & Okazaki, 2006b; and as discussed in Chapter 5). Thus, having CM, in turn, can negatively affect the ethnic identity development of young Filipino Americans.

The same can be said about Filipinos in the Philippines, wherein parents, grandparents, or other relatives with CM may already be teaching their children the English language (sometimes, speaking exclusively in English to their children) so that their children will become better prepared for school, where English is the language used for instruction (as discussed in Chapters 4). Children may also be exposed to popular Filipino culture wherein the celebrities are mostly lighter-skinned folks and hear their parents and other relatives refer to such celebrities as beautiful. Such children may also be asked by their parents or other relatives to stay away from the sun because their skins might get too dark, or perhaps even see their parents and other relatives use skin whitening products to appear more White. They may even begin to hear the desires of many of their relatives to move to the United States to live a better life, see their relatives treat Filipino American relatives and friends (balikbayans) who are visiting the country in a more special manner, and observe their relatives fight over American made products brought home by their balikbayan relatives and friends as *pasalubongs* (homecoming gifts). Indeed, recent data suggests that 85-90% of Filipino immigrants in the United States witnessed their relatives, friends, and other Filipinos in the Philippines display attitudes and behaviors that denigrate the Filipino culture and ethnicity (David & Nadal, under review). These findings suggest that CM is highly ubiquitous in the Philippines, and supports the notion that the denigration of the Filipino ethnicity and culture is commonly experienced by Filipinos in the Philippines and by Filipino American immigrants long before their arrival to the U.S. Thus, Filipinos in the Philippines also receive the message that anything American or Western is better than anything Filipino very early in their lives. Filipinos and Filipino Americans, therefore, may already begin to perceive and regard the Filipino ethnicity and culture, and other Asian Americans or minorities who are darker-skinned, in a negative, deprecating, and even discriminating way, and regard the dominant White group and their characteristics in a very positive manner. In other words, Stage 2 of the PAID model may already be Stage 1 for many young Filipinos and Filipino Americans, even if their exposure to environmental factors outside their families or exposure to the mainstream culture that pressure them to assimilate (David, 2011; Roccas, Horenczyk, & Schwartz, 2000) may still be limited during their early years (e.g., because they still do not go to school, etc.).

Furthermore, if one perceives historical and contemporary discrimination and oppression as the natural cost for progress or civilization (colonial debt, one aspect of CM or internalized oppression; discussed in Chapters 2 and 5), then it will be difficult for that person to experience social and political awakening (Stage 3 of the PAID model). In other words, a person with CM – specifically colonial debt – will be unlikely to stand up against the discrimination that they, their group, other Asian Americans, and other oppressed groups experience. Such a negative relationship between CM and ethnic identity has been supported by empirical data, as recent research have shown that higher CM levels are related to lower levels of ethnic identity development (David, 2008; David, 2010b; David & Okazaki, 2006b). With CM, it is difficult for Filipinos and Filipino Americans who possess such a colonized ethnic identity formation to escape it or move beyond from it, and such a colonized ethnic identity may last their entire lifetime.

The loss or the dilution of the sense of Kapwa among Filipinos and Filipino Americans, due to CM or internalized oppression (as discussed in Chapter 7), may influence the manner to which they are able to escape the colonized type of ethnic identity that they may have developed and progress to the other ethnic identity stages in the PAID model. Indeed, if one's sense of Kapwa is already damaged or gone, it will be difficult for a person to feel a connection with other people, especially other Filipinos and Filipino Americans. Without Kapwa, it will be difficult for a Filipino or a Filipino American person to display Pakikisama and participate in Filipino events, celebrations, gatherings, or projects. Such a lack of Pakikisama, participation, and involvement in family, community, or other social gatherings may lead to the person being regarded negatively by his or her community, friends, and family, because such a person may now be perceived as someone who does not have Hiya, Utang na loob, or Pakikisama. For example, Liebkind and Jasinskaja-Lahti (2000) reported that parental support and obedience to traditional Filipino values improve psychological well-being. Highly assimilated or Americanized Filipino American youths may not receive such familial support because of their failure to adhere to Filipino values, which, in turn, may contribute to their distress. The survey by the Filipino American Council of Chicago reported that 33% of their respondents had experienced parent-child conflicts because of the cultural clash between Filipino and American values (Cimmarusti, 1996). Furthermore, Heras and Revilla (1994) found that mothers of highly assimilated Filipino American youths who may no longer adhere to values such as Hiya, Utang na loob, and Pakikisama reported lower family satisfaction than mothers of more enculturated Filipino American adolescents. Consequently, Filipinos or Filipino Americans who are regarded as not having Hiya, Utang na loob, or Pakikisama may become avoided, marginalized, or negatively regarded by others, including important characters such as parents and other relatives. Such a marginalization makes it difficult for the Filipino or Filipino American to make connections with other Asian Americans, other minorities, and other Filipinos and Filipino Americans. It is more difficult for Filipinos and Filipino Americans with a damaged or lost sense of Kapwa, or those who fail to adhere to values such as Hiya, Utang na loob, and Pakikisama, to see the similarities between their oppressed experiences and the oppressed experiences of other Filipinos, other Asian Americans, and other minority groups.

For Filipinos in the Philippines, without Kapwa it will be difficult for them to acknowledge the oppression that many non-Manilan, non-Catholic, non-Christian, and non-educated Filipinos experience contemporarily. It will be difficult for them to make connections between their oppressed realities and the oppressed realities of other groups around the world, whether they are Asians, Africans, Latinos, Native Americans, or whatever else. It will be difficult for them to acknowledge, respect, and value the strong but oppressed indigenous groups in the Philippines such as the Ifugao, the Negrito, the Bagobo, the Kalinga, and the Tboli peoples, among others. Without Kapwa, they will constantly look for ways in which they can differentiate or separate themselves from others. It will be difficult for them not to discriminate against the non-Manilan, non-Christian, non-educated, or non-Westernized Filipinos. It will be difficult for them not to discriminate against the darker-skinned Filipinos, or just darker-skinned peoples more generally (e.g., Africans, Latinos, etc.).

Consequently, it is almost impossible for Filipinos and Filipino Americans with a damaged or lost sense of Kapwa to develop a panethnic Asian American consciousness (Stage 4 of the PAID model) and achieve ethnocentric realization (Stage 5 of the PAID model). With this logic, it is almost impossible for Filipinos and Filipino Americans to achieve the last, most ideal, and theoretically most beneficial stage of the PAID model – the incorporation stage (Nadal, 2004). Thus, CM and the consequent loss of or damage to one's sense of Kapwa, may keep many Filipinos and Filipino Americans from progressing beyond the assimilation to dominant culture stage (Stage 2 of the PAID model).

Chapter Summary

This chapter discussed the manner in which Filipinos and Filipino Americans may develop their sense of ethnic identity using the seminal Pilipino American Identity Development (PAID) model proposed by Nadal (2004). With this framework, I have theoretically explored how the psychological consequence of historical and contemporary oppression – CM or internalized oppression – may influence Filipinos' and Filipino Americans' ethnic identity. Briefly, the ethnic identity of Filipinos and Filipino Americans may have already been negatively affected by historical and contemporary oppression even very early in their lives if their parents and other relatives hold CM and pass on to them a general negative regard of anything Filipino and superior regard of anything American or Western. Thus, Stage 1 of the PAID model may not be true for many Filipinos and Filipino Americans. Also, CM may lead many Filipinos and Filipino Americans to lose or damage their sense of Kapwa, leading them to not participate, contribute, or attend many Filipino, community, family, or other social events, gatherings, or celebrations. Their lack of participation and contribution to such important events may lead to others, especially other Filipinos and Filipino Americans, to regard them negatively because of their failure to display or practice other important Filipino values such as Hiya, Utang na Loob, and Pakikisama. Not adhering to such Filipino values may lead to them being marginalized from other people, especially from other Filipinos and Filipino Americans. Such marginalization may only serve to reinforce the negative attitudes they already hold toward other Filipinos and Filipino Americans, as well as toward other minorities or non-Western peoples. Thus, based on the CM-contextualized identity development model discussed in this chapter, many Filipinos and Filipino Americans may be stuck in the assimilation to the dominant culture stage (Stage 2 of 6) of the PAID model, and it may be difficult for them to progress in their ethnic identity development formation toward more beneficial and desired stages. Future empirical and data-based research is needed to investigate such theoretical possibilities, and further our understanding of the dynamics between historical and contemporary oppression, CM, Kapwa, and ethnic identity formation among Filipinos and Filipino Americans.

*   *   *

In addition to exploring the theoretical relationships between CM, Kapwa, and ethnic identity among Filipinos and Filipino Americans, this chapter has also introduced us to concepts such as acculturation and enculturation. These concepts, along with other related psychological constructs such as personal and collective self-esteem, have been found to significantly contribute to various mental and behavioral health variables in several psychological research, and thus, are regarded as important mental and behavioral health-related variables to consider especially for ethnic and cultural minorities. Also, as discussed in this chapter as well as in Chapter 7, CM and the loss of Kapwa may lead many Filipinos and Filipino Americans to become negatively regarded, avoided, and marginalized by other members of their community or family. As a result, many Filipinos and Filipino Americans may not have strong, positive, and reliable social support networks that may serve as buffers or protective factors against many mental and behavioral health concerns. Thus, CM and the consequent loss or dilution of Kapwa that may negatively affect the ethnic identity of many Filipinos and Filipino Americans may play a significant role in their mental and behavioral health. The mental and behavioral health implications of CM or internalized oppression among Filipinos and Filipino Americans are discussed in more detail in the next chapter.

Chapter 9

Mental Health Implications of Colonial Mentality

ᜋᜒᜈ᜔ᜆᜎ᜔ ᜈᜅ᜔ ᜃᜎᜓᜐᜓᜒᜌᜎ᜔ ᜈᜅ᜔ ᜃᜆᜓᜆᜓᜐᜈ᜔
ᜈ᜔ ᜋ ᜈ᜔ ᜃᜆᜒᜐᜈᜆ᜔

The findings from the relatively few mental health-related research among Filipinos and Filipino Americans suggest that this group faces several alarming issues. For instance, Filipino American adolescents have one of the highest rates of suicidal ideation in the United States (President's Advisory Commission on Asian Americans and Pacific Islanders, 2001). Indeed, the Center for Disease Control and Prevention reported that 45.6% of Filipina American adolescents have thought about suicide – the highest rate among all ethnic groups (as reported by Agbayani-Siewart & Enrile, 2003; Wolf, 1997). Among Filipino American adults, Kuo (1984) found a higher rate of depression for this group (19.1%) than for White Americans (15.6%). Relatedly, a study among Filipino American adults in California showed that only 20% of Filipino Americans reported feeling satisfied with their lives, compared to a

32% life satisfaction rate among the general population (Cabezas, 1982). Tompar-Tiu and Sustento-Seneriches (1995), using the Center of Epidemiological Studies Depression Scale (CES-D) among Filipino American adults in California, revealed a depression rate (27.3%) that was higher than rates reported for the general United States population (10%-20%). Based on a national sample of Filipino Americans also using the CES-D, my mentor and I (David & Okazaki, 2006b) found a similarly high depression rate (30.0%) for this group. More recently, I (David, 2008) found a 29.8% depression rate in a separate national sample of Filipino Americans. Despite such evidence showing high rates of distress by Filipino Americans, however, members of this group have been reported to seek mental health services at a much lower rate than the general population and even compared to other Asian American groups (Gong, Gage, & Tacata, 2003), suggesting that many Filipinos and Filipino Americans may have unmet mental health needs.

Based on the discussions in the previous chapters, it is now clear that historical and contemporary oppression has influenced how Filipinos and Filipino Americans think about, feel about, and behave toward themselves, other Filipinos and Filipino Americans, and other racial or ethnic groups (e.g., the dominant White group). We now understand that because of colonialism and contemporary oppression, many Filipinos and Filipino Americans may have developed CM or internalized oppression and this may be expressed by regarding anything of the Filipino culture or ethnicity as inferior to anything American or European (Chapter 5). Such a consequence of oppression can influence the extent to which Filipinos and Filipino Americans still have *Kapwa* (Chapter 7) and the manner in which they develop their ethnic identity (Chapter 8). The presented materials thus far support the notion that colonialism and contemporary oppression has influenced the psychological experiences of Filipinos and Filipino Americans, as well as their sense of identity and personhood (pagka-tao). Although already significant as is, it is important to further address the question of why it is necessary to pay attention to CM. In other words, *so what if Filipinos and Filipino Americans have colonial mentality? So what if they are no longer connected with their heritage and no longer subscribe to their culture? So what if they do not value their heritage? So what if they do not regard the Filipino ethnicity and culture in equal regard as the American culture? Does colonial mentality or CM have an effect on the concerning indicators of Filipino and Filipino American mental health such as low rates of life satisfaction, and high rates of depression and suicide?* This chapter will address the *so what* questions by discussing in detail how the consequence of historical and contemporary oppression – CM or internalized oppression – has negatively affected the mental health and psychological well-being of Filipinos and Filipino Americans.

Colonial Mentality and Acculturation

The two previous chapters have made it clear that it is important for many Filipinos and Filipino Americans to stay connected with their heritage ethnicity and culture. In the field of psychology, the extent to which an individual is connected with, comfortable in, and can appropriately function within his or her heritage culture is called *enculturation*. The extent to which an individual does or does not stay connected with one's heritage culture, or the degree to which an individual connects or does not connect with another culture, is called the process of *acculturation* (David, 2006). Many factors can influence the process of acculturation, including larger sociopolitical factors such as the economy, immigration status, discrimination, and oppression. As acculturating individuals experience such sociopolitical factors that force them to change or adapt, stress may come about. Researchers in ethnic minority psychology have found that *acculturative stress* and how acculturating individuals respond to such stress is related to their mental health (for a review, see Balls Organista, Organista, & Kurasaki, 2003). Berry (2003) argued that persons may acculturate in four different ways: *assimilation* (high adherence to dominant culture and low adherence to heritage culture), *integration* (high adherence to both cultures), *separation* (low adherence to dominant culture and high adherence to heritage culture), and *marginalization* (low adherence to both cultures). Although there is no current consensus as to which strategy is the most beneficial (Rudmin, 2003), high levels of enculturation (i.e., the extent to which one adheres to one's heritage culture), either alone (i.e., Berry's separation) or in combination with high dominant culture adherence (i.e., Berry's integration), often contribute to better well-being and mental health (e.g., Balls Organista et al., 2003; David, Okazaki, & Saw, 2009; LaFromboise, Coleman, & Gerton, 1993; Sands & Berry, 1993; Tsai, Chentsova-Dutton, & Wong, 2002; Ying, 1995). Enculturation is theorized to lead toward the development of a *positive ethnic identity,* which is associated with psychological well-being (e.g., Gong, Takeuchi, Agbayani-Siewart, & Tacata, 2003; Phinney, 1992; Phinney, Chavira, & Williamson, 1992).

Using the CMS (as presented in Chapter 5) as the measure of CM or internalized oppression, there is scientific evidence suggesting that higher levels of CM is related to lower levels of enculturation and higher levels of assimilation among Filipinos and Filipino Americans (David, 2008; David, 2010b; David & Okazaki, 2006b). These studies also show that higher CM levels are related to lower levels of ethnic identity development. That is, Filipinos or Filipino Americans who have CM tend to not be connected with their Filipino heritage (low enculturation), tend to be more likely to assimilate (adhere only to the dominant American culture), and are less likely to value, understand, and participate in their heritage Filipino culture (low ethnic identity). As discussed in Chapter 7, low enculturation and low ethnic identity among Filipinos and Filipino Americans may be influenced by ignoring, devaluing, or losing their sense of Kapwa due to historical colonialism and contemporary oppression. In other words, CM may be negatively influencing Filipinos' and Filipino Americans' sense of Kapwa and adherence to other indigenous Filipino values, which in turn leads to lower levels of enculturation and ethnic identity development. Furthermore, these studies also provided empirical evidence connecting CM with levels of life satisfaction, such that Filipinos and Filipino Americans with CM tend to be less satisfied with their lives (lower levels of psychological well-being). The same relationships between CM, enculturation, assimilation, ethnic identity, and life satisfaction among Filipinos and Filipino Americans were found using the implicit association test (as discussed in Chapter 6) as the tool to measure CM or internalized oppression (David, 2010b).

Colonial Mentality and Self-Esteem

Although most of our current understanding of the self is focused on the personal aspect or *personal self-esteem* (i.e., how positively one evaluates one's personal characteristics), scholars argue that developing a *positive collective self* and having a positive *collective self-esteem* (i.e., how positively one evaluates the social groups to which one belongs) is also vital for mental health (Crocker & Luhtanen, 1990; Crocker, Luhtanen, Blaine, & Broadnax, 1994; Tajfel & Turner, 1986). Our self-concept is not just composed of the individual or personal self. Instead, self-concept is composed of both a personal and a collective component and each component can be associated with either positive (or pleasant) or negative (or unpleasant) attributes (Tajfel & Turner, 1986). The manner in which we associate positive or negative attributes to our personal characteristics (e.g., being tall, being athletic, being good a math, etc.) and the characteristics of the groups we belong to (e.g., my family is supportive, my group of friends are never serious, my church is helpful to a lot of people, etc.) is influenced by our experiences, what we learn, and what we have been taught. If personal self-esteem is the extent to which individuals evaluate their personal selves positively, collective self-esteem is the extent to which individuals evaluate the social groups they belong to positively (Crocker & Luhtanen, 1990, Luhtanen & Crocker, 1992).

Among Filipinos and Filipino Americans, Kapwa is the core of their personhood which connects their self to the self of others – it is a shared inner self – a recognition that the self and the other are one and the same (Enriquez, 1994). If some Filipinos and Filipino Americans no longer have Kapwa or they are consistently ignoring or devaluing their sense of Kapwa, then they are in danger of ignoring and devaluing their shared connectedness with other people – in essence devaluing the other half of their self-concept (i.e., their collective self), a part of their self-concept that is just as vital for psychological well-being and mental health as the personal aspect of the self.

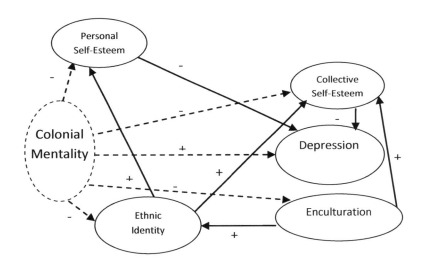

Figure 10. The Colonial Mentality Model of Depression

One important social group or collective identity for ethnic minority individuals is their ethnic or cultural group. The extent to which ethnic minority individuals evaluate their heritage ethnic or cultural group is one aspect of their collective self-esteem. For a collectivistic and especially people-centered culture such as Filipinos and Filipino Americans, for whom the value of Kapwa is considered to be the most important concept and part of being a person or Filipino, being connected to and having high regard for the Filipino culture and ethnicity is essential. However, for Filipinos and Filipino Americans, their experiences of centuries of classical and internal colonialism may have resulted into CM, which in turn, may negatively influence their sense of Kapwa and collective self-esteem. Empirically, using the CMS as the tool to measure CM or internalized oppression, such a speculation was supported as we (David & Okazaki, 2006b; David, 2008) found CM to be related to lower levels of personal and collective self-esteem among Filipinos and Filipino Americans. That is, Filipinos and Filipino Americans who have CM tend to have more negative evaluations of their personal characteristics and the characteristics of the Filipino culture and ethnicity. The same relationships between CM, personal self-esteem, and collective self-esteem among Filipinos and Filipino Americans were found using the implicit association test (as discussed in Chapter 6) as the tool to measure CM (David, 2010b).

Colonial Mentality and Depression

The literature on ethnic minority psychology suggests that psychological constructs that are especially salient to minorities (e.g., enculturation, ethnic identity, collective self-esteem) are potential contributors to their mental health. More specifically, various studies consistently show that such constructs are related to symptoms of depression (for a review, see Balls Organista, Organista, & Kurasaki, 2003). The solid variables and paths in Figure 10 represent the relationships between these psychological constructs and depression symptoms. Based on the studies described above, such psychological constructs among Filipinos and Filipino Americans are influenced by CM or internalized oppression. Other studies using both the CMS (David, 2008; David & Okazaki, 2006b) and the implicit association test (David, 2010b) to capture CM or internalized oppression also show that higher levels of CM are related to more depression symptoms among Filipinos and Filipino Americans. In other words, Filipinos and Filipino Americans who have CM tend to experience more depression symptoms than Filipinos and Filipino Americans who do not have CM (Figure 11). Thus, it is possible that CM or internalized oppression is also related to depression symptoms through its connections with other psychological constructs such as enculturation, ethnic identity, and collective self-esteem (through the devaluing and loss of Kapwa). The variables and paths represented by dashed lines in Figure 10 compose the effects of CM or internalized oppression on depression.

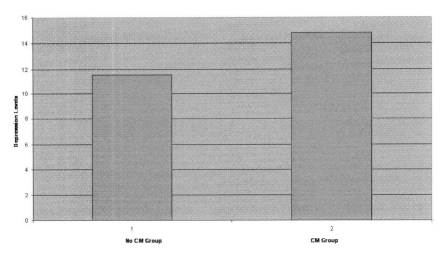

Depression Levels Between CM and No CM Groups

Figure 11. Levels of Depression (as measured by the Center for Epidemiological Studies-Depression Scale; CES-D; Radloff, 1977) of Individuals With and Without CM. CES-D scores of 16 or above may suggest clinical depression.

Using *structural equation modeling*, I (David, 2008) tested the CM model in Figure 9 and found CM to be negatively related to enculturation, ethnic identity, personal self-esteem, and collective self-esteem. I also tested a conceptual model of depression symptoms that included CM versus a model that did not include CM and found that the CM-model better captured Filipino Americans' experience of depression, that the CM-model accounted for a large percentage of the experienced depression symptoms (62% of the variance in depression), and that CM had a direct and significant effect on depression symptoms above and beyond the effects of other variables such as enculturation, ethnic identity, personal self-esteem, and collective self-esteem on depression. Thus, it is clear that CM can significantly contribute to the depression symptoms that many Filipinos and Filipino Americans experience. Given what we know regarding the strong link between depression and suicide, CM may also be an important factor to consider when addressing the high rates of suicide ideation among Filipinos and Filipino Americans.

Colonial Mentality and Other Mental and Behavioral Health Concerns

Given CM or internalized oppression's documented relationships with variables such as personal and collective self-esteem, satisfaction with life, as well as with depression symptoms, it is not too farfetched to hypothesize that CM may also be negatively related to other mental health concerns facing Filipinos and Filipino Americans, primarily because low self-esteem and depression typically go hand in hand or co-occur with other problem behaviors and conditions (e.g., Clark, Watson, & Reynolds, 1995; Owens, 2001). For instance, through CM's negative effects on self-esteem, Nadal (2009) provided case studies that linked CM or internalized oppression to clinically-diagnosable conditions such as eating disorders and social anxiety or social phobia. Recent research also suggest that experiences of oppression may lead oppressed individuals to experience maladaptive emotional and cognitive states such as rumination, emotional avoidance, negative self-schemas, and feelings of hopelessness in response to such experiences, all of which may increase the likelihood of oppressed individuals to develop clinically diagnosable disorders or for them to engage in high-risk behaviors (Hatzenbuehler, 2009). Furthermore, not having Kapwa, having low levels of enculturation, and not positively identifying with one's heritage ethnicity and culture can lead one to become avoided and, thus, marginalized, even by others who are important characters in the person's life (e.g., family, relatives, friends, etc.). Not having a strong and positive social support system may lead to many high-risk and problematic behaviors such as alcohol and drug use, unprotected sex, delinquency, and school drop-outs (e.g., Kim, & Goto, 2000; Newcomb, & Bentler, 1988; Peirce, Frone, Russell, Cooper, & Mudar, 2000; Solomon, & Liefeld, 1998; Steptoe, Wardle, Pollard, Canaan, & Davies, 1999). Thus, although there are various factors that may contribute to such problematic and health-risk behaviors, and although CM-specific empirical research still needs to be conducted, CM may also be one of such important factors that may contribute to the development of behavioral and mental health concerns according to theory and based on the empirical literature on other related variables.

Also, the psychological literature on other historically and contemporarily groups such as African Americans, Alaska Natives, and American Indians or Native Americans suggest that, among these groups, internalized oppression is related to domestic violence and other violent crimes, substance use and abuse, school drop-out rates, and high-risk behaviors that may lead to sexually-transmitted diseases and unwanted teen pregnancies (e.g., Duran & Duran, 1995; Harrell, 1999; McBride, 2002; Tatum, 1994). Interestingly, findings from the small body of Filipino American-focused research indicate similar alarming issues for this community as well, including high rates of HIV/AIDS, unintended pregnancy, eating disorders, sexually transmitted infections, alcohol and drug use (Nadal, 2000; Nadal, 2009), school drop-outs (President's Advisory Commission on Asian Americans and Pacific Islanders, 2001), and low rates of college admission and graduation (Okamura, 1998). High rates of incarceration, delinquency, and gang membership and involvement in gang violence have also been reported for Filipino American adolescents throughout the United States, especially in areas where there are large concentrations of Filipino -/ Americans (see Nadal, 2009 for a review). One main similarity between Filipino -/ Americans and other groups such as African Americans, American Indians or Native Americans, and Alaska Natives is that they all have experienced centuries of historical and contemporary oppression (as discussed in Chapters 3, 4, and 5). Given: (1) the abundance of psychological literature linking low self-esteem to symptoms of depression, suicide, gang involvement, poor vocational and educational performance, alcohol and other drug use, and other high-risk behaviors that may lead to unintended pregnancies and sexually-transmitted diseases; (2) the literature on other oppressed groups linking internalized oppression to various mental and behavioral health outcomes; and (3) the literature on CM among Filipinos and Filipino Americans linking CM or internalized oppression to low levels of self-esteem and higher depression symptoms, it is reasonable to hypothesize that CM or internalized oppression may also be contributing to the high rates of other mental and behavioral health concerns experienced by Filipinos and Filipino Americans.

Cultural Mistrust: Another Consequence of Oppression

Another psychological consequence of historical and contemporary oppression – *cultural mistrust* – may also play a role in Filipino and Filipino American mental health. Initially conceptualized for African Americans, cultural mistrust is defined as a psychological construct that describes the general distrust among African Americans of White Americans and mainstream American institutions including the legal system, political system, government agencies, educational system, health care system, employment settings, and other entities that are governed or staffed by White Americans, primarily because of the centuries of oppression that African Americans have experienced (Carter, 2007; Terrell &

Terrell, 1981; Whaley, 2001). Thus, cultural mistrust may be considered as another reaction to oppression that is the complete opposite of CM, and some Filipinos and Filipino Americans have been shown to also experience cultural mistrust (David, 2010c). Although cultural mistrust is theoretically the opposite of CM, cultural mistrust is still a reaction to, and therefore an effect, of historical and contemporary oppression. Thus, it is important to briefly discuss its mental health implications here.

It is widely accepted in the field of psychology that racism and racism-related stress are associated with the experience of paranoia and schizophrenia (e.g., Combs, Penn, & Fenigstein, 2002). Furthermore, although racism-related stress can lead to psychopathology, an adaptive, logical, and even healthy form of paranoia (i.e., cultural mistrust) among African Americans may be misunderstood by many clinicians as pathological paranoia, which may contribute to the overdiagnoses of paranoid schizophrenia among this racial group (Whaley, 2001). Similarly, Filipinos' and Filipino Americans' extensive experiences of oppression, which may lead to higher levels of cultural mistrust, may also contribute to the development of psychopathology or overdiagnoses of paranoia and schizophrenia. Indeed, some researchers have reported that Filipino Americans have higher rates of schizophrenia than other Asian American ethnic groups (Sanchez & Gaw, 2007; Young & Kinzie, 1974). A recent large-scale study of mental health service use among all racial and ethnic groups in California (Barreto & Segal, 2005), where Filipinos compose the largest Asian American ethnic group, have even reported that schizophrenia was more frequently diagnosed among Filipino American clients (23.8%) than African American clients (20.0%). Thus, cultural mistrust – another psychological consequence of historical and contemporary oppression – may also be playing a role in Filipinos' and Filipino Americans' experiences with schizophrenia, especially the paranoid type (David, 2010c).

Covert Colonial Mentality and Mental Health

It has been my experience, in many years of conducting research on CM or internalized oppression and presenting such research in professional and community events, that people frequently raise the possibility that just because they have some aspects of CM does not necessarily mean that they are ashamed of being Filipino, feel depressed, or have low self-esteem. In other words, many Filipinos and Filipino Americans may discriminate against FOBs or desire to look, talk, and act more Westernized or Americanized, but they also report being highly proud of their heritage and do not experience mental health concerns. Indeed, I myself know plenty of Filipinos and Filipino Americans who express similar experiences. In such cases, what I believe is happening is that different aspects of CM have differential effects on mental health. That is, research seems to suggest that it is the covert components of CM that is especially linked with poorer mental health than the overt CM components.

Using the CMS as the measure of the overt manifestations of CM and the implicit association test as the measure of the covert manifestations of CM (as discussed in Chapter 6), I (David, 2010b) found that covert CM is moderating the link between overt CM and depression symptoms. That is, Filipinos and Filipino Americans who have overt CM manifestations such as discriminating against FOBs and desiring to look and act more White or American, and also hold covert CM manifestations such as feeling inferior, ashamed, or embarrassed of their Filipino heritage, tend to experience more depression symptoms. The mental health of Filipinos and Filipino Americans who have overt CM manifestations but do not have the covert CM manifestations do not seem to be negatively affected. Thus, it is possible that some Filipinos and Filipino Americans may hold and display overt CM manifestations not because they are ashamed or embarrassed of their Filipino heritage, but because of external pressures to fit in with the majority. Their efforts and perhaps success in fitting-in with the majority, in turn, may lead to fewer instances of discrimination and marginalization for such individuals, which may benefit their mental health.

Such findings also call for a slight modification of CM theory. According to CM theory as discussed in Chapter 5, covert CM is externally-driven or driven by factors outside the person. That is, one's experiences of oppression, which is an external factor, may eventually lead to the development of feelings of inferiority, shame, and embarrassment toward the Filipino ethnicity and culture, which are covert CM manifestations. Once Filipinos and Filipino Americans develop covert CM, it may create an internal desire among individuals to display overt CM such as changing one's physical characteristics and discriminating against less Americanized Filipinos (overt CM manifestations). Thus, overt CM was initially conceptualized as internally-driven or driven by factors inside the person, and that overt CM develops after, or as a result of, covert CM. However, given recent scientific evidence (David, 2010b), CM theory (as discussed in Chapter 5) is incomplete in that covert CM may also develop as a result of overt CM. Furthermore, overt CM may also develop as a result of factors outside the person such as one's experiences of oppression. Individuals who commonly observe others being discriminated against, made fun of, or teased (in psychology, this example is called *vicarious learning*) may eventually learn to display overt CM manifestations such as wanting to be lighter skinned, speak English without a Filipino accent, or discriminate against Filipinos who are perceived to be *too Filipino* as an effort to "fit in" and not be subjected to such maltreatments themselves. Within such individuals, however, they may still feel proud of their Filipino heritage. In other words, they are outwardly displaying one set of behaviors (i.e., overt CM) but internally they hold a different set of attitudes. Thus, individuals need not develop covert CM first before developing and displaying overt CM. Instead, individuals may display overt CM without covert CM or without their overt behaviors being driven by internal factors. Indeed, their overt behaviors may also be driven by external factors such as the pressure to "fit in" and avoid being maltreated.

In terms of mental health implications, these recent results suggest that *internally-driven overt CM* (overt CM with covert CM) may be negatively related to mental health. *Externally-driven overt CM* (overt CM without covert CM) by itself, on the other hand, may not be immediately detrimental to Filipino and Filipino American mental health. In fact, overt CM with no covert CM may even serve as a protective factor against mental health concerns. Such individuals may be displaying overt CM not because of covert CM, but because of learned behaviors (through vicarious learning, etc.) that they believe will allow them to "fit in" better and not be subjected to maltreatments. That is, some Filipinos and Filipino Americans may simply be making fun of FOBs because they have learned that this is one manner in which to be accepted by the mainstream or dominant group. This may possibly be how overt CM may function as a protective factor against depression, because individuals with externally-driven overt CM may indeed be more Westernized, and thus, are less likely to experience oppression that may negatively affect their mental health (David, 2010b).

Despite the seemingly innocuous or harmless effects of externally-driven overt CM, however, this does not mean that Filipinos and Filipino Americans with such a form of overt CM will not develop covert CM. It is possible that individuals with externally-driven overt CM may eventually develop covert CM with continued exposure to and practice of overt CM. That is, individuals with externally-driven overt CM may begin to internalize the oppressive messages about one's cultural group with continued exposure to and practice of overt CM. Furthermore, such individuals may begin to feel conflicted and distressed about the contradictions between their behaviors (overt CM) and feelings or attitudes (covert CM) (*Cognitive Dissonance Theory* [CDT]; Festinger, 1957). Thus, consistent with CDT's contention that it is easier to change one's attitudes than to change one's behaviors (Aronson, 1969), individuals with externally-driven overt CM may eventually change their attitudes and feelings (i.e., develop covert CM such as feelings of inferiority and embarrassment for being of Filipino heritage) to make them more consistent with their behaviors. Finally, such overt displays of CM may still be detrimental to the community as a whole as it creates division within the community and prevents Filipinos and Filipino Americans from being united and from speaking out against oppression. Furthermore, such overt acts of CM may also be injurious to future generations of Filipinos and Filipino Americans who witness such behaviors, which in turn, may contribute toward the development of covert CM such as feelings of shame, embarrassment, and inferiority for being Filipino, the component of CM that is strongly linked with various mental health concerns (David, 2010b).

Chapter Summary

This chapter has addressed the *so what?* questions surrounding the existence, salience, and influence of CM or internalized oppression on the psychological experience of Filipinos and Filipino Americans. Not only does CM play a major role in how Filipinos and Filipino Americans think about, feel about, and behave toward themselves, other Filipinos and Filipino Americans, and other racial or ethnic groups, not only does CM influence the extent to which Filipinos and Filipino Americans retain their cultural values, the extent to which they still value and express Kapwa, and the extent to which they identify with the Filipino ethnicity and culture, but CM also plays a significant role in Filipino and Filipino American mental health and other behavioral concerns. More specifically, this chapter has presented empirical and theoretical literature suggesting that CM is strongly and consistently related to various mental health and mental health-related outcome variables such as self-esteem, depression, suicide, anxiety, life satisfaction, ethnic identity, acculturation, general psychological distress, and other behavioral health concerns such as substance use and abuse, school drop-outs, and delinquency. This chapter also further refined our understanding of CM as experienced by Filipinos and Filipino Americans, in that we now have a more complex understanding of the different components of CM and how they differentially relate to mental health variables. More specifically, empirical evidence suggests that it is the covert component of CM that is especially linked to the mental health and psychological well-being of Filipinos and Filipino Americans. We now also have a more complex understanding of CM theory by knowing the difference between externally-driven and internally-driven overt CM manifestations, with the internally-driven type being the one linked to mental health and psychological being among Filipinos and Filipino Americans. By discussing the mental and behavioral health implications of CM among Filipinos and Filipino Americans, this chapter has connected historical and contemporary oppression to very real concerns that many in the Filipino and Filipino American community struggle with on a daily basis. It is hoped that by doing so, more attention and efforts toward better understanding and addressing CM will come about.

*   *   *

Despite all of the serious mental and behavioral health concerns facing the Filipino and Filipino American community, however, members of this group tend to not seek professional services for such concerns. Indeed, one major and consistent finding in Asian American/Pacific Islander (AAPI) mental health research is that, as low as the rate of help-seeking is among AAPIs, Filipino Americans seek mental health services at a much lower rate even compared to other AAPIs (Gong, Gage, & Tacata, 2003). Using thousands of data from the Filipino American Community Epidemiological Study (FACES) dataset, the largest epidemiological study with Filipino Americans thus far, Gong and colleagues (2003) found that 75% of their sample have never used any type of mental health service, with an additional 17% receiving help from their friends, relatives, priests, ministers, herbalists, spiritualists, or fortune-tellers only. Thus, many Filipinos and Filipino Americans may not be receiving the appropriate services that they may need. One commonly cited reason for such an underutilization of mental health services is the lack of cultural sensitivity of existing services (Sue & Zane, 2006). Furthermore, despite clinical psychology's efforts to develop and promote *empirically-supported treatments* (ESTs) (Chambless & Hollon, 1998; Chambless, et al., 1996), the applicability and appropriateness of such treatments for non-White or non-Western peoples still remain to be a controversial issue. Indeed, various researchers have commented that there is not one EST for ethnic minority populations (Bernal & Scharron-Del Rio, 2001; Chambless, et al., 1996; Sue & Zane, 2006; Zane, Hall, Sue, Young, & Nunez, 2003). Among Filipinos and Filipino Americans, cultural mistrust or regarding existing mental health services as culturally insensitive or inappropriate for their needs may contribute to lower likelihood of seeking and using such services (David, 2010c). Consequently, there has also been a recent push toward making psychological treatments more culturally appropriate and, thus, more effective for non-Western or non-White individuals (e.g., Sue & Zane, 1987). In the next and last part of the book (Part III), I provide a discussion of culturally-sensitive and culturally-appropriate interventions and strategies that are intended to address CM or internalized oppression among Filipinos and Filipino Americans.

PART III:

DECOLONIZATION IN A MODERN WORLD

Upon realizing that Spanish and American colonialism brought immense damages to the Filipino and Filipino American peoples, cultures, identities, and mental health, are modern day Filipinos and Filipino Americans supposed to reject anything American or Western? Is it beneficial for modern day Filipinos and Filipino Americans to perceive Western or American culture – along with its many influences – as automatically bad and evil, and regard anything Filipino as better, superior, or more desirable? When we talk about decolonization today, do we mean that modern day Filipinos and Filipino Americans literally have to give up their current lives and go back to the indigenous Tao's pre-colonial culture and ways of life (as described in Chapter 1)? Now that we have a better understanding of the historical and contemporary experiences of Filipinos and Filipino Americans, how such experiences may have led to CM or internalized oppression, and how CM or internalized oppression have influenced Filipino and Filipino American psychology and mental health, this final part of the book will discuss some ways in which the consequences of historical and contemporary oppression – CM or internalized oppression – may be addressed by modern day Filipinos and Filipino Americans.

In brief, the answer to all of the questions above is "no." Although this book has presented aspects of American or Western history and culture that are less than positive, and although this book has delineated how Filipinos' and Filipino Americans' culture, psychology, and mental health may have been damaged by Western colonialism and oppression, it is still undeniable that there are some positive influences of Spanish and American colonialism and that there are many Filipinos and Filipino Americans today who value many things about the Western or American culture. In fact, for many Filipinos and Filipino Americans today, the Western or American culture is an important part of their social or collective selves as well, especially those who are of mixed race (22% of the Filipino American population; Nadal, 2009). Thus, automatically rejecting this important component of their self-concept can also be as damaging to their psychological experiences, identities, and mental health (as discussed in Chapters 8 and 9). In essence, what I believe needs to take place is for Filipinos and Filipino Americans to develop an accurate and realistic understanding of the Filipino and the American histories, cultures, and societies, and not simply and automatically regard one part of their self-concept as superior or inferior to the other (similar to the Incorporation stage as discussed in Chapter 8). An equal regard of both cultures – both of which are important parts of their self-concept that equally contribute to a positive mental health (as discussed in Chapter 9; David, Okazaki, & Saw, 2009; LaFromboise, Coleman, & Gerton, 1993) – is likely to be the most psychologically beneficial approach to, and goal of, any decolonization effort.

To this end, Part III of the book will discuss some programs or interventions that essentially attempt to facilitate among Filipinos and Filipino Americans a more complete, accurate, and realistic understanding of their histories and contemporary experiences. With such a complete, accurate, and realistic perception of the Filipino and the American culture and society, I believe, comes a better-informed regard of both cultures. Perceptions, attitudes, and beliefs about both the Filipino and American cultures that are better-informed, in turn, can lead to fewer instances of automatically regarding anything American as superior, desirable, or pleasant, and automatically regarding anything Filipino as inferior, undesirable, or unpleasant. In other words, there will be fewer instances of CM or internalized oppression among Filipinos and Filipino Americans. To me, this is what psychological decolonization means.

Let us begin Part III with a discussion of clinical services for CM.

*   *   *

Chapter 10

Clinical Services For Colonial Mentality

ᜃᜓᜎᜒᜈᜒᜃᜎ᜔ ᜐᜒᜎ᜔ᜊᜒᜐᜒᜐ᜔ ᜉᜓᜇ᜔ ᜃᜓᜎᜓᜈᜒᜌᜎ᜔ ᜋᜒᜈ᜔ᜆᜎᜒᜆᜒ

There are plenty of viable approaches to psychotherapy in the field of psychology. More specifically, there are plenty of psychotherapeutic orientations and techniques that may be used to conceptualize and address CM or internalized oppression. For instance, the humanistic approach (Rogers, 1980) to therapy may be useful in facilitating personal growth among Filipinos and Filipino Americans, improving their sense of self or self-esteem, and encouraging them to selflessly serve their communities (self-actualization). Even Freud's psychodynamic approach to therapy may be used to conceptualize some aspects of CM or internalized oppression, such as desiring to look more White or discriminating against FOBs, as ego defense mechanisms functioning to hide one's unconscious feelings of inferiority or insecurities for having Filipino heritage. However, this chapter is going to focus on Cognitive-

Behavioral Therapy (CBT) and its general approach and techniques toward addressing psychopathology or psychological distress, beginning with why I believe this psychotherapeutic approach holds the most promise in terms of easily integrating our understanding of CM into existing mental health models and systems of care, which may contribute toward improving the cultural sensitivity, cultural appropriateness, and consequently, effectiveness of our services for Filipinos and Filipino Americans.

The Potential of Cognitive-Behavioral Therapy

The primary reason for why I am focusing on a discussion of how CBT may be used to address CM or internalized oppression is that CBT is the most popular form of psychotherapy today (Norcross, Hedges, & Prochaska, 2002). Furthermore, there is a growing body of scientific literature suggesting that CBT is effective for addressing a wide range of psychopathology including mood disorders (e.g., depression), anxiety disorders (e.g., social phobia), eating disorders (e.g., bulimia), and severe mental disorders (e.g., schizophrenia). Indeed, CBT seems to be the most effective and most popular form of treatment today, even compared to other forms of interventions in the list of Empirically Supported Treatments (ESTs), a list of treatment modalities that is typically used by clinicians, health care facilities, insurance companies, funding agencies, and policy makers to guide their decisions in terms of determining what forms of treatments are considered to have satisfactory evidence supporting their effectiveness and therefore, are appropriate for use. Given CBT's documented effectiveness for a variety of disorders, its popularity and familiarity among mental health service providers, officials, and policy makers, and its inclusion in the list of ESTs, I believe CBT is the best and easiest avenue through which our understanding of CM may be incorporated into existing conceptualizations of and services for mental health concerns among Filipinos and Filipino Americans. Consequently, it is possible that such an ease of integration into existing models and systems will contribute toward the increased culturally sensitivity, cultural appropriateness, and effectiveness of our interventions for Filipinos and Filipino Americans. It should be noted, however, that my advocacy for CBT does not mean that I am arguing that it is the best approach to address CM. It would be nice, for instance, if we can easily use indigenous forms of healing in existing systems of care or make health care providers use indigenous forms of healing when working with Filipinos and Filipino Americans. The reality, however, is that this is not immediately possible. My advocacy for CBT is driven by practicality given our current sociopolitical conditions, in that CBT is most familiar and mostly used in existing systems of care by health care providers. My advocacy for CBT is driven by the desire to increase health care systems' and providers' attention to CM, which may assist them in providing better services for Filipinos and Filipino Americans. However, such an advocacy for CBT should not be misinterpreted as an advocacy for CBT to replace indigenous forms of healing, nor should it be misinterpreted as suggesting that CBT is the best way to address CM, as promising as it may seem. Let us now turn our attention to a brief orientation and discussion of CBT.

Cognitive-Behavioral Therapy

In general, proponents of CBT consider five components to any problem, concern, or issue: the (1) cognitions (thoughts); the (2) moods or affects (emotions); the (3) physiological reactions (physical sensations or symptoms such as increased heart rate); the (4) behaviors; and (5) the environment (Padesky & Greenburger, 1995). Therapists who subscribe to CBT believe that individuals' environmental contexts, such as how they were raised and what messages about the world, about themselves, and about others they constantly receive, can lead to the development of general patterns of thinking (*mental schemas*). These general patterns of thinking are highly influential in producing the automatic thoughts or cognitions that individuals have as they interact with the world. In turn, cognitive-behavioral therapists theorize that a person's thoughts or cognitions influence that person's mood, behavior, and physical sensations in response to his or her environmental context. Thoughts or cognitions that are distorted, inaccurate, or false may lead to unhealthy or maladaptive moods, behaviors, or physical sensations, whereas thoughts or cognitions that are accurate, true, or realistic contribute to healthy and adaptive moods, behaviors, and physical sensations (Beck, 1995). The relationships and interconnectedness between these five components of any distress, problem, concern, or issue are explained to the client during CBT. The goal of CBT is to help facilitate within clients the recognition or realization that the client's experiences in his or her environment can create inaccurate, distorted, or unrealistic thoughts or cognitions within the client, which can lead to psychological distress in the form of undesired physical symptoms, maladaptive behaviors, and intense undesirable emotions that may seem uncontrollable and inescapable. Therapists who use CBT, therefore, attempt to help clients develop improved problem solving skills, stronger social support networks, and more realistic, accurate, and consequently, adaptive cognitions or thoughts about one's environment (Hays & Iwamasa, 2006).

As popular, effective, and promising as it is, however, CBT is not without limitations. For instance, an overwhelming majority of the literature on the use and effectiveness of CBT involves only people of European American identities (Suinn, 2003). Thus, it remains to be proven if CBT is in fact effective as a psychotherapeutic intervention for non-White individuals. Furthermore, CBT is often criticized for being value-neutral and its overreliance on science, logic, and rational thinking makes it appear to be valuing dominant cultural perspectives such as individualism and objectivity (Kantrowitz & Ballou, 1992). Also, CBT's strong emphasis on changing internal factors (e.g., cognitions and behaviors) has been viewed as potentially reinforcing the notion of victim blaming and limits its ability to consider and change external and sociopolitical factors (Hays & Iwamasa, 2006). This limitation is especially relevant when addressing CM or internalized oppression, where external factors are argued to be the cause of such conditions. However, such limitations of CBT are not insurmountable, and a closer look at its major tenets reveals that CBT may be highly appropriate for various ethnic and cultural minority groups. First, CBT emphasizes the need to tailor interventions to the unique contexts of individuals, and recognizes that psychological distress may be sparked by environmental factors outside the individual. Second, cognitive-behavioral therapists work toward empowering the client by recognizing the client as the expert regarding his/her experiences. Finally, cognitive-behavioral therapists pay attention to and utilize the client's strengths and support systems. Indeed, CBT has been shown to be culturally-modifiable and effective for various minority clients (for examples, please see Hays & Iwamasa, 2006). Thus, the commonly cited criticisms and limitations of CBT may be addressed by carefully modifying it to fit clients' unique historical, cultural, and environmental contexts. Next, I describe how CM or internalized oppression among Filipinos and Filipino Americans may be conceptualized using CBT terms and theories.

Conceptualizing Colonial Mentality in CBT Terms

Using CBT terms and theories, CM or internalized oppression may be conceptualized as a set of *self-defeating cognitions, attitudes, and behaviors* that have been developed over time as one consistently experiences an unjust and oppressive environment. Furthermore, CM or internalized oppression may be conceptualized as a distorted view of one's self and of others that is a consequence of how one experiences his or her environment. One of the most basic tenets of CBT is that thoughts that occur most frequently and are most easily accessible in memory are the ones we tend to believe. Historically oppressed groups have been, both in subtle and overt ways, consistently receiving the message that they are inferior to the dominant group. Eventually, members of historically oppressed groups may no longer need the dominant group to perpetuate such inferiorizing messages; they begin telling themselves in overt and subtle (and automatic) ways (David, 2009).

Consistent with the literature on cognition and culture (Hong, Morris, Chiu, & Benet-Martinez, 2000; as discussed in Chapter 6), members of oppressed groups may eventually internalize the cultural oppression they experience in such a deep way that it creates within them a cultural knowledge system that is characterized by automatic negative cognitions and perceptions of their heritage group. For the Filipino experience, due to the extensive historical and contemporary oppression they have faced, Filipinos' and Filipino Americans' cultural knowledge systems may now be developed in such a way that ideas of inferiority, undesirability, and unpleasantness may now be a part of their Filipino knowledge system, whereas ideas of superiority, desirability, or pleasantness may now be a part of the American or Western knowledge system. Recently, as discussed in Chapter 6, my mentor and I (David & Okazaki, 2010; David, 2010b) used methods such as the implicit association test and the lexical decision priming task among multiple samples of Filipino Americans and found empirical evidence supporting the notion that members of this group have automatically associated undesirable, unpleasant, and negative thoughts with the Filipino culture and desirable, pleasant, and positive thoughts with the American culture, suggesting that oppression has been internalized deeply enough by members of this group for a distorted cognitive system to be developed and automatically operate.

Consistent with CBT theories on psychopathology development (e.g., Beck, Rush, Emery, & Shaw, 1979), underlying such automatic thoughts, attitudes, (e.g., "Lighter skin is more attractive or desirable") or behaviors (e.g., discriminating against less-Westernized Filipinos or Filipino Americans) are *maladaptive general beliefs* or mental schemas (e.g., "Being White or American is better than being Filipino") that have been developed from previous experiences (e.g., colonialism, contemporary oppression, seeing others display CM). Such thoughts and beliefs contribute to the creation of *dysfunctional self-schemas* (e.g., "I'm Filipino, therefore I am not attractive and I am inferior to Whites") that may lead to psychological distress and psychopathology (David, 2009). For a historically and contemporarily oppressed group such as Filipinos and Filipino Americans, centuries of ethnic and cultural subjugation may have created a general belief that their culture and ethnicity are somehow inferior to those of their Western colonizers. Such a belief may underlie the automatic self-deprecating thoughts and behaviors that many members of this group display today. However, given the implicitness and automaticity of CM, as discussed in Chapter 6, Filipino and Filipino American clients may not be able to explicitly report CM-consistent automatic thoughts, general beliefs, and schemas such as the ones mentioned above. Thus, assessment tools such as the Colonial Mentality Implicit Association Test may be useful for clinicians as a tool to tap into CM-consistent automatic negative cognitions and attitudes when hypothesizing that CM may be contributing to their clients' distress. Such automatic negative cognitions, attitudes, and related behaviors are likely damaging to clients' self-esteem and may contribute to the development of various forms of psychopathology, including depression and anxiety (as discussed in Chapter 9). Figure 12 is a pictorial example of how CM may operate and lead to psychological distress and psychopathology using CBT concepts.

In the next section, I provide two examples of how CM or internalized oppression may lead to psychological distress and psychopathology among Filipinos and Filipino Americans. I also discuss how commonly used CBT techniques can be utilized to address such psychological concerns. It should be noted, however, that the focus on psychological disorders such as depression and social anxiety in the following section should not be misinterpreted as suggesting that these are the only instances wherein the effects of CM becomes deserving of clinical attention. As discussed in Chapter 9 and as supported by recent research on the negative psychological effects of internalized oppression (Hatzenbuehler, 2009), the historical and contemporary forms of oppression experienced by various minority groups may lead to higher likelihoods of maladaptive emotional and cognitive states such as rumination, emotional avoidance, negative self-schemas, and feelings of hopelessness, as well as to other concerns such as low self-esteem, alcohol and drug use, and other health risk behaviors. All of these possible outcomes are serious enough and are highly distressing enough to warrant attention whether or not they eventually lead to the development of clinically diagnosable psychological disorders such as depression, anxiety, and substance use disorders.

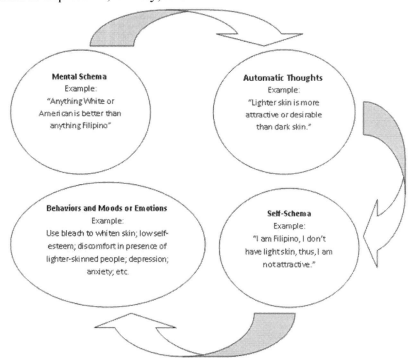

Figure 12. An example of how CM-consistent schemas and automatic thoughts can lead to distress and psychopathology.

Colonial Mentality and Depression

In brief, internalized oppression may lead to depression in the following manner: A Filipino person internalizes the idea that he/she is worthless, stupid, or undeserving due to his/her group membership (e.g., being of Filipino heritage), an idea that has been consistently imposed and reinforced by the person's experiences with his/her environment. More specifically, because of the negative connotations attached to the characteristics of one's social group (e.g., Filipinos are ugly), the person may eventually distance and isolate himself/herself from other members of the social group, many of whom may be significant characters in the person's life (e.g., parents, siblings, cousins, best friends, etc.). Moreover, given that it may be impossible for this Filipino person to completely rid himself/herself of his/her respective group identities (i.e., others can unmistakably know he/she is Filipino, their skin is always going to be darker, etc.), the person may develop what cognitive-behavioral psychologists call *learned helplessness* (Peterson & Seligman, 1984). That is, the Filipino person may develop the attitude that there is nothing he/she can do to rid himself/herself of the negative attributes he/she possesses because it is intrinsically linked to their social group (e.g., dark skin, flat nose, short stature, etc.). This is consistent with what Peterson and Seligman (1984) called having a *pessimistic explanatory style*, which is the tendency to perceive the assumed inferior characteristics of their group as permanent or stable (e.g., "I will never be able to completely rid myself of my dark skin"), personal or internal (e.g., "It's my fault or my ethnic groups' fault"), and pervasive or global (e.g., "All of the characteristics of my ethnic group are inferior"). Thus, the person may altogether "give up" and stop trying to improve the adverse situation. Such feelings of inferiority, isolation, and helplessness, in turn, may create within the person a sense of guilt or self-blame for being a member of an allegedly inferior social group (e.g., being Filipino). The combination of such feelings of worthlessness, isolation, guilt, and lack of motivation may contribute to the development of a major depressive episode, dysthymia, or an anxiety disorder (American Psychiatric Association, 2000).

CBT may be utilized to address CM or internalized oppression, which may be contributing to the experienced depression and other negative emotions, in the following manner: Homework may be assigned testing the client's *distorted core belief* that the social group to which he/she belongs (e.g., Filipino culture and ethnicity) possesses mostly (if not all) undesirable characteristics (in CBT terms, *magnification of negatives* and *minimization of positives* regarding one's social group). The client may be asked to list the characteristics of the Filipino culture and ethnicity that are desirable or positive. The client may also be asked to speak with other Filipino and Filipino American community members (e.g., elders, community leaders, etc.), attend Filipino or Filipino American social events (e.g., Filipino culture nights, Filipino dance performances, etc.), or conduct literature search (e.g., books about Filipino history, culture, etc.) to help facilitate the identification of positive Filipino and Filipino American characteristics. Furthermore, the distorted or inaccurate core belief that he/she is worthless may be challenged by asking the client to list positive attributes that he/she possesses. The list of positive attributes may be generated by the client or the client may ask relatives, friends, co-workers, or other people to provide positive attributes they think the client has. One of the main purposes of these tasks is to make more positive information about the client and about the client's social group more frequently available and salient to the client, which may eventually challenge the negative automatic cognitions about himself/herself and about his/her group that the client had developed over time. In other words, these tasks are specifically assigned to address the low personal and collective self-esteem of the Filipino client.

Another goal of such tasks is to encourage the client to interact with other members of the Filipino and Filipino American community in order to reduce the client's sense of isolation and improve the client's appreciation of the Filipino and Filipino American culture and ethnicity. Participating in and contributing to

Filipino and Filipino American community events, gatherings, celebrations, or projects may improve or revive the sense of Kapwa within the client – the recognition that the client shares an inner self with others and that the client is not alone. Increased participation in such events and gatherings, as well as recognizing the similarities between one's self and others through the development of Kapwa, may help improve the client's social support network, which in turn can be instrumental in facilitating client progress. Also, it is likely that as the client learns more about Filipino and Filipino American history either through increase community involvement or through independent explorations, he/she will learn more about the historical and contemporary oppression of Filipinos and Filipino Americans. This may contribute toward the identification of where inferiorizing messages are coming from and the eradication of the self-blame that has been developed. This cognitive restructuring is challenging because Filipinos and Filipino Americans will likely continue to have experiences that reinforce their distorted core belief that being Filipino or Filipino American is inferior, undesirable, or unpleasant. However, the realization that such inferiorizing messages are inaccurate and the increased salience of positive messages about the Filipino ethnicity and culture may provide Filipinos and Filipino Americans the needed tools to resist the internalization of the inferior messages that are perpetually reinforced by society. In other words, increased understanding of the Filipino ethnicity and culture may serve as a *protective factor* against the internalization of the inferiorizing messages that Filipinos and Filipino Americans may receive from the general society. It is likely that a more accurate perception (i.e., a cognitive system consisting of both positive and negative attributes) of his/her personal characteristics and of his/her social group's characteristics may reduce, and eventually eradicate, the feelings of depression that the client has for being of Filipino heritage.

Colonial Mentality and Social Anxiety

Internalized oppression may lead to social anxiety in the following manner: A Filipino person internalizes the notion that he/she is incapable of performing a particular task due to his/her social group membership (e.g., being Filipino), a notion imposed on him/her repeatedly and a notion that he/she had eventually learned. Thus, this Filipino person may experience heightened levels of anxiety when faced with performing such a task in front of other people and may choose to completely avoid the task and such a social situation altogether, primarily because of fears that others will judge him/her negatively when he/she performs such a task. If this task is significantly important to the Filipino person's personal, professional, educational, or overall functioning, then the avoidance of such a task due to the excessive anxiety the person feels over such a task may warrant a diagnosis of social anxiety (American Psychiatric Association, 2000).

For example, given the stereotype about Filipinos and Filipino Americans that they are not good at sports, then a person with Filipino heritage who repeatedly hears such a message may eventually believe it. Consequently, this person may experience heightened levels of anxiety when performing various athletic tasks and may learn to avoid being in such situations altogether. The person may believe that if he/she does not do well in these athletic events, other people will judge him/her negatively. Given that he/she believes other people have an a priori tendency to assume that Filipinos and Filipino Americans are not good at sports, he/she believes it is more likely for other people to judge him/her negatively because he/she is of Filipino descent. If participation in sporting events is a significant part of this person's personal, professional, or overall functioning (e.g., the person is married to someone who enjoys playing in community leagues and would like the client to participate; the person's job has a company sports team that is viewed by the company as an essential tool for improving company morale and efficiency, etc.), then this person warrants a diagnosis of social anxiety.

CBT may be utilized to address CM or internalized oppression, which may be contributing to the social anxiety, in the following manner: Homework may be assigned testing the client's developed core beliefs that Filipinos or Filipino Americans are not good at sports and that others are more likely to judge his/her athletic performance negatively because he/she is of Filipino descent. This can be accomplished by having the client identify successful Filipino and Filipino American athletes and list their accomplishments. It may also be worth it for the client to look for explicit evidence (e.g., verbal comments, etc.) that other people are more likely to judge his/her athletic performance in a negative manner than they are to others. Both of these tasks will systematically test the client's developed and distorted core beliefs and cognitions of himself/herself, of his/her social group, and of others. Furthermore, these tasks are likely to provide the client with systematically-derived evidence that is contrary to his/her distorted beliefs and cognitions, which may help facilitate cognitive restructuring efforts in therapy. It is also of importance that the client does not develop an extremely positive but still inaccurate and distorted perception of society, because this may also contribute to maladaptive behaviors (e.g., believing that racism and other forms of oppression no longer exist). Instead, the goal is to help the client develop an accurate and realistic understanding of society, consisting both of positive and negative attributes. Developing a more accurate and realistic view of his/her self (e.g., "I am not bad at sports just because I am of Filipino descent."), ethnic group (e.g., "Not all Filipinos or Filipino Americans are bad at sports, actually, there are many very successful Filipino or Filipino American athletes in the world."), and of other people (e.g., "Not all and only a few people hold the stereotypical belief that all Filipinos are bad at sports" or "Most people are not more likely to judge me negatively just because I am of Filipino descent.") may consequently reduce the client's experienced anxiety while participating in athletic events or activities.

Despite the strong emphases given by the American Psychological Association (APA) to research and training efforts surrounding ESTs, a national survey of Masters- and Doctoral-level psychologists revealed that very few clinicians utilize ESTs in their work (Steir, Lasota, & Christensen, 2007). This finding led the authors to conclude that ESTs "...are not yet fully embraced by the psychological community. Although therapy such as Cognitive Behavioral Therapy...work(s), the data to date suggests that many therapists...do not utilize these approaches." (pp. 63-64). Furthermore, the researchers also found that only 23% of therapists have had formal training in ESTs, supporting their speculation that one main reason for the low levels of EST utilization is the lack of such training on the part of the therapists. In addition to many current psychologists not having training in ESTs, it is also very likely that even more current and future psychologists do not have training in culturally appropriate applications of ESTs. Thus, in my discussion of how CBT may be used to conceptualize and address CM as it relates to depression and social anxiety, I have explicitly laid out and clarified how a very popular EST (i.e., CBT) may be applied in a sociopolitically and culturally appropriate manner to conceptualize and address CM or internalized oppression, a factor that may influence psychopathology development among Filipinos and Filipino Americans. For the remainder of this chapter, I would like to present other clinical considerations that service providers need to take into account when attempting to incorporate and address CM in their work.

First, clinicians or service providers should conceptualize CM or internalized oppression as an individual-differences variable and to not assume that all Filipinos and Filipino Americans have internalized the oppression they have experienced or regard oppression as a primary stressor in their lives, or that CM is the factor that is heavily contributing to their disorders. As discussed in

Chapter 6, many Filipinos and Filipino Americans may not even be aware of, or may not even acknowledge that, historical colonialism, contemporary oppression, and/or CM is part of their psychological distress. Although assessment tools such as the Colonial Mentality Implicit Association Test (discussed in Chapter 6; David, 2010b; David & Okazaki, 2010) and even the Culturally Informed Functional Assessment Interview (Tanaka-Matsumi, Seiden, & Lam, 1996; Okazaki & Tanaka-Matsumi, 2006) may be used to obtain more culturally complete conceptualizations of clients' psychological experiences, even possibly contributing to the identification of historical colonialism, contemporary oppression, and/or CM as important antecedent factors that shaped clients' maladaptive core beliefs which, in turn, leads to distress, it is important to remember that not all psychological distress has its basis in oppression. Also, it is important to note that there are multiple pathways leading from CM to distress (as discussed in Chapter 9) and multiple intervention pathways of decolonization. For example, among Filipino and Filipino American clients who may not have CM as their main stressor, or who may not acknowledge that historical and contemporary oppression contributes to their distress, focusing on more general issues or issues that they themselves identify in treatment may increase their personal and collective self-esteem, as well as levels of ethnic identity and awareness, which may in turn facilitate awareness of historical and contemporary oppression and empower them to address issues of oppression among themselves and in the greater community.

It is also important to note that the goal in therapy is not to help clients develop an extremely positive but still distorted and inaccurate perception of society (e.g., believing that oppression is not present) because this may invalidate clients' experiences of oppression and may lead clients to blame themselves for feeling unjustly treated. Clinicians should keep in mind that the essential goal of CBT as applied to CM or internalized oppression, or of CBT in general, is to help clients develop a realistic and accurate perception of themselves, of others, and of the world they live in. Given that a realistic perception of society will likely involve the identification that oppression is still present in today's world, an accompanying goal for the client may be to develop a more adaptive perception of reality (i.e., they must learn that although oppression is real and powerful, it is not an insurmountable obstacle), and clinicians may work with their clients to develop strategies to cope with the oppression they experience (e.g., the client learns how to directly confront racial microaggressions in a way that feels empowering, the client learns about legal options if they experience work discrimination, etc.). Again, the experiences of oppression and the construct of CM or internalized oppression may vary among Filipinos and Filipino Americans, and the goals and techniques of interventions should be personalized and tailored to the individual needs of each Filipino or Filipino American client. Nevertheless, clinicians who keep an eye for CM or internalized oppression as potentially contributing to their Filipino or Filipino American clients' concerns may demonstrate to their clients that the therapist is genuinely attempting to understand clients' historical and contemporary sociopolitical experiences. Thus, in addition to potentially identifying a major etiological variable for their clients' psychopathology or psychological distress, paying attention to CM or internalized oppression may also improve rapport between client and therapist. Such an improved rapport, which may begin to eradicate cultural mistrust on the part of the Filipino or Filipino American client (David, 2010c), and a more complete understanding of clients' experiences, may lead to improved intervention strategies and better therapeutic outcomes. Finally, eradication of cultural mistrust and improved therapeutic outcomes, in turn, may lead toward reducing the disparities in help-seeking and psychological distress among Filipinos and Filipino Americans (Gong, Gage, & Tacata, 2003).

Also, in addition to being open to incorporating the notion of CM in our conceptualizations of Filipino and Filipino American mental health and psychological experiences, researchers and service providers should collaborate in designing, implementing, and evaluating intervention programs that are specifically intended to decolonize Filipino and Filipino American mentalities (e.g., Halagao, 2004; Strobel, 2001). Having a culturally- and sociopolitically-sensitive conceptualization of Filipino and Filipino Americans' psychological experiences and developing culture-specific interventions may contribute toward addressing the underutilization of mental health services by Filipinos and Filipino Americans. Indeed, as mentioned earlier in Chapter 9, studies have found that members of this group are less comfortable seeking mental health services even compared with other Asian American groups (Gong, Gage, & Tacata, 2003; Ying & Hu, 1994). This low rate of help-seeking from professional mental health services among Filipinos and Filipino Americans cannot be attributed to lower rates of distress and psychopathology, as research also shows that members of this group experience psychological distress and mental health concerns just as much, if not more frequently, than other Asian Americans and other racial groups (as discussed in Chapter 9). Along with stigma, poor service quality and cultural mistrust may also contribute to Filipinos' and Filipino Americans' disinterest in seeking mental health services (David, 2010c).

For various minority groups, several efforts have since been implemented to improve services and eradicate cultural mistrust. In the process, culturally sensitive practices for various minority groups have gained wide popularity in research and service settings. However, there is yet to be a clinical service or intervention developed specifically to meet the cultural and sociopolitical complexities of Filipinos and Filipino Americans. As one way to be culturally competent and effective, it is recommended that researchers and service providers develop interventions that specifically target CM or internalized oppression. Not only may CM-specific interventions lead to an improved understanding of Filipinos' and Filipino Americans' experiences, but they may also improve rapport, reduce cultural mistrust between service providers and clients, and lead to better therapeutic outcomes. Such a culture-specific intervention may contribute toward improving the effectiveness of mental health services for Filipinos and Filipino Americans, which in turn, may contribute toward reducing the disparity in service utilization.

Finally, another implication for mental health service providers working with Filipinos and Filipino Americans is to be cognizant of how Filipinos and Filipino Americans may perceive the clinician's race or ethnicity and, consequently, their competence. Given that previous studies' (David, 2010b; David & Okazaki, 2010) results suggest that superior or pleasant perceptions are activated by mere exposure to American-related stimulus and that inferior or unpleasant perceptions are activated by mere exposure to Filipino-related stimulus, initial contact by clinicians with their Filipino or Filipino American clients may already begin to shape their clients' attitudes and behaviors. More specifically, Filipinos and Filipino Americans may initially have a more positive perception of a White clinician, whereas Filipinos and Filipino Americans may initially doubt the competence of a non-White or Filipino clinician who is perceived to be not very Americanized or westernized. Thus, it seems that it is more imperative for non-White providers or professionals with Filipino heritage to establish their credibility and demonstrate their competence to their Filipino and Filipino American clients early than for White mental health service providers. However, although mental health service providers are recommended to be aware of how their race or ethnicity may influence their Filipino and Filipino American clients, service providers should again keep in mind that CM is an individual differences variable and not automatically assume that every Filipino or Filipino American person holds CM or internalized oppression, and thus are judging their clinical competence in a way that is consistent with CM.

Chapter Summary

This chapter has begun to elucidate how CM or internalized oppression as experienced by Filipinos and Filipino Americans may be conceptualized using terms and theoretical models that are familiar to many mental health service providers. Furthermore, this chapter also presented some suggestions regarding how commonly-used psychotherapeutic techniques and strategies may be applied to address CM or internalized oppression. More specifically, this chapter discussed how compatible CBT techniques and theories are to the conceptualization and eradication of CM or internalized oppression. By using CBT – a very popular and effective type of psychotherapy that is familiar to, known to, and accepted by many mental health providers and systems of care – as a vehicle to conceptualize and address CM and other cultural factors such as Kapwa, perhaps mental health service providers and existing systems of care will become more accommodating of CM, Kapwa, and other related factors and find it easier to incorporate such cultural factors in their services for Filipinos and Filipino Americans. By doing so, it is believed that the cultural sensitivity, cultural appropriateness, and consequently, effectiveness of existing clinical interventions may also benefit. It is possible that by improving the cultural sensitivity and appropriateness of our services, the existing disparities between Filipino and Filipino American mental health help-seeking and their levels of psychological distress will also begin to be addressed. Finally, this chapter also suggested some other clinical considerations for mental health service providers working with Filipinos and Filipino Americans, one of which is to always regard CM as an individual differences variable whose existence and strength within Filipinos and Filipino Americans greatly vary. Thus, service providers should always control the tendency to overgeneralize and assume that all Filipinos and Filipino Americans hold CM or regard CM as a factor that contributes to their distress.

*   *   *

The CBT techniques described in this chapter as applied to CM or internalized oppression reveal that such techniques and the CBT theories behind them are very compatible with the goals of prior decolonization programs. In general, decolonization programs attempt to eradicate CM by teaching individuals a more accurate understanding of the historical and contemporary experiences of Filipinos and Filipino Americans, as well as by identifying what CM is and how it develops. Thus, CBT as applied to CM or internalized oppression and decolonization programs have as their ultimate goal the development of a critical and accurate understanding of Filipino history, culture, and contemporary experiences. Furthermore, CBT techniques may facilitate cognitive restructuring and help individuals realize connections between one's social experiences and mental health, as well as making connections between historical and contemporary experiences, one's experiences and other Filipinos' experiences, and Filipinos' experiences and the experiences of other historically oppressed groups – all of which are common goals of existing decolonization programs for Filipinos and Filipino Americans. Moreover, as discussed in this chapter, in addition to incorporating CM in existing models and systems of mental health, another way to address the disparities between levels of psychological distress and rates of mental health service utilization among Filipinos and Filipino Americans is to develop CM- or culture-specific interventions for this group. In the next chapter, I provide a discussion of how CBT techniques and strategies may be combined with decolonization programs to specifically address CM or internalized oppression and, consequently, facilitate empowerment in the Filipino and Filipino American community.

CHAPTER 11

FILIPINO -/ AMERICAN DECOLONIZATION EXPERIENCE (FADE): FADE-ING AWAY OUR COLONIAL MENTALITY

ᜓᜌ᜔ᜌᜒᜈ᜔ᜊᜒᜌᜓ ᜐᜒᜈ᜔ ᜊᜒ ᜇᜒᜌᜓ
ᜓᜈ᜔ᜌᜓᜈ᜔ᜋ ᜊᜒᜏᜒᜓᜌᜒᜋᜒ ᜐᜒᜈ᜔ᜌᜒᜎ ᜋᜒ
ᜊᜒᜌᜓ ᜋᜒ ᜐᜒᜊᜊᜊᜒᜊᜒ

Due to the prevalence of CM and the emerging empirical literature documenting the adverse psychological effects of CM (as described in Part II), several decolonization efforts have begun in various Filipino American communities. Decolonization is the process of reducing CM by critically examining common feelings, attitudes, and behaviors that are indicative of CM among Filipinos and Filipino Americans and tracing it back to Filipinos' historical and contemporary experiences of oppression. This follows Freire's (1970) notion of *conscientization*, which is defined as freeing oppressed individuals' minds by helping them develop a critical consciousness in which the reality of their oppression is recognized. In psychological terms, this concept is often referred to as *psychological liberation*. Once oppressed individuals develop a realistic and accurate understanding of their oppressed historical and contemporary experiences, then they may begin to confront those oppressive social conditions, a concept called *political liberation*. Two Filipino American-focused decolonization efforts have appeared in the published literature thus far and both share the characteristics of helping Filipinos and Filipino Americans: (1) develop a more accurate understanding of Filipino history and culture; (2) make historical and contemporary connections; (3) become aware of CM in oneself and others; and (4) take social action. I provide a brief summary of both decolonization efforts below.

Existing Decolonization Efforts

Leny Strobel (2001) gathered eight Filipino Americans willing to participate in an in-depth decolonization process for more than a year. The group was exposed to Filipino history and culture and each member kept journals and participated in interviews, dialogues, and discussions. Strobel identified common themes experienced by the group as they underwent decolonization: (1) *Naming* the historical oppressors and identifying the effects of oppression on one's identity; (2) *Reflection* about the effects of colonialism on one's life, family, and community, as well as developing a desire to do something about the realized injustices; and (3) *Action* toward assisting others in their decolonization journey, as well as assisting one's community to rise and challenge oppression. In essence, Strobel's proposed framework for decolonization includes the acquisition of historical and cultural knowledge, improved consciousness regarding contemporary experiences, awareness of CM and how it develops, improved connection to and pride with the Filipino culture, and giving back to the community through social action. Regarding the exploration of mental health-related variables,

Strobel identified denial, shame, insecurity, loneliness, and feelings of inferiority as common experiences and found that decolonization allowed participants to explore and eventually resolve such feelings and heal the damages of historical and contemporary oppression.

Another published decolonization effort is described by Patricia Espiritu Halagao (2004). Halagao interviewed six Filipino Americans who engaged in a semester-long experience that involved intensive education on Filipino history and culture. Similar to Strobel's (2001) work, Halagao's (2004) decolonization effort included extensive discussions, dialogues, and journaling. Halagao identified: (1) making connections (between historical and contemporary experiences, as well as between the experiences of Filipinos and the experiences of other oppressed groups); (2) becoming aware of CM; (3) enhancing ethnic identity consistent with those proposed in the Pilipino American Identity Development Model (Nadal, 2004; as discussed in Chapter 8); and (4) inspiring social action to be the most important goals and results of the experience. In terms of mental health-related findings, she noted that participants experienced enhanced self- and community-awareness, and felt a strong sense of personal and community empowerment, after the decolonization experience.

Combining Decolonization with Conventional Clinical Practice

The described decolonization efforts above are definitely culturally-sensitive and both efforts had great success in facilitating improved understanding of the Filipino ethnicity and culture, as well as of the historical and contemporary experiences of Filipinos and Filipino Americans. Both efforts also facilitated the identification and eradication of CM. Both efforts seriously incorporated Filipino culture in their development and implementation, and the content of the interventions were contextualized appropriately within the historical and contemporary experiences of Filipinos and Filipino Americans. As groundbreaking as they were, however, both efforts did not specifically and explicitly make connections to how it can be incorporated into conceptual models and services that are more familiar among mental health service providers.

Given evidence that CM is an important risk-factor for low self-esteem, depression, suicide, substance use and abuse, and other mental and behavioral health concerns among Filipinos and Filipino Americans (as described in Chapter 9), perhaps it is important to make decolonization goals and strategies more clearly compatible with existing mental health services, and more palatable to the providers who deliver such services. Perhaps it is essential that we conceptualize and present decolonization goals and strategies in a way that is understandable and compatible to existing service providers and systems of care, so that the likelihood that Filipinos and Filipino Americans will receive culturally-appropriate services is increased. The initial attempt to conceptualize CM in Cognitive-Behavioral terms as described in Chapter 10 may be considered as a start. Perhaps by explicitly integrating the techniques of conventional clinical psychology with those of decolonization programs, culturally-sensitive and appropriate services for Filipinos and Filipino Americans will become more frequent. Thus, it may be necessary to develop a decolonization program that incorporates existing mental health services and techniques, or vice versa (i.e., making services culturally-sensitive), to better understand the psychological experiences of Filipinos and Filipino Americans and better serve members of this group. A pilot test for how conventional clinical psychology techniques were utilized and combined with components of previous decolonization programs (Halagao, 2004; Strobel, 2001) to facilitate the process decolonization among a sample of Filipino Americans is described next.

The Filipino American Decolonization Experience

Combining knowledge obtained from previous decolonization programs and recent efforts to conceptualize CM or internalized oppression in cognitive-behavioral terms (David, 2009; as described in Chapter 10), I gathered a group of eight Filipino Americans to engage in an experience that incorporated key decolonization and Cognitive-Behavioral Therapy (CBT) components. Data obtained from this project included qualitative and quantitative information that provided evidence for a decolonizing effect of the intervention. Participants went through a 20-session experience that combined the study of the existing literature on CM with CBT techniques, participatory action research, and social action surrounding decolonization practices (Halagao, 2004; Strobel, 1997, 2001). This experience was intended to foster within participants a more accurate and empowering view of their personal and social selves, of society, and how they may create social change. During the first 10 sessions, participants were encouraged to develop a deeper and more critical understanding of themselves as Filipino Americans, of their historical and contemporary relations and situations with and within the United States, and how such experiences shape the ways they think, feel, and behave. The next 10 sessions involved designing and implementing workshops facilitated by the participants themselves. As an example of the collaborative nature of this experience, the participants themselves came up with a name for the program, which they unanimously entitled the Filipino American Decolonization Experience (FADE).

Similar to the experiences of other Filipino Americans in prior decolonization efforts, FADE participants did not find the journey of decolonization easy. The beginning of FADE composed of didactic lectures, discussions, and dialogues about Filipino and Filipino American history, as well as the participants' personal and family histories as they relate to the experiences of other Filipinos and Filipino Americans. As they began developing a deeper and more complete understanding of their personal history relating to the Filipino culture and ethnicity, as well as of the collective history of the Filipino people, many participants experienced intense emotions such as anger, pain, and identity confusion, similar to Strobel's

(2001) descriptions. Below are some examples of FADE participants' reactions as they began their decolonization journeys:

> "Many of the topics discussed about Filipino history caught me by surprise. I never realized how much the Filipinos were subjected to the cruelty and unfairness by other countries. It angered me because it seemed like the only reason it was not exposed was because they were the actions of the United States. Why is it that the United States can order the killings of innocent people and replace a group of people's culture and pay no consequence? Why is it that the United States seems to believe that they are higher than any other country in the world, therefore have the right to do whatever they choose? If it was any other country, the whole world would know, but since it was the United States, it was like they had the right to keep it undercover." (Expressed by a 20-year old Filipina American)

> "Instead of being prideful and excited about my history and ethnicity, I can't. As I started learning much about the Filipino culture and their relationship with America, I began to realize how hard it is to walk around being a minority and with everyone else having preconceived notions about my own ethnicity: 'dog eater,' 'island people,' etc. It hurts." (Expressed by a 21-year old Filipino American)

The two examples above reflect the realization that the United States – an important and salient part of each participants' identities – is not perfect. It speaks to the realization of these two individuals that American policies and practices, both historically and contemporarily, are not perfect and have damaged another important part of their identities – the Filipino part. In a way, this can be seen as the starting point of when the legacies of the Thomasites' teachings (as described in Chapter 3) begin to unravel. It is when the intergenerational effects of inferiorization and miseducation begin to fall apart. Once aware of the imperfections of the United States, the FADE participants began to critically examine their own experiences with American institutions, leading to the identification of more examples that provide evidence for the injustices that Filipinos and Filipino Americans have faced historically and are facing contemporarily. Below is an example:

> "This experience presented me with larger amount of Filipino history in two hours than I have acquired in 19 years. Growing up my knowledge on Filipino history was limited with the only sources being family and friends. I was not taught any Filipino history unless it was the bare minimum in a high school history class, offering a trivial amount of information for the sake that the students at least acknowledged the Philippines exists. In college, I choose to be a part of taking some Filipino classes in hopes of catching up on the history I've been deprived of. Seeing that Filipino Americans are a heavy minority population, the amount of history taught in schools is very disproportional. It does upset me that we are not taught enough." (Expressed by a 19-year old Filipina American)

Not only did FADE participants began to question American institutions such as schools, but also other Filipinos and Filipino Americans who are perceived to not care about the historical and contemporary injustices they experienced or are currently experiencing. FADE Participants also began to feel a sense of loss, and of being cheated, for believing in and practicing what they thought to be authentic Filipino cultural values and behaviors, but are now realizing to be the products of the painful colonial history they just learned. Similar to Halagao's (2004) *Cultural Collisions*, FADE participants began to question what their parents shared with them, and what messages about Filipino history, ethnicity, and culture their parents sent them. They began to realize that even their parents – and even their grandparents and beyond – were also miseducated and were victims of colonialism and oppression.

> "It is a discomforting thought that the Filipino culture that I participate in, and even what my family generations' past practices are, to be historically accurate, not genuinely Filipino. The influence and seemingly permanent effects of our historical aggressors is what I actually consider to be Filipino culture. The mention of colonialism now only sends unsettling vibes to me. If Filipino Americans are not aware of this and have no interest in educating themselves as of why their culture is the way it is, it will be lost in the past. I don't feel that many Filipino Americans are very interested in their historical culture...I find this to be unfortunate and a bit shameful." (Expressed by an 18-year old Filipina American)

> "I had the chance this weekend to talk to my parents about colonialism in the Philippines...my dad indefinitely defeated me in all aspects of debate. Hating to lose to my dad, I brought up the notion that America is trying to colonize Iraq, just as they did to the Philippines. 'No they didn't (colonize the Philippines)' my dad replied unhesitatingly, 'America saved them (the Filipinos).' I was at a loss of words—I didn't expect that kind of reply at all. His main argument was that the United States was

trying to protect us from Japan…My persistence in explaining how America oppressed and colonized Filipinos minimally fazed my dad." (Expressed by a 20-year old Filipino American)

"I don't know if my parents would have wanted me to learn about my ethnicity (when I was younger), especially since they were new immigrants and they wanted my sister and I to fit in. They didn't even give us my mom's maiden name as one of our middle names, which is customary with Filipinos. They were worried about teachers and peers mispronouncing our names." (Expressed by a 18-year old Filipina American)

"I asked my dad if he knew about the Battle of Manila Bay. Then, I proceeded to ask him if he knew it was a set up, that it was actually a 'mock battle.' He completely denied what I was telling him, saying that it was a real battle and asking me how it could be a set up. I tried to explain it to him, but I did not know what else to say. So, I kind of thought I failed in my mission to convince my dad that the battle was a set up. Nevertheless, I think I showed my family more so this weekend than any other time, that I am interested in the Filipino culture and that I do have questions to ask." (Expressed by a 21-year old Filipina American)

The initial phase of FADE is similar to the early stages of change – both in the personal (Prochaska & Vellicer, 1997) and community (Plested, Edwards, & Jumper-Thurman, 2005) levels – which is to bring or raise awareness that there was and is a problem within the Filipino and Filipino American community. Once FADE participants realized that there was a historical problem, it is important to make sure that they were able to make connections between the past and their current experiences. To facilitate such a connection, the participants took part in a CM assessment using the CMS (as presented in Chapter 5) in order for them to start becoming aware of their attitudes, emotions, and behaviors toward the Filipino culture and ethnicity that may reflect CM. Raising individual and community awareness about the existence of CM is important, especially given the fact that CM may exist and operate outside of intention, control, or awareness (as discussed in Chapter 6). This individual assessment strategy is commonly used in typical clinical psychology work, in order to facilitate self-understanding among clients and help clinicians in diagnoses, treatment planning, and treatment evaluation. Furthermore, this next phase of the FADE program also utilized techniques often used with CBT such as psychoeducation and daily logs to make participants more aware of their environment. More specifically, psychoeducation was conducted to inform participants of the psychological and mental health consequences of colonialism and contemporary oppression (as discussed in Part II). Also, FADE participants were asked to keep track of any experiences they have that relates to contemporary oppression and CM, as well as record any cognitive and emotional reactions to such experiences to make participants become aware of the connections between such experiences and their mental health, a technique very common in CBT. The following are some examples from their CM, oppression, and mental health logs:

> "Upon visiting the Philippines I realized how modernized and Americanized the society was; from the mega malls to the traffic to the businesses. It seems wrong to be too Americanized but it is also impossible to go back to what we used to be before colonization. Watching Filipino made movies, many actors have white skin. Pop culture embraces looking American; which further affects Filipino

society as a whole." (Expressed by a 20-year old Filipina American)

"I called my sister this week. We got into an argument, and I was winning. I guess to get back at me, she told me that I had an accent. This came out of nowhere. What a weird way to put someone down. Then, she proceeded to tell me to get 'white friends.' I didn't even know how to respond to this. I have friends of all colors. I didn't get it. It made me really upset. I don't think I have an accent. What difference does it make? Accent or not, I'm still the same person." (Expressed by a 21-year old Filipina American)

"I was walking home with my friend and we were just talking, and then all of a sudden, I said something funny and my Filipino accent came out. She then called me a FOB. It was sort of embarrassing since the word FOB has a negative connotation to it. Another day, I was hanging out with one of my friend's group of friends and I was very annoyed by one of his friends because he was doing some funny things, but at the same time mocking the Filipino culture. He was mocking the way Filipino's talked and just doing Filipino stereotypes. It was very upsetting, so I just left the room and hung out somewhere else. It's so sad to know that even Filipinos make fun of other Filipinos, and it's unfortunate to say that I think I participate in this type of situation. I don't know how I feel about this. I think I'm somewhat confused, but I'm slowly realizing what I must do to make things better for EVERY Filipino, not just Filipino Americans who have assimilated to the

American culture." (Expressed by a 18-year old Filipino American)

"I went to the Bayanihan performance last week, and it was amazing. I was VERY excited. They were so fun to watch. Their costumes were beautiful, and their dances were very well choreographed. Even the sets and the lighting added to the mood and the stories. I did notice something else: none of the dancers were really brown. In the Igorot scene, the lighting made the dancers look darker and fierce. In all of the other dances, however, I noticed that every one of the dancers, male and female, were really light-skinned. I just think it's a shame that Bayanihan is a world-renowned dance company, and even the National Philippine Dance Company, and they don't represent all colors of a Filipino. It's like they pick and choose to make their group more recognizable, or more marketable. Or more like an American dance company..." (Expressed by a 21-year old Filipina American)

"I know that I was never one of those who did the whole skin lightening thing, but my mom uses them though. But I never was fond of the sun. I didn't like growing dark. Something that was light tan but not too dark. I don't know. I just think I don't look pretty really dark. I don't know if it was the whole I want to be 'white' thing. Could it have been? And I've always been sort of jealous of my mom's lighter skin. And I've always sort of teased my brother for being darker than me. I don't know why. So now I guess he has a complex about it. And I don't remember how I teased my brother, I just did. I just did. And now he has a complex about it but whatever. Now he's not so big on playing outside, enjoying the sun, etc. I think when I go to the Philippines, I'm going to make sure to lie out in the sun… or maybe not. I'm still… not big on the sweat… and ok, the getting too dark. Unless it's at a beach, that I can do. But then I'd want to stay under a kubo-thing… but I don't want to get burned! I guess I really don't want to be dark!" (Expressed by an 18-year old Filipina American)

"My mom refers to those seemingly uncivilized as the 'people in the mountains'. Is 'uncivilized' synonymous with living as our ancestors did"? (Expressed by a 21-year old Filipino American)

"As a young child, I kind of always knew I was different from the kids on my block just because of the type of environment I was immersed in. I was the only minority within my group of playmates. I was probably one out of the two or three Asians in my elementary school. Within my group of friends, I noticed that I was always spending time at their homes but never the other way around. However, on occasion, whenever my friends would come into my house they would always ask me weird questions like 'What's that smell?' or 'What's this?' and 'What's that?' while referring to the various Filipino decorations we would have in our house. As a child, I was embarrassed to have to explain to my friends what all those things meant. However, now that I look back on it, I ask myself 'What's the big deal?' Why does something so little and irrelevant to my friendships have to make me feel so embarrassed?" (Expressed by a 20-year old Filipina American)

The quotations above speak to the realization of FADE participants that historical oppression has negative influences on their contemporary experiences. Such quotations were facilitated by the CM logs, oppression logs, mental health logs, and CM assessment (using the CMS). Participants were able to identify that inferiorizing messages about the Filipino ethnicity and culture are still being propagated both in the Philippines and in the United States. They were able to make connections between historical colonialism and contemporary oppression, between the postcolonial societal context in the Philippines and the internal colonial context in the United States, and between their experiences of CM and those of other Filipinos and Filipino Americans. They were able to make connections between the existence of CM within them, and those of other Filipinos and Filipino Americans, including their families and friends. They were able to connect their CM and those of others, to how they feel, their well-being, and their mental health. Furthermore, participants were also able to make connections between the Filipino and Filipino American experience and the experiences of other historically and contemporarily oppressed groups, as further shown by the following quote:

> "In reality, when we learn about American history and their global relations, we are not presented with their ethical short-comings. Seeing that we are Americans, we apparently must hold the...view that America is the 'good guy' in it all. Seeing that historically the United States miseducated Filipinos, it is not a coincidence that we are not even being educated today. A similar historical example is Native Americans and their relations with the United States. I do feel that I've been taught a good amount of what 'really' happened—the cheating, lies, abuse, and disrespect, victimizing the Native Americans. Native Americans suffered so greatly under the

United States..." (Expressed by a 19-year old Filipina American)

Also, giving way to the initial feelings of anger and resentment toward the United States and the American culture, participants realized that just like how Filipinos and Filipino Americans were taught to believe that they are inferior, Americans were also just a product of the messages they receive in their environments as well. In essence, from being angry and ethnocentric, FADE participants learned to be sympathetic with White Americans. In addition to all of the other connections they made, FADE participants were also able to connect their experiences with White or mainstream Americans.

> "If we have to go back to the early stages, the development of civilization, it's all about conquering, developing, and religion. Those three things are what advancement was about. Rulers wanted to develop their kingdoms and expand their territories. At the same time rule through the name of their god (eg: pharaohs, God, Zeus, etc). Now that I think about it, colonization is just a more modern version of this concept. Americans, or the conquerors do it or did it because this is the very foundation of their culture. This is the very establishment of their mind. They were brought up to believe they are superior." (Expressed by a 21-year old Filipino American)

> "It seems like Americans have very little knowledge of Filipino American history or culture. I think that in general, Americans regard Filipino Americans the same as they regard any Asian group. Ideally, it would be nice if Americans in general were more aware of Filipino American history, if only as it

pertains to America. I mean, it would be nice if Americans in general had a desire to know more about other cultures, but I feel that it is a necessity to at least have an accurate knowledge of our own (American) history with other cultures, even if the American history with other cultures involves colonialism and subjugation. The truth should not be hidden. It would also be ideal if they could regard their (White American) culture as different but equally valuable. This would also be an ideal viewpoint for Filipino Americans to have about themselves." (Expressed by a 22-year old Filipina American)

The vast amount of personal and collective learning that FADE participants experienced created within them a strong desire to do something about the identified problems. This is similar to the effects of Strobel's (2001) and Halagao's (2004) findings that many of their participants were inspired to take social action.

"If we could only have a real dialogue about it…if we could just share…then maybe we could find even more ways to relate to each other…find more ways to unite and find our voice and perhaps more importantly, our identity as Filipino Americans…shed our 'invisible minority' status and let everyone know what it MEANS to be who we are." (Expressed by a 23-year old Filipino American)

An in-depth data analysis of the information collected from the FADE participants' journals, logs, one-on-one interviews, and group discussions – some of which were presented above –revealed important CBT and decolonization components that facilitated decolonization among the participants. First, components of past decolonization efforts such as historical and cultural education, making historical and contemporary connections, and CM education were identified as the key components of FADE that decreased levels of CM (decolonization) and improved levels of ethnic identity (and thus, mental health) among the participants, similar to the findings of past decolonization efforts (Halagao, 2004; Strobel, 2001). What is unique about FADE, however, is the use of CBT-influenced techniques such as keeping journals, creating a positive Filipino list, maintaining discrimination logs, CM logs, mental health logs, and receiving CM assessment and feedback, which were identified as common CBT techniques that helped facilitate decolonization among the participants and, thus, improving their ethnic identity and mental health. Receiving CM assessment and feedback allowed participants to become aware of CM manifestations that they may hold but may not be aware of (as discussed in Chapter 6), and paved the way for identifying more adaptive behaviors and cognitions that may begin to challenge and eliminate such CM manifestations. The positive Filipino list made positive Filipino ethnic and cultural characteristics more salient among participants which, in turn, helped facilitate cognitive restructuring of the distorted belief that there is little positive about the Filipino culture and ethnicity that one can be proud of. Discrimination logs allowed participants to develop a more accurate understanding of their current experiences as minority individuals and the experiences of others like them (other Filipinos and other oppressed groups). CM logs allowed participants to gain better understanding of CM manifestations among themselves and others, including their loved ones, as well as to realize how prevalent CM is among Filipinos and Filipino Americans. Mental health logs allowed participants to make connections between their social experiences (e.g., positive interactions with other Filipinos, experiences of discrimination, experiences of CM, etc.) and how these experiences influence how they feel about themselves, their ethnic and cultural heritage, and other Filipinos. Making connections between one's social experiences and mental health (Mental Health Connections) paved the way for identifying and practicing more adaptive cognitive and behavioral responses when individuals face similar situations in the future.

Individual level empowerment seems to have been fostered, as participants eradicated self-blame and feelings of inferiority and confusions by better understanding how such feelings, attitudes, and behaviors were taught and reinforced by their environment; by inferiorizing environmental messages that may not be obvious or blatant but instead may be very subtle (i.e., microaggressions, as discussed in Chapter 4). Further, collective empowerment was fostered as participants were able to make connections and see similarities between their historical and contemporary experiences, between their experiences and those of other Filipinos (Within-Group Connections), and between the Filipino experience and those of other historically oppressed or colonized groups (Inter-Group Connections). Fostering collective empowerment seems to be especially important, as it may also increase if not revive the sense of Kapwa (discussed in Chapter 7) among the participants – the recognition that they are not separate from others, that they have similarities with others, and that they can identify themselves in other peoples. Thus, based on FADE data, making (1) Historical/Contemporary Connections, (2) Within-Group Connections, (3) Inter-Group Connections, and (4) Mental Health Connections were facilitated by the CBT tasks and group discussions that took place during every session of FADE.

Below is an example of how common CBT techniques and group discussions that are typical of prior decolonization efforts (Halagao, 2004; Strobel, 2001) complemented each other during FADE and jointly facilitated making Historical/Contemporary Connections, Within-Group Connections, Inter-Group Connections, and Mental Health Connections among the participants (parenthetical comments added for emphasis):

"I increasingly understand the implications of colonial mentality and its psychological effects on the Filipino community. In general, I realize how its historical context has evolved into a psychological issue as well (*Mental Health Connection*). The effects of colonial mentality were not limited to its initial victims, rather those initial victims reflected their acquired feelings of inferiority in their interpersonal relationships (*Intergenerational Effects Through Socialization*). Holding values of their colonizers, the colonized bestows his or her family with this colonial mentality and these messages and values are passed on to further generations. Facts about being colonized was watered down or didn't even exist. Seeing that historically the United States miseducated Filipinos, it is not a coincidence that we are not even being educated today. A similar historical example is Native Americans and their relations with the United States *(Inter-Group Connections)*. These effects are reflected in the Filipino community today *(Historical and Contemporary Connections; Within-Group Connection).* I never realized how much the Filipino's were subjected to the cruelty and unfairness by other countries. It was like a whole other Holocaust, a 'cultural holocaust,' that no one knew about *(Inter-Group Connections).* It angered me because it seemed like the only reason it was not exposed was because they were the actions of the United States. I felt angered when I learned about the losses associated with colonization. I had feelings of denial and shame when I learned about all the things that Filipinos lost. Before, I had no opinion about the Filipino community's everyday use of the term "FOB." I never really took the time to analyze whether or not I was actually making someone feel offended by calling them a fob or even just using the word *(Becoming aware of CM in oneself and in others; Within-Group Connection).* Now I realized that the term "FOB" has many negative connotations behind it. In the past, I would have never thought of taking the time to reconnect with my past just to understand the present *(Historical and Contemporary Connections)*. I never knew the importance of what is was to have knowledge beyond what my parents told me and what I learned from the textbooks in high school, to really analyze the truths and separate them from the myths of Filipino history. It never occurred to me that without the knowledge of true Filipino history, I really would never know myself." (Expressed by a 20-year old Filipina American)

In sum, making Historical/Contemporary Connections allowed participants to trace CM or internalized oppression to factors outside of themselves, which helped in facilitating the eradication of self-blame. Making mental health connections also allowed participants to become aware of how oppressive external factors and experiences can influence their mental health and psychological well-being. In a way, these two forms of connections are examples of *personal empowerment*. Participants making Within-Group Connections and Inter-Group Connections, on the other hand, allowed them to realize that they are not alone, unique, or *weird* in their experiences. Such connections allowed participants to see similarities between themselves and other Filipinos and Filipino Americans, as well as between themselves and other members of historically and contemporarily oppressed groups, which may foster the sense of

Kapwa (discussed in Chapter 7) within the participants. These two forms of connections are examples of *collective empowerment*. Thus, it seems like this initial attempt at integrating decolonization and CBT goals and strategies is successful in reducing CM (i.e., decolonization) and promoting psychological well-being through personal and collective empowerment. Table 4 briefly summarizes the decolonization and CBT components found to be important in reducing CM and improving mental health based on the FADE data.

Table 4. Decolonization and CBT Components of FADE

The Past: Understanding personal and collective histories. (Lecture and Discussion)
• This allows individuals to develop a complete and accurate understanding of their heritage culture and its history. (A major component of prior decolonization efforts and similar to raising awareness in personal and community change models)
The Present: Understanding our contemporary experiences. (CBT Intervention Techniques: Use of CM-Logs, Positive Filipino List, CM assessment and feedback, and Oppression Logs)
• This allows individuals to develop a complete and accurate understanding of their contemporary experiences as Filipino Americans, and a more complete and accurate perception of their personal and collective selves. (This is a major component of prior decolonization efforts and also a goal consistent with CBT)
Making Connections: Understanding how our past may have shaped our present (CBT Intervention Techniques: Mental Health Logs; Group Discussion; Psychoeducation; Cognitive Restructuring)
• This allows individuals to trace the origins of CM as external and eliminate self-blame, normalize their experiences of CM and oppression, and eliminate feelings of loneliness; make connections between historical and contemporary oppression, make connections between their experiences and their mental health and well-being, make connections between their experiences as Filipino Americans and the experiences of other historically oppressed groups. (These are major components of prior decolonization efforts and a goal consistent with CBT)

Finally, based on FADE data, participants seem to have developed a strong desire to continue learning more about Filipino history and culture, further enhancing their ethnic identity and potentially maintaining cognitions and behaviors developed during the experience over a long period of time. Below is an example of the strong desire to learn more and maintain a more adaptive set of cognitions and behaviors that were developed as a result of FADE, as expressed by a 21-year old Filipino American:

> "The more I learn about how colonization has implications other than just historical I just get more confused and upset, but above all, wanting to know more. I truly believe that you can't just find your ethnic identity in one day, and it never really ends. We are always learning about who we are and discovering where we came from. Through this experience, I learned about the ugly histories of colonization and oppression. All of this is helping me form a base ethnic identity. It transforms as we grow and learn, and if we can start the process earlier, we can help the younger generation of Filipinos take charge of who they are and make others aware of our true culture." (Expressed by a 22-year old Filipino American)

Chapter Summary

This chapter described the experiences of Filipino Americans who participated in the process of decolonization through FADE. FADE is very similar to other prior decolonization efforts such as those of Strobel's (2001) and Halagao's (2004), which attempts to promote the achievement of the Incorporation stage of the Pilipino American Identity Development Model (Nadal, 2004; as discussed in Chapter 8). Indeed, just like other decolonization efforts, FADE included intensive dialogues, interviews, and discussions about Filipino and Filipino American history and culture. Furthermore,

FADE's goals of improving Filipinos' and Filipino Americans' understanding of themselves and of their world, historically and contemporarily, are the same as those of prior decolonization efforts and consistent with the ideal ethnic identity development stage proposed by Nadal (2004). Even the recognition and facilitation of Kapwa in FADE is similar to the goals and effects of prior decolonization efforts among Filipinos and Filipino Americans. What makes FADE different, however, is that it explicitly incorporates techniques and concepts widely known and accepted in the field of psychology in its effort to facilitate decolonization among Filipinos and Filipino Americans. Thus, it is possible that FADE may be more understandable and palatable to clinicians and other service providers, and making FADE components and strategies easier to incorporate into existing forms of services or systems of care. Although the contents, strategies, and techniques used in FADE still need to be further developed, refined, and empirically tested to provide more evidence for its clinical utility, efficacy, and effectiveness, preliminary evidence thus far as presented in this chapter suggests that they hold promise in terms of facilitating the process of decolonization among Filipinos and Filipino Americans. Preliminary evidence also suggest that FADE has promise as serving as an example of how commonly-used clinical interventions such as CBT can be modified so that it is more culturally-sensitive and appropriate for Filipinos, Filipino Americans, and members of other historically and contemporarily oppressed groups. Indeed, FADE can be further developed and tested so that it can be considered as an example of what Hall (2001) termed as Culturally Sensitive Therapies or Treatments (CSTs).

*   *   *

Thus far, Part III of the book has focused on eradicating, or at least, reducing the effects of historical colonialism and contemporary oppression among Filipinos and Filipino Americans. More specifically, Part III has discussed in some detail some possible interventions and strategies that may be useful in addressing CM or internalized oppression – the psychological consequence of colonialism and historical oppression – among Filipinos and Filipino Americans. Such discussions are highly relevant to the work of many professionals in the field of psychology such as clinical, counseling, and community psychologists. However, I believe that decolonization should not just happen in the individual level. I also do not believe that decolonization in psychological terms should be contained only in the clinical context or in other fields of psychology that are interested in intervening against undesirable outcomes or in promoting well-being. Instead, I believe that decolonization needs to happen in all aspects of psychology. In the next and final chapter, I will discuss the colonization and decolonization of the main foundation of the field of psychology as a whole – research. More specifically, in the next chapter I discuss the colonized nature of psychological research around the world, with a focus on Filipino psychology, as they have been historically dominated by Western or American psychological theories, methods, and concepts. I also present some ideas as to how we can decolonize the manner in which we conceptualize, conduct, and interpret psychological research, especially for Filipinos and Filipino Americans, and other historically and contemporarily oppressed groups.

CHAPTER 12

POSTCOLONIAL
PSYCHOLOGICAL RESEARCH

ᜎᜂᜊ᜔ᜊ᜔ᜎ ᜊ ᜊᜒᜆ᜔ ᜃᜆ᜔ᜎ

When Dr. Virgilio Enriquez, the father of Filipino indigenous Psychology or *Sikolohiyang Pilipino*, obtained his Ph.D. from Northwestern University in Illinois, he was very proud to go back to the Philippines and was very excited to celebrate with his father. When he got home, however, one of the first things his father told him was that he should not celebrate just yet because he is not done – his father wanted him to explain his doctoral dissertation in Tagalog (Pe-Pua & Protacio-Marcelino, 2000). The sense of his work not being done goes beyond this father-son interaction, however, as Enriquez quickly realized as he began his career in the Philippines that many of the psychological models, theories, concepts, and methods that he learned over many years while studying in the United States were not applicable or appropriate for the Philippine and Filipino contexts. In essence, he realized that the field of psychology in the Philippines was also colonized, with many scholars regarding Western or American theories, concepts, and methods as automatically better and adapting them inappropriately for use among Filipinos. In other words, the field of Filipino psychology was also affected by colonial mentality. Examples of such a colonized manner of psychological work in the Philippines were the simple translations of concepts, theories, and tests or measurement tools into the local language, without regard to the sociopolitical realities of Filipinos, a method that is referred to as *indigenization from without* (Enriquez, 1994). Also, the practice of psychological research was usually conducted by outsiders (mostly Westerners), and thus, were usually biased by the outsiders' worldviews. In the words of Pe-Pua and Protacio-Marcelino (2000) as they quoted Enriquez (1992):

> "…in the area of personality, the Western approach in research of not being enmeshed and bound by the culture being studied has resulted in a characterization of the Filipino from the 'judgmental and impressionistic point of view of the colonizers' (Enriquez, 1992, p. 57). For example, the predisposition to indirectness of Filipino communication was regarded as being dishonest and socially ingratiating and reflecting a deceptive verbal description of reality… rather than a concern for the feelings of others…Thus, using American categories and standards, 'the native Filipino invariably suffers from the comparison in not too subtle attempts to put forward Western behavior patterns as models for the Filipino' (Enriquez, 1992, p. 57)." (Pe-Pua & Protacio-Marcelino, 2000, pp. 49-50)..

Indeed, psychological research in the Philippines was being colonized by the dominant Western or American approach to scientific psychology. With this harsh realization, Enriquez's work was just beginning instead of being done, as he developed an intense desire to decolonize the psychological field in the Philippines and develop an approach to psychology that is appropriate, accurate, relevant, meaningful, and empowering for the Filipino people. Hence, Sikolohiyang Pilipino or Filipino Indigenous Psychology was born.

To this end, this chapter will discuss how we may begin to decolonize the field of psychology itself – with mentions of Filipino and Filipino American psychology – analogous to how the two previous chapters (Chapters 10 and 11) have discussed some concepts, strategies, and techniques that may help us facilitate decolonization and the eradication of CM or internalized oppression among Filipino and Filipino American individuals. In other words, this chapter will discuss how we can help the field of psychology eradicate its colonial mentality. However, unlike the other chapters in the book, this final chapter will focus more on the field of psychology in general and less so on the specifics of Filipino and Filipino American psychology. Although this chapter will discuss Sikolohiyang Pilipino as an example for how to decolonize the field of psychology, this chapter is more focused on the field of indigenous psychology in general and how it can lead to the decolonization of psychology in non-Western cultures and countries worldwide. Also, although this chapter will discuss some research methods that are deemed to be more appropriate for Filipinos and Filipino Americans – methods that may facilitate more accurate understanding of the psychological realities of Filipinos and Filipino Americans and empowerment such communities – such methods may also serve as examples for how psychological research with other historically and contemporarily oppressed groups may be conducted in a more culturally-appropriate, meaningful, and applicable manner. Finally, this chapter will also make connections between the goals and methods of indigenous psychology (including Sikolohiyang Pilipino) and the goals and methods of a subfield of Western or American psychology – Community Psychology – with the intention of outlining a conceptual model for how we can truly achieve a balanced and decolonized global field of psychology. Thus, this chapter is not only relevant for Filipino and Filipino American psychology, but also to the psychology of other historically and contemporarily oppressed groups, as well as to conventional Western or American psychology itself. Let us begin the chapter with a description of the history and goals of indigenous psychology.

Indigenous Psychology

The indigenous psychology movement began in the 1970s due to the dissatisfaction of many psychologists in other countries and cultures with Western or American psychology's extreme adherence to logical-positivistic, natural sciences-patterned, highly quantitative, hypotheses testing-oriented, universal-seeking, and western culture-dominated research paradigms (e.g., Enriquez, 1977, 1993; Church & Katigbak, 2002; Kim, 2000; Kim, Park, & Park, 1999; Pe-Pua & Protacio-Marcelino, 2000; Shams, 2002; Sinha, 1997; Yang, 2000). Instead, in its efforts to make psychology more ecologically or culturally appropriate (Sinha, 1997), indigenous psychology strives toward developing a "system of psychological knowledge based on scientific research that is sufficiently compatible with the studied phenomena and their ecological, economic, social, cultural, and historical contexts" (Yang, 2000, p. 245). Proponents of the indigenous psychology movement believe that indigenously deriving and applying psychological knowledge equally recognizes and values the complexities and differences of psychological experiences throughout the various cultures and countries of the world, making indigenous psychology the best path toward a genuine global psychology in their eyes (e.g., Yang; Sinha; Enriquez; Kim; Shams; Adair, 1999; Diaz-Loving, 1999).

In addition to arguing against the American dominance on, or westernization of, other psychologies in other parts of the world, Yang (2000), who is one the leaders of the indigenous psychology movement, also presented an argument about the limitations of the field of cross-cultural psychology in appropriately and accurately understanding psychological phenomena in other countries and cultures. Yang asserted that because cross-cultural psychology is a subdiscipline of mainstream American or Western psychology, cross-cultural psychology still has a tendency to utilize and impose highly positivistic paradigms and natural sciences-based theories and methods in its search for universal psychological laws. Thus, Yang referred to this type of cross-cultural psychology as *cross-cultural westernized psychology* (CCWP). CCWP is argued to have led to the imposition of American or Western beliefs and assumptions on the psychology of non-American or Non-Western peoples, leading to the development of a *monocultural westernized psychology* (MCWP) or a field of psychology that has colonial mentality. In turn, such inappropriate or ill-fitting psychological theories and methods have hindered the holistic and accurate understanding of the psychology of non-American or non-Western individuals and groups (Poortinga, 1999), which is argued to be a form of scientific imperialism, scientific ethnocentrism, or colonization of the mind (e.g., Diaz-Loving, 1999; Enriquez, 1993; Kim, 2000; Shams, 2002). Similarly, Yang also criticized the subdiscipline of cultural psychology for its seemingly extreme adherence to human sciences-based theories and methods, and its generally strong rejection of natural sciences-based theoretical and methodological models. Yang argued that both natural science- and human science-based theories and methods present valuable contributions to our understanding of psychology, and that overly adhering to one model at the expense of the other is just as limiting.

Instead, Yang (2000) advocated for indigenous psychology, a discipline that does not limit its theoretical and methodological toolbox. Consistently, Kim and Berry (1993) also asserted that an indigenous approach does not assume that any particular theoretical and methodological paradigm is superior to others. In other words, indigenous psychology is willing to use any type of approach in its derivation and interpretation of research questions, approaches, and results as long as such practices are appropriate for the phenomena and contexts in question. Due to its unique theoretical and methodological inclusiveness, Yang argued that indigenous psychology is the best-equipped and most appropriate paradigm in psychology's quest of accurately understanding the diverse psychological experiences of our highly diverse world. In his support for the development of multiple indigenous psychologies as the paths toward the establishment of a genuinely balanced global psychology, Yang proposed a conceptual framework of how each of the non-American, non-dominant, or less-established indigenous psychologies should develop: (1) establish an independent, non-westernized, or decolonized *monocultural indigenous psychology* (MCIP) instead of a monocultural westernized psychology (MCWP); and (2) to transform cross-cultural westernized psychology (CCWP) into a *cross-cultural indigenous psychology* (CCIP). These two suggestions are further elaborated below.

As mentioned above, Yang (2000) recognized the continuously unquestioned dominance and imposition of American or Western psychological thoughts and methods over the rest of the world that arguably led to westernized psychologies in other countries, a situation he believed to be hindering psychologies in such countries and cultures from being genuinely appropriate, culturally and contextually. For example, although Turkey and the former USSR (Ongel & Smith, 1999) have established what are supposedly their own indigenous psychologies, a closer look reveals a persistent orientation toward American or Western theories and methods, suggesting that such countries have a monocultural westernized psychology (MCWP). Similarly, this is perhaps the type of Filipino psychology that Virgilio Enriquez encountered when he returned to the Philippines after getting his doctorate from Northwestern University. Thus, what Yang suggested to be the first step toward a proper establishment of a genuinely independent and indigenously derived psychology, which he calls monocultural indigenous psychology (MCIP) or a decolonized psychology, is that researchers in other societies need to use the *monocultural indigenous approach* (MCIA) in their research, service provisions, and teaching. As an example, for research to be considered as adhering to the MCIA, "...the investigators' research activities (including topic selection, conceptual analysis, research design, and theory construction) must be sufficiently congruous with the native people's studied psychological or behavioral elements, structures, mechanisms, or processes as rooted in their ecological, economic, social, cultural, or historical contexts" (Yang, 2000, pp. .249-250).

In addition, the MCIA involves the critical examination of the appropriateness of American or Western paradigms within the local contexts and topics of interest. This is not to say, however, that other indigenous psychologies should totally reject American or Western paradigms. Instead, Yang proposed critically examining such paradigms first instead of simply and unquestionably regarding them as superior or "the" paradigm. If after such a critical examination a researcher still finds American or Western approaches to be most appropriate for his or her research questions, then such approaches should be utilized. In other words, it is only suggested that other indigenous psychologies need to regard American psychology, although more established, as simply another type of indigenous psychology and not as the only, legitimate, or superior type of psychology. In short, Yang proposed that other indigenous psychologies, which are likely to be victims of American psychological imperialism or colonization, needs to transform their monocultural westernized psychology (MCWP) into a monocultural indigenous psychology (MCIP) by using the MCIA (as shown in Figure 13). Yang's descriptions of MCWP, MCIP, and MCIA are exactly the ways in which Virgilio Enriquez (1994) decolonized the field of Filipino psychology, as will be discussed below. More specific suggested developments within other indigenous psychologies that may assist in its de-westernization or decolonization processes are: training and hiring locally-trained psychologists (e.g., Adair, 1999); focusing on topics that are of local concern and not on American-imposed topics (e.g., Adair, 1999); production of locally-written and locally-relevant textbooks and other teaching materials (e.g., Adair, 1999; Pe-Pua & Protacio-Marcelino, 2000; Church & Katigbak, 2002); production of local psychological academic journals (Adair; Pe-Pua & Protacio-Marcelino, 2000; Church & Katigbak, 2002); and the use of the local language in teaching and writing about psychology (Pe-Pua & Protacio-Marcelino, 2000).

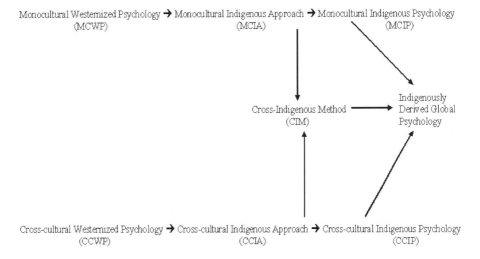

Figure 13. Yang's Framework for Decolonizing Psychology

Once multiple psychologies that do not have deferential tendencies toward American psychology have been established (multiple MCIPs or several decolonized fields of psychology), Yang (2000) suggested that the next step is to integrate or compare research findings from multiple MCIPs for making cross-cultural generalizations and, in the process, create an indigenously derived body of cross-cultural knowledge. What Yang suggested to be the method for such an undertaking is what Enriquez (1993) called the *cross-indigenous method* (CIM). At this point, it is deemed necessary to point-out that Enriquez never had the chance to describe the characteristics and purposes of the CIM in detail before his death. However, it seems as though Yang was interpreting what limited understanding we have about the CIM as the method in which multiple MCIPs are compared and analyzed to contribute to an indigenously derived cross-cultural knowledge system.

In addition to the CIM, Yang (2000) also proposed another and more detailed method that he believes will contribute to the establishment of a cross-cultural indigenous psychology (CCIP) – the *cross-cultural indigenous approach* (CCIA) (as shown in Figure 13). The CCIA is not the same as the CIM because the CIM is interpreted as a comparison of already conducted research and their findings from multiple MCIPs, whereas the CCIA describes the process of designing, conducting, and interpreting research in a cross-culturally collaborative and indigenous manner. Furthermore, in contrast to the high ethnocentrism and quantitative cross-cultural equivalence-seeking approaches that usually characterize the cross-cultural westernized methods used by cross-cultural westernized psychology (CCWP), the CCIA is a bottom-up process that is based on individual studies that are indigenously derived, conducted, and interpreted; and it places importance on collaborations between various indigenous researchers from the involved cultures in the development, execution, and discussion of qualitative research. Therefore, similar to how the MCIA is a method of transforming a MCWP into a MCIP, the CCIA is a method of transforming a CCWP into a CCIP. Because of the high cross-cultural indigenous compatibility of research done with the CCIA, CCIP is regarded by Yang as the "real" cross-cultural psychology that will lead to the establishment of an indigenously derived and balanced global psychology. In his own words:

> "(Some scholars) have suggested that indigenous psychologists are against cross-cultural psychology.

Actually, indigenous psychologists do not reject all kinds of cross-cultural psychology, only the ones that has been based on questionable knowledge created by the pervasive application of Western-dominated imposed-etic or partial imposed-etic procedures. What is needed is a new kind of cross-cultural psychology as a knowledge system with high cross-cultural indigenous compatibility. This (CCIP) is exactly the type of cross-cultural psychology to be established by adopting the CCIA and the cross-indigenous method as the major ways of creating genuine cross-cultural knowledge. The final goal of cross-cultural indigenous psychology (CCIP) is to construct an indigenously derived global psychology." (p. 257).

Sikolohiyang Pilipino

Consistent with the history and goals of indigenous psychology, Sikolohiyang Pilipino or Filipino Indigenous Psychology also developed out of the dissatisfaction of many psychological scholars in the Philippines – led by Virgilio Enriquez – with Western or American theories, concepts, and methods that have been forced upon inappropriately to fit the psychological realities of Filipinos. In fact, it is perhaps more accurate to say that the psychological realities of Filipinos were forcibly fit into Western or American theories, concepts, and methods of psychology – *indigenization from without*. Instead, consistent with indigenous psychology, Sikolohiyang Pilipino's main goals is to also generate psychological knowledge in a culturally-appropriate manner, using methods that are more congruent and compatible with indigenous Filipino behaviors and worldview – *indigenization from within* or *cultural revalidation* (Enriquez, 1992; Pe-Pua & Protacio-Marcelino, 2000) – which it believes will lead to a more accurate understanding of the Filipino psychological realities. In the words of Virgilio Enriquez (1994),

> "Sikolohiyang Pilipino is the embodiment of the systematic and scientific study, appreciation, and application of indigenous knowledge for, of, and by the Filipinos of their own psychological make-up, society, and culture, rooted in their historical past, ethnic diversity, and the dynamic interaction of Filipinos with forces within and outside their social and physical boundaries…Sikolohiyand Pilipino only seeks to put things in their proper perspective and check the imbalance resulting from extreme reliance on Western models as a basis for analyzing (Filipino) social realities…Sikolohiyang Pilipino seeks to explain (Filipino) realities from the Filipino perspective, taking into account the peculiarities and distinct values and characteristics of the Filipino which the Western models invariably fail to explain or consider." (p. 27).

With such goals, Sikolohiyang Pilipino advocates for the use of research methods that are deemed to be more culturally-appropriate for the Filipino people, methods that are more empowering of the Filipino people and ones that may lead to more accurate understanding of their psychological realities, and thus, more effective interventions for their social concerns. In addition to, if not instead of, using common Western or American psychological research methods such as experiments and surveys to obtain psychological data, Enriquez (1994) argued for the use of information gathering strategies that are more natural and appropriate for Filipinos such as *pagtatanong-tanong* (asking around), *pakikiramdam* (using one's shared inner perception), *panunuluyan* (staying with), and *pakikipamuhay* (living with). As can be noticed, these Filipino information gathering methods vary in terms of the depth of involvement a researcher may have with the participants, and thus, the depth of the gathered information will vary as well. In other words, a researcher who is still considered an outsider will only be able to use the method of pagtatanong-tanong and obtain very surface level information as a result, whereas a researcher who has developed rapport with the participants and has gained the community's trust by developing Kapwa, may use methods such as panunuluyan and pakikipamuhay and gather more in-depth and accurate information. To this end, it becomes clear that the extent to which a researcher is considered to be trustworthy by the community determines which research methods can be used and, consequently, the quality of the information obtained.

Santiago and Enriquez (1976) organized the levels of natural social interactions in the Filipino culture into two categories: the Outsider or *Ibang-Tao* category; and the One of us or *Hindi Ibang-Tao* category. Individuals, including researchers, who have yet to establish rapport with the community by developing Kapwa and consistently practicing other values such as Utang na Loob and Pakikisama (as discussed in Chapter 7), are considered to be Ibang-Tao. Thus, community members will only be comfortable in a limited way spending time with Ibang-Tao and sharing information with them only to a certain extent – community members may only display *pakikitungo* (being civil, but still uninvolved), *pakikilahok* (participating), *pakikibagay* (conforming), or *pakikisama* (adjusting). Consequently, the quality of information that researchers may obtain in such interactional contexts will also be limited. Individuals, including researchers, who consistently practice the Ibang-Tao social interactions above, and do so respectfully and appropriately, may begin to develop rapport and trust with the community over time. Eventually, such an individual or researcher may be perceived as someone who is developing Kapwa and Pakiramdam, and thus, be considered by the community as Hindi Ibang-Tao.

Individuals, including researchers, who are now considered to be Hindi Ibang-Tao may start experiencing a deeper level of social interaction with the community, as the community may now be more comfortable with them to the extent that the community members may now display *pakikipagpalagayang-loob* (mutual trust/rapport, confiding), *pakikisangkot* (getting involved), and *pakikiisa* (fusion, oneness, and full trust). These Hindi Ibang-Tao levels of social interactions may result into the collection of information that are very rich, accurate, and meaningful. Most important, however, is that these methods of information gathering are more natural and culturally-appropriate in the Filipino culture than surveys or lab-based experiments. Having said this, however, Sikolohiyang Pilipino is not against science nor is it non-scientific. Similar to Yang's (2000) assertion that indigenous psychology only asks that Western or American theories, concepts, and methods be critically examined first before using and applying them on non-Western or non-American peoples, instead of automatically assuming that such approach to psychological research is better or the "standard," Sikolohiyang Pilipino is also open to the use of such approaches and concepts among Filipinos when it is deemed that they are the most appropriate. As Virgilio Enriquez (1994) argued,

> "Sikolohiyang Pilipino utilizes scientific methodology in the study of psychological phenomenon. However, it goes beyond the cold and impartial methods employed by science…(it) aims to use science to enhance, not to dehumanize, (humankind)…Sikolohiyang Pilipino uses both phenomenological and behavioristic concepts. But unlike its Western counterpart, which gives emphasis to individual experience, it puts greater weight on the collective experience of a people with a common bond of history…In analyzing the results of a social science study…it relies not only on the scientific analysis of the findings but also takes into

account in its interpretation other equally, if not even more, important variables like the historical background, social context, political implications and cultural meaning of the study." (pp. 28-29).

Thus, Sikolohiyang Pilipino acknowledges the value of Western methods, concepts, and theories. However, Sikolohiyang Pilipino also recognizes the limitations of Western methods, concepts, and theories, especially when ill-fittingly applied to the Filipino context. Also, Sikolohiyang Pilipino has a broader understanding of what the terms *science* and *scientific* mean, extending it beyond notions of objectivity to also include the importance and values of subjective realities. Sikolohiyang Pilipino is open to all methods, theories, and concepts, so long as it generates accurate and empowering knowledge about the psychological realities of Filipinos. Sikolohiyang Pilipino is open to Western or American methods, theories, or concepts, so long as those who are involved (researchers and participants) do not automatically regard such methods, theories, and concepts as better or more sophisticated than other methods, theories, and concepts, especially the Filipino ones. It is a scientific field that seeks to conduct psychological research and projects that are culturally, socially, politically, and historically meaningful and beneficial to Filipinos. To this end, Sikolohiyang Pilipino is: (1) a sikolohiyang malaya (liberated psychology) as it is against a psychology that promotes Filipino colonial mentality; and a (2) a sikolohiyang mapagpalaya (liberating psychology) as it denounces an elite-, Western-, or American-oriented psychology that ignores the realities of many oppressed or dominated peoples (Enriquez, 1994). Therefore, through its values and principles, the openness to multidisciplinary approaches to research, and the use of culturally-appropriate methods which may be considered to be examples of the MCIA, Sikolohiyang Pilipino is an example of how a MCWP can turn into a MCIP.

With such goals of developing accurate, empowering, and culturally-appropriate, meaningful, and applicable psychological knowledge and understanding of Filipinos, the use of Sikolohiynag Pilipino methods when conducting Filipino and Filipino American psychology research seems promising. For instance, the use of such methods have led Enriquez (1994) to better conceptualize and understand the core Filipino value of Kapwa and how it is related to a variety of Filipino values, cognitions, and behaviors (as discussed in Chapter 7). An improved understanding of Kapwa and the indigenous Filipino value structure has led to a more empowering understanding of the psychological realities of Filipinos, which may contribute to more culturally-appropriate, effective, and longer-lasting social changes that may promote the well-being of Filipinos. Thus, it is possible that the use of Sikolohiyang Pilipino methods when studying the psychological realities of Filipinos and Filipino Americans may also bear similar fruit. It is unfortunate, but the reality is that the usage of such methods in Filipino and Filipino American psychological research are currently very rare. In fact, even the majority of the studies and experiments presented in this book were conceptualized, conducted, and interpreted in ways that are consistent with the paradigm of the dominant Western or American psychology. This is not to say that such studies and experiments are value-less, however, as even the strongest proponents of indigenous psychology (Enriquez, 1994; Yang, 2000) see value in such works. Nevertheless, there is definitely an imbalance in terms of the concepts, theories, and methods that are currently used in Filipino and Filipino American psychology, with those of the Western or American paradigm continuing to be dominant. However, there is hope that such a strong dependence on typical Western and American scientific paradigms will begin to weaken, as an entity within the dominant Western and American psychological field itself have risen to challenge the field as a whole.

Community Psychology as America's Indigenous Psychology

Similar to the proponents and founders of indigenous psychology, many psychologists within the dominant mainstream American psychology itself have expressed equal dissatisfaction with such traditionally or conventionally western, and usually uncriticized, scientific assumptions, orientations, and practices that propagate the field of psychology (e.g., Marsella, 1998; Trickett, 1996; Camic, Rhodes, & Yardley, 2003; Howarth, 2001; Fuks, 1998). These psychologists argue that such a paradigm often lead to non-contextualized and, thus very limited, research questions, methods, results, and interpretations. This dissatisfaction within American or mainstream psychology is arguably expressed the strongest by the subdiscipline of community psychology. As an alternative, community psychology endorses a highly context-based derivation of research questions, methods, findings, interpretations, and theories (e.g., Trickett; Rappaport; 1977; Kelly, 1990) – highly similar to and consistent with those advocated by indigenous psychology (Gregory, 2001). Due to such culturally and contextually sensitive characteristics of community psychology, its strong potential to be American psychology's vehicle toward a truly balanced global psychology has been recognized (e.g., Marsella, 1998; Wingenfield & Newbrough, 2000; Roesch & Carr, 2000), analogous to how the development of multiple independent indigenous psychologies has been regarded as other countries' "royal road to the development of a balanced global psychology" (Yang, 2000, p. 241).

As a response to the emerging high levels of connectedness between the different countries and cultures of the world, which is the result of rapid changes in global telecommunications, transportation, and political and economic ties, Marsella (1998) suggested that American psychology needs to respond to the presenting challenges brought about by such an emerging "global village" (p. 1282). However, he quickly added that responding to such global challenges does not mean further imposing traditional American cultural beliefs and Western psychological assumptions on

America's rapidly diversifying population, and on the rest of the world, because American/Western assumptions that highly emphasize "the individual, objectivity, quantification, narrow disciplinary orientation, and universal 'truths' may be irrelevant and meaningless for non-Western (or non-White) people and their life contexts" (p. 1285). Instead, he suggested that American Psychology needs to reconsider its assumptions and methodologies and develop a discipline that is responsive, inclusive, and respectful to such an emerging global connectedness and its resulting multiethnic, multicultural, and multinational conditions and contexts. In Marsella's words:

> "It is time to reexamine Western (or American) psychology within the global-community context of our lives, with all that this may imply for new assumptions, methods, and interventions. It is time for a global-community psychology. Psychologists, throughout the world, can develop and advance psychologies by using the wisdom and knowledge of their cultures, and they can evaluate the applicability of these psychologies in various arenas and forums across the world" (pp. 1286-1286)"

Although not explicitly stated, Marsella (1998) seems to advocate for the paradigm of community psychology as American psychology's best answer to such global challenges because of his visions' and suggestions' many similarities with the goals, intentions, approaches, and methods of community psychology. Also, it is probably not by accident that Marsella included the word "community" in the title of his vision of a global psychology. In other words, Marsella seems to consider community psychology as American psychology's best path toward the establishment of what he calls a Global-Community Psychology (GCP) - "a superordinate or meta-psychology concerned with understanding, assessing, and addressing the individual and collective psychological consequences of global events and forces by encouraging and using multicultural, multidisciplinary, multisectoral, and multinational knowledge, methods, and interventions...(a psychology that) prizes diverse psychologies and (resists) the inequities imposed by any power asymmetries" (Marsella, 1998, p, 1284). In addition to acknowledging and encouraging the developments of other indigenous psychologies (as previously mentioned), GCP also: (1) challenges local socialization values and forces and introduces the emergence of global socialization forces; (2) strives toward minimizing ethnocentricity and cultural bias by repositioning traditional Western psychology from being "the" psychology, or dominant psychology, into regarding it as simply being one of many psychologies worldwide; (3) emphasizes the importance of highly-contextualized research, services, and education to more appropriately respond to our rapidly diversifying societies; (4) encourages the use and development of complex and nonlinear theories and orientations, and the utilization of interdisciplinary and multidisciplinary approaches; and (5) welcomes the use of qualitative research methodologies such as narratives, ethnographic analysis, interviews, ethnosemantic analyses, and many others.

Marsella's (1998) vision of what should constitute a global psychology is highly consistent with Yang's (2000) idea of an indigenously derived global psychology. Furthermore, Marsella's implicit endorsement of community psychology as America's vehicle toward his vision of a global psychology is also highly consistent with Yang's support for the establishment of multiple monocultural indigenous psychologies as other countries' road toward the development of his idea of a global psychology. In other words, community psychology may be considered as America's version of a monocultural indigenous psychology.

Indeed, there is substantial compatibility and overlap between the characteristics, visions, and proposed global potentials of community and indigenous psychologies (Gregory, 2001). Furthermore, because of the many similarities between the two psychologies in terms of their paradigms and global-psychological intents, it is arguable that the two psychologies might only differ in name and may essentially be the same. For instance, Yang (2000) coined the term "indigenous compatibility" (IC) to refer to the degree to which research is "conducted in a manner such that the researcher's concepts, theory, methods, tools, and results adequately represent, reflect, or reveal natural elements, structures, mechanisms, or process of the studied phenomenon embedded in its context" (p. 250); and that the concept of IC may be used "for judging the degree of indigenousness of the approach, research, and psychology" (p. 251). Community psychology has put an emphasis on research and intervention methods that are socioplotically-contextualized, culturally-appropriate, and responsive to the people they work with, as exemplified by its increased utilization of *community-based participatory research* (CBPR) or *participatory action research* (Wallerstein & Duran, 2003), which are collaborative research approaches "that equitably involves all partners in the research process and recognizes the unique strengths that each brings. CBPR begins with a research topic of importance to the community with the aim of combining knowledge and action for social change to improve community health and eliminate health disparities" (a definition developed by the W.K. Kellogg Community Scholars Program based on the definition provided by Israel, Shulz, Parker, & Becker, 1998). Thus, because of its high IC level, community psychology may be regarded as American psychology's version of indigenous psychology.

Creating a Decolonized, Indigenously-Derived, and Balanced Global Psychology

Both Marsella (1998) and Yang (2000) called for the reexamining, critical questioning, and de-centering of the dominant American or Western scientific assumptions and paradigms in their efforts to make the discipline of psychology more culturally and contextually sensitive, responsive, inclusive, and appropriate. However, Marsella's proposals are coming from within, and intended for, American or Western psychology itself, whereas Yang's suggestions are for other countries' and cultures' developments of their own decolonized psychologies. Marsella's proposal of de-centering the dominant American or Western psychological methods, concepts, and theories seems to focus on creating a higher level or superordinate type of psychology – his Global-Community Psychology (GCP) – a psychology that is higher than American or Western psychology, and a psychology that encourages equality among all types of psychologies. In other words, Marsella seems to be proposing the re-centering of psychological thoughts and methods, from American or Western psychology to a higher order psychology (GCP). At the same time, Marsella seems to imply that the characteristics of community psychology provide American psychology the best tools for creating a GCP. On the other hand, Yang proposed that other psychologies need to break out of its "American psychology equals superior psychology" mentality in order to critically question and de-center American or Western psychological paradigms and establish their own independent and non-American dominated indigenous psychologies. In other words, instead of creating a higher level or superordinate psychology to de-center American or Western psychology, Yang focused his proposals on a change of "mentality" among those psychologies that regard American or Western psychology as superior. These two proposals, however, are not contradictory of each other. Instead, Marsella's and Yang's proposals are highly complementary and a conceptual connection and combination of these two proposals creates a framework that displays how American and other psychologies need to simultaneously and collaboratively develop in order to accomplish the goal of establishing a truly balanced and decolonized global psychology – one that is not affected by colonial mentality.

Figure 14 begins with brief descriptions of the dominant positivistic paradigm within American or Western psychology. However, as previously discussed, such a paradigm may not be appropriate for the varying psychological experiences of America's diverse population, making psychological research and service provisions performed under such a paradigm as having low levels of indigenous compatibility (IC). Furthermore, such low IC level research and practices have been arguably adapted by cross-cultural westernized psychology (CCWP) in its endeavors outside of America or the West, which likely influenced the development of psychologies in other countries and cultures of the world. Such American or Western influences on the development of other psychologies, in turn, made other psychologies what Yang called monocultural westernized psychologies (MCWP) – or psychological fields that are affected by colonial mentality. As MCWPs developed in other countries and cultures, it is a natural tendency that cross-cultural psychologies that develop from such psychologies are also going to be westernized, or CCWP. Needless to say, MCWP and CCWP research and services in other parts of the world are likely to possess low IC levels, which likely contributes to the previously mentioned dissatisfaction of many American and non-American psychologists about the lack of cultural and contextual appropriateness and sensitivity of research questions, approaches, and interpretations, as well as of psychological services provisions. Furthermore, CCWP from America and the West, as well as from the other countries and cultures of the world, leads to the development of a Western-dominated and colonizing form of global psychology.

At this point, Marsella's (1998) and Yang's (2000) proposals are inserted into the framework (as shown in Figure 14). Within American psychology, Marsella called for a paradigm shift from highly positivistic, exclusive, quantitative, and often non-contextualized research and service practices into a more inclusive, qualitative, and culture- or context-sensitive theories and methods utilized by community psychology. As mentioned in the beginning, community psychology's highly context-based research, service provision, and teaching practices indicate high IC levels, making such practices consistent with Yang's (2000) monocultural indigenous approach (MCIA). Thus, community psychology is considered to be American psychology's version of indigenous psychology, or using Yang's term, monocultural indigenous psychology (MCIP). Therefore, because of the existence and strong presence of community psychology, American psychology already has a well-established MCIP within its realm in community psychology. For instance, community psychology already has multiple avenues for disseminating and sharing its research and ideas (i.e., journals, handbooks, organizations, conferences, etc.), and for training community-oriented psychologists. Community psychology and its methods, along with its broader understanding of what "science" means (Rappaport, 2005), has also made some headway in terms of convincing funding agencies of the scientific merit or rigor of research methods that may be more appropriate for non-White peoples. However, within other indigenous psychologies such as Sikolohiyang Pilipino, such discourses, training opportunities, and funding are fewer or are yet to be established (e.g. Rodriguez, Bravo, & Moreno, 1999; Sanchez, 1999). Thus, the transformation of MCWPs within other countries and cultures, the ones that have developed in such countries and cultures due to the influences of low IC American psychology, into MCIPs through the MCIA requires plenty of work and will likely take years, unlike American psychology which already has a well established MCIP in community psychology. However, once an MCIP has been well established within a particular country or culture, such as community psychology within American psychology, the cross-indigenous method (CIM) may be used to contribute to an indigenously derived body of cross-cultural knowledge. American indigenous psychology (community psychology) may begin comparing, analyzing, or synthesizing its indigenously derived theories and knowledge with the indigenously derived theories and knowledge of other well-established MCIPs. However, as previously mentioned, other countries and cultures do not yet possess as much indigenously derived understanding about their cultures and contexts as America's community psychology does about its cultures and contexts. Instead, what other countries and cultures have are highly westernized or Americanized understanding of psychology. Thus, it is likely that it will also take some time before mass integration, comparison, analyses, or syntheses between multiple independent and indigenously derived psychological systems of knowledge takes place.

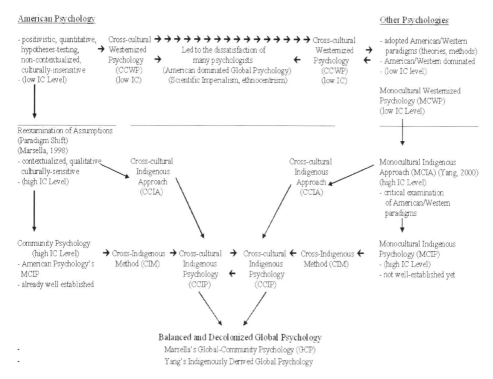

Figure 14. A Framework Toward a Decolonized Global Psychology

In addition to the presented differences between American indigenous psychology and other indigenous psychologies in terms of MCIP developments, it seems like an equal amount of work is necessary for both American and other psychologies to transform their CCWPs, which are low in IC level, into cross-cultural indigenous psychologies (CCIP) through the use of the cross-cultural indigenous approach (CCIA). However, another roadblock that hinders the immediate application of the CCIA to contribute to CCIP is the lack of indigenous researchers from, and indigenous psychological knowledge about, other countries and cultures. The CCIA requires that "each individual study is conceptualized, designed, and carried out to maximize its indigenous compatibility within a particular culture" (Yang, 2000, p. 256), but if a particular culture lacks indigenously knowledgeable researchers or indigenously derived knowledge due to a weak MCIP status, then a CCIA research is more difficult to conduct. In other words, a study cannot maximize its IC level if the researchers in such studies are not aware of what indigenous is in the country or culture of interest. If the indigenous knowledge is not balanced, that is, more indigenous knowledge is known about one country or culture (A) than is known about the other (B), the tendency to impose indigenous knowledge from country or culture A on country or culture B will be too high. Therefore, such an indigenous knowledge imbalance is likely to follow the familiar course of scientific imperialism, ethnocentrism, or colonization of the mind. Thus, it seems as though the proper establishment of a CCIP through the CCIA requires a solid and well-established MCIP within the involved countries or cultures. In other words, it seems necessary that before a particular country or culture attempts to cross other cultures, it needs to first establish a body of knowledge within and about itself.

At this point of the framework, Marsella's (1998) Global-Community Psychology (GCP) seems to be the type of psychology created once Yang's (2000) conceptual framework for non-American psychologies has been developed and once Marsella's call for American psychology to reexamine its assumptions and refrain from imposing on other psychologies is accomplished, simultaneously (as shown in Figure 14). GCP will be the type of psychology developed as a result of the indigenously derived contributions of multiple indigenous psychologies, making GCP consistent with Yang's Indigenously Derived Global Psychology. At the same time, GCP is also a global psychology that encourages the developments of multiple indigenous psychologies while resisting any type of indigenous psychology from becoming dominant or imposing of its values and paradigm. It is believed to be the type of psychology that can best respond to the dissatisfaction of many with the lack of cultural or contextual sensitivity and scientific imperialism tendency of the current global psychology. GCP is also likely to provide the needed time and assistance for non-American indigenous psychologies to develop and establish themselves independently of, and non-deferentially toward, American or Western psychology. In other words, Marsella's GCP is believed to be the type of psychology that provides and protects the opportunity for multiple monocultural indigenous psychologies to properly develop as proposed by Yang. Furthermore, GCP also seems to be the type of global psychology that equally values the different psychological experiences, theories, and methods from all the different cultures of our diverse world, creating a balanced global psychology in the process. Finally, Marsella's GCP also seems to be type of psychology that can most appropriately assist in answering the emerging global challenges, challenges and influences that affect not only a particular society, but challenges and influences that has significance to all countries and cultures.

Chapter Summary

In contrast to other chapters in the book, this chapter focused less on the specifics of Filipino and Filipino American psychology and instead discussed the colonizing and colonized nature of the field of psychology as a whole. This chapter, however, still presented some specific Filipino and Filipino American concepts and ideas (e.g., Sikolohiyang Pilipino and its methods) to serve as examples for how we can decolonize the field of psychology throughout the world. Similar to how many Filipinos and Filipino Americans may have developed colonial mentality due to centuries of Western imposition and domination, the field of psychology in many non-Western cultures and countries around the world, such as the Philippines, have developed colonial mentality as well because of the dominance and imposition of Western and American psychology. Such a colonial mentality is evident in the automatic preference for and utilization of Western or American theories, methods, and concepts on non-Western or non-American peoples and cultures. This led many scholars to recognize that such a psychology is inappropriate for many peoples, which led to the birth and growth of the subfields of indigenous and community psychologies. For instance, Virgilio Enriquez (1994) spearheaded the decolonization of the field of psychology in the Philippines, which led to the creation of Sikolohiyang Pilipino. One take home message from this chapter is that the manner in which Sikolohiyang Pilipino was developed and the goals, methods, and ideals that it advocates may serve as examples for how psychological research among Filipinos and Filipino Americans, as well as among other historically and contemporarily oppressed groups, may become decolonized and decolonizing, liberated and liberating, and more culturally-appropriate, meaningful, and applicable.

This chapter also discussed what the field of psychology as a whole needs to do in order to correct its colonizing tendencies and decolonize psychological fields in other cultures and countries that may have colonial mentality. Marsella's (1998) proposal is for the reconsideration of American or Western psychological paradigms by American or Western psychology itself, whereas Yang's (2000) proposals are for the critical examination of such dominant assumptions and practices by non-American or non-Western psychologies. In Marsella's vision, he suggested that a paradigm shift is needed for American psychology to sufficiently respond to the emerging global challenges presented by our highly inter-connected world: from a non-contextualized, exclusive, specialized, positivistic, and highly quantitative paradigm into a more context-based, multidisciplinary, and qualitative one. In the process, Marsella seems to advocate for the goals and methods of community psychology. Yang, on the other hand, proposed that other psychologies need to de-westernize or de-Americanize their paradigms and utilize methods, theories, and other practices that are more fitting and appropriate for their culture and context. With this suggestion, Yang advocated for the development of multiple independent indigenous psychologies for the creation of a genuinely balanced and decolonized global psychology.

It is believed that a non-separated discussion and analysis of the proposed needed developments within American and non-American psychologies are necessary in order to provide a clearer picture of the needed simultaneous and collaborative developments within multiple psychologies. To this end, a conceptual framework combining and connecting Marsella's (1998) Global-Community Psychology and Yang's (2000) Indigenously Derived Global Psychology has been presented. This conceptual integration of Marsella's and Yang's proposals reveals that these two proposals are highly complementary and one that provides a clearer picture of the needed simultaneous and collaborative developments within and between the dominant American psychology and the dominated non-American psychologies in order to reach the goal of establishing a genuinely balanced and decolonized global psychology. It is argued that the dominant American or Western psychological paradigm needs to cease such dominance and allow other indigenous psychologies to independently develop and establish themselves. Marsella argued that community psychology is the best-equipped American psychological discipline to make and let this happen. Simultaneously, non-American or non-Western psychologies need to cease its uncritical acceptance or superior regard of American or Western psychological thoughts and methods and work toward establishing their own indigenous psychologies. In other words, non-Western and typically dominated psychologies need to address their colonial mentalities and decolonize their psychological field.

*   *   *

We have now journeyed from understanding the life and culture of the indigenous Tao, how historical colonialism and contemporary oppression has damaged such indigenous cultures and contributed to the development of colonial mentality or internalized oppression, how such a condition negatively affects various aspects of Filipino and Filipino American psychology including Kapwa, identity, and mental health, to how colonial mentality among Filipinos and Filipino Americans may be addressed in both the clinical and community contexts, and ended with how the field of psychology as a whole was affected by Western domination and colonial mentality while exploring some ways in which we can decolonize the field of psychology itself. There are plenty of materials to digest, both historically and contemporarily, and there are plenty of needed developments that need to take place, both within individuals and in the larger systems of psychology and society, in order for us to fully understand the psychological realities of and address internalized oppression among Filipinos and Filipino Americans, as well as among other historically and contemporarily oppressed groups. It is hoped, however, that the vast amount of theories and concepts that need to be understood and talked about, as well as the vast amount of individual and systemic changes that need to be sparked and carried out, do not paralyze us from working toward the changes that are clearly needed.

Understanding the concepts covered in this book such as colonialism, contemporary oppression, colonial mentality or internalized oppression, distorted cognitions, Kapwa, enculturation, and collective self-esteem, among many others, and recognizing the needed individual and systemic changes that this book hopefully helps in clarifying for us, as difficult as they may be to undergo and accomplish, are developments and changes that need to take place in order for Filipinos and Filipino Americans, as well as for other groups with similar experiences, to decolonize themselves. Because the concept of colonial mentality or internalized oppression may exist and operate outside of our intention, control, or even awareness (as discussed in Chapter 6), this book may serve to raise individual, community, and global awareness of such an insidious and negative consequence of historical and contemporary oppression. Becoming aware of colonial mentality is the first step toward the decolonization of individuals and systems. For those who are members of dominant or agent groups, understanding such concepts and recognizing the need for individual and systemic changes, are also crucial for their efforts to serve as allies for dominated and oppressed groups, as well as to also facilitate decolonization within themselves – as difficult as they may be to undergo and to accomplish. Together, we can all do our parts toward decolonizing ourselves, the people around us, and the systems and institutions that we are all parts of. Together, we can strive toward achieving social justice and equality for all peoples and cultures around the world.

Epilogue

In the process of reading this book, the reader may have noticed a few things. First, the terms "Filipino" and "Filipino American" appear almost always together, and the title of the book even uses the term "Filipino -/ American," implying that I am referring to both Filipinos in the Philippines and Filipinos in the United States. Second, there are several parts of the book wherein I spent considerable time discussing the experiences of other historically and contemporarily oppressed groups, which may lead some readers to wonder about the reasons why. Third, some readers may be wondering why the title of the book includes the term "postcolonial" when the contents of the book mostly focus on "pre" colonial history and the effects of colonial history. Such possible questions actually provide a nice framework to express my intentions and goals for writing this book. To this end, this section of the book will provide clarifications to such possible questions while expressing my goals in the process, and I will end by sharing my own overall impression of the book as well as my hopes.

Filipino, Filipino American, and Filipino -/ American

Although there are key differences between the experiences and realities of Filipinos in the Philippines and those of Filipinos in the United States, I believe that the main premise of the book – which is to discuss how historical colonialism and contemporary oppression may have affected the psychological experiences and mental health of Filipinos and Filipino Americans – makes these two groups very much intertwined and almost impossible to separate. For instance, the effects of internal colonialism on the psychological experiences of Filipinos in the United States are similar to the effects of colonial and postcolonial oppression on the psychological experiences of Filipinos in the Philippines (as discussed in Chapters 4 and 5). Also, a large percentage of Filipinos in the United States are immigrants from the Philippines (approximately 60%), and large numbers of Filipinos from the Philippines (approximately 60,000) enter the United States every year. Thus, the majority of Filipinos in the United States have experienced the inferiorization of the Filipino culture and ethnicity both in the Philippines and the United States. Furthermore, Filipino Americans who were born in the United States have experienced the oppression of their ethnicity and culture in this country as well. In addition, many Filipinos in the Philippines have a relative or know someone who lives in the United States, and many Filipinos in the United States regularly visit the Philippines as balikbayans. These facts, along with improved technology (internet, telephone, airplanes, etc.) that makes intercultural exposure between the Philippines and United States significantly easier and more common, contribute to a phenomenon called "transnationalism" (Espiritu, 2003) among many Filipinos in the United States, definitely blurring the line between Filipinos in the Philippines and Filipinos in the United States (as mentioned in Chapter 8). Relatedly, Filipinos in the Philippines may actually be considered to be bicultural, and perhaps even transnational, due to their extensive historical and contemporary exposure to American culture, in addition to the increased intercultural exposure brought on by technology. Moreover, many concepts discussed in this book – such as Hiya, Utang na loob, Pakikisama, Pakiramdam, and especially Kapwa – which have their roots in the Philippines, may be highly meaningful, relevant, and applicable to many Filipinos in the United States. The same thing can be said about Sikolohiyang Pilipino. Similarly, many models and concepts in this book which have their roots in the United States such as the Pilipino American Identity Development model, collective self-esteem, and Cognitive-Behavioral Theory may also be meaningful, relevant, and applicable to many Filipinos in the Philippines. Lastly, many Filipinos in the United States today still refer to themselves or consider themselves to be "Filipinos." Thus, if I simply used either the term "Filipino" or "Filipino American" in this book, especially in the title, I would have ignored or excluded the experiences of many individuals for whom the contents of this book may be highly relevant, meaningful, applicable, and empowering. To this end, I hope that the book was able to accomplish one of its main goals, which is to reach as many individuals as possible for which the concepts of colonial mentality may be relevant or meaningful.

The Experiences of Other Historically and Contemporarily Oppressed Groups

Historical colonialism and contemporary oppression are not unique to Filipinos and Filipino Americans. The concept of colonial mentality or internalized oppression is not unique to Filipinos and Filipino Americans. The negative mental and behavioral health effects of colonial mentality are not unique to Filipinos and Filipino Americans. Indeed, as covered throughout this book, such experiences, concepts, and alarming mental and behavioral health concerns are also applicable to many historically and contemporarily oppressed groups within the United States (e.g., American Indians or Native Americans, African Americans, etc.) and around the world (e.g., the Maori of New Zealand; Lawson-Te Aho & Liu, 2010; Sibley, 2010; Smith, 1999). The main rationale for the relatively heavy emphases on these facts throughout the book is to explicitly make connections between the experiences of Filipinos and Filipino Americans to the experiences of other groups. By doing so, I hope that readers will come to appreciate the widespread negative effects of colonialism and contemporary oppression, and thus, realize the enormity of this problem, which may facilitate a desire to make individual and systemic changes happen. Furthermore, by making such connections between the experiences of various racial, ethnic, and cultural groups around the world, perhaps collaborations between these different groups in advocating for changes toward addressing this problem may also be sparked. The attempt of this book to highlight the connections between the Filipino and Filipino American experience and the experiences of other groups may also facilitate the re-birth (if it has been lost) or the growth (if it has been damaged) of Kapwa among many Filipinos and Filipino Americans. As discussed in Chapter 7 and in other places throughout the book, Filipinos and Filipino Americans who may have lost or damaged their sense of Kapwa because of colonial mentality may find it beneficial to remember and foster their connectedness to all other peoples – those with Filipino heritage and those without. Simultaneously, the re-birth or growth or Kapwa may also lead many Filipinos and Filipino Americans to re-connect with their heritage, as well as toward a more positive regard and understanding of the Filipino culture and ethnicity. Lastly, by repeatedly discussing the similarities between the experiences of Filipinos and Filipino Americans and those of other groups, I hope to at least make it clear to and remind Filipino and Filipino American individuals who may be struggling with colonial mentality or internalized oppression, that they are not alone.

Postcolonial

After reviewing the growing literature on the psychological study of colonial mentality, while heavily citing the work that my mentor (S. Okazaki) and I have conducted, Volpato (2010) concluded that "Today, research on colonial mentality represents a promising path for studying the consequences of the asymmetrical relationships imposed by colonial, later neocolonial, policies on the psychological wellbeing of individuals" around the world (pp. 7-8). This statement and compliment, I believe, speaks to the fact that by studying the psychological consequences of historical colonialism and contemporary oppression, we are in essence conducting postcolonial work. This is primarily because postcolonial studies is the systematic analyses of the various effects of Western colonialism throughout the world (Bhatia & Ram, 2001), with the recognition that such experiences of colonialism have typically been characterized by unequal power relationships between the colonizing West and the colonized "other" (Said, 1979; 1983). Having said this, however, postcolonial scholars do not simply regard colonialism as "over" when a colony ceases being a colony. Instead, postcolonialism also refers to the realization that many systems and conditions that are experienced by various groups around the world today are still colonial. In other words, postcolonial thought acknowledges that oppressive systems that mirror those of what is typically established in a colonial society (as discussed in Chapter 5), still exists today in various parts of the world even though such parts may no longer be, or were never, an official colony of some Western or European country. Through the analyses of colonialist or oppressive pasts and presents, highlighting the unequal power distributions between the oppressed (colonized) and the oppressor (colonizer), and consequently illuminating the negative effects of such historical and contemporary forms of oppression, postcolonial studies attempt to drive the global society or global community toward a more peaceful and balanced future – a world where all cultural, racial, ethnic, and other social groups are equally valued and respected. Thus, postcolonialism attempts to liberate the world from its colonized past and present, and decolonize both the present and the future world. To this end, this book is postcolonial because it analyzes the effects of historical colonialism and contemporary oppression among Filipinos and Filipino Americans. The presented histories in the book (Part I) are presented in a way that it may spark awareness that may lead toward decolonization – to liberation. It is postcolonial because it directs our attention to the unheard and painful contemporary realities of Filipinos and Filipino Americans, thus it is advocating for social justice and asking for individual and social change. The book is postcolonial because it combines indigenous psychological methods and concepts with Western methods and concepts to understand, lift, and empower Filipinos and Filipino Americans, especially as it concerns colonial mentality. The book is postcolonial because it attempts to eradicate colonial mentality (as discussed in Part III), which is the internalization of the power imbalances in our world – the internalization of the oppressive world. It is postcolonial because it attempts to facilitate within Filipinos and Filipino Americans a more balanced regard of the Filipino culture and the American culture. In other words, the book attempts to facilitate decolonization among Filipinos and Filipino Americans. I hope that the book is at least able to accomplish some of these postcolonial goals.

Conclusions

In the process of writing this book, and editing it, revising it, and modifying it, both after personal critiques and after receiving the peer reviewers' recommendations, I came to realize that the entire book is almost like a storyboard for my own personal decolonization journey – a journey that is not perfect and a journey that is by no means finished. Similarly, this book is not perfect. This book does not provide a complete picture of Filipino and Filipino American history. This book does not contain everything we need to know about colonial mentality or internalized oppression. This book does not cover all the possible psychological and mental health implications of colonial mentality. This book does not discuss all the possible changes that need to take place in the individual, community, and systemic levels for decolonization to be facilitated. Furthermore, although I may have finished writing this book and the reader may have finished reading it, it does not mean that our work – or our journey – is done. This book is only a very small part of a very large and complex issue. Furthermore, Filipino -/ American psychology and the Filipino -/ American community still have a long ways to go and plenty more directions to take, and plenty more successes and plenty more struggles to experience in our journeys (David, 2010d). Having said these, however, one of the things that I hope this book does is to spark the decolonization journeys of individuals, communities, and systems by raising awareness about the existence and effects of colonial mentality – an insidious consequence of historical and contemporary oppression that may exist and operate within us without our intention, control, or even awareness (as discussed in Chapter 6).

The contents presented in the book are some of the personal, historical, sociopolitical, psychological, and cultural knowledge that I have gained over the last 15 plus years, which helped in my decolonization journey. I hope that by presenting and sharing what I have learned to other people, that such contents may also have a similar effect on them, and that they may also begin their decolonization journeys. The contents of this book are products of my desire to answer questions about myself, my family, my friends, and everyone else who are close to me. Thus, the contents of this book – much of what I have learned – are products of my MEsearch. In the process of doing my MEsearch, however, I learned that the questions I had about myself, my family, my friends, and everyone else who are close to me are the same questions that many other Filipinos and Filipino Americans have asked, are currently asking, or may ask in the future. Thus, I hope this book may serve as a catalyst, a source, or even a supplement for others as they conduct their own MEsearches. Hopefully, as we all conduct our own individual and collective MEsearches – our journeys – we realize that the effects of historical and contemporary oppression have been negatively affecting us and our loved ones for many generations. I hope that this book may serve as a tool for remembering the past and as a tool for awakening to address the present. Hopefully, through such remembrance and awakening, we all develop a desire to stop colonial mentality or internalized oppression with us, and not pass it on to future generations.

Makibaka at Mabuhay Tayong Lahat!

E.J.R. David

ᜐᜒᜆᜓᜏᜒᜆᜎᜒ ᜇᜓᜅᜒᜇ

꠸꠸꠲ ꠛꠣ3

AFTERWORD

By

Kevin L. Nadal, Ph.D.

THE REVALUING OF INDIGENOUSNESS IN A POSTCOLONIAL WORLD

As a young Filipino American boy who grew up in the United States, I distinctly remember learning that colonialism was a good thing. As early as first or second grade, my classmates and I were taught in our American History classes that the United States was built on colonialism. We learned how the English settlers had heard of this "New Land" where they could settle and build a better life. We were taught they eventually met the American Indians (that was the term that was still used in the 1980s), and that these "Pilgrims" and "Indians" peacefully celebrated Thanksgiving together. Allegedly, these Pilgrims acquired the Native Americans' ways of farming and hunting, while the Natives were taught European ways and how to become "civilized." And thus, the United States was born.

In our World History classes, we learned similar messages about colonialism. We were forced to memorize that in 1492, Columbus sailed the Ocean Blue. In an attempt to prove that the world was not flat, he was allegedly commissioned by Queen Isabella of Spain to travel to the Far East, where he could bring back foreign goods and products. He accidentally landed in the Caribbean on October 12, 1492. There, he happened upon brown-skinned people, who he called Indians because he believed he was in Asian India. Following

Columbus' explorations, Spain ended up colonizing most of South America and even went off to "discover" the Philippines. Other countries followed suit and began their journeys to conquer "new" land. Eventually there were French, British, Dutch, and Portuguese empires in Asia and Africa, as well as in North, South, and Central America. Again, our history books and teachers taught us that colonialism was necessary and that the natives in all of these lands were better off in being colonized by these groups. In retrospect, I don't know how an educator could even teach that conquering and enslaving other people, for any reason, was a positive thing.

It wasn't until college that I learned that most of these "facts" were untrue. The book *Lies My Teacher Told Me* was one of the first texts I read that encouraged me to think critically about everything I learned. Despite this, I recognize that my journey of questioning and searching for truth began at an even earlier age. When I was in fifth grade, I vehemently remember a classroom debate, where I was asked to take the position that American colonization was a positive thing. I was dumbfounded because I didn't believe in this opinion at all and was only prepared to take the anti-colonialism stand. I couldn't comprehend how killing Native Americans and stealing their land was acceptable. But in two minutes, I had to come up with something. The competitive nature in me found myself saying things I didn't believe in just so that I could win the debate. And I did. Ironically, I would later learn this value of competition was actually an American colonial value in itself.

When I was in the eighth grade, I remember being encouraged by a teacher to apply for a scholarship from our local Knights of Columbus chapter. We had to write an essay about the wonderful contributions of Christopher Columbus. I wrote about how without him (and the colonizers that followed his lead), my life would definitely not be the same. Because I was the child of Filipino immigrant parents who searched for a better life in the US, my life was significantly impacted by colonialism. If the Philippines was not colonized by Spain, my family wouldn't be Catholic. If the Philippines was not colonized by the US, my family wouldn't speak English and my parents likely would not have immigrated. Despite these seemingly pro-Columbus sentiments, the bulk of my essay revolved around the fact that despite Columbus's contributions, the massacre of American Indians, either through war, brutality, or disease was atrocious. Needless to say, I didn't get the scholarship.

As I reflect upon these experiences, I am comforted in knowing that my passion for social justice and activism were rampant since my earlier years. But I must also remember that there were also struggles and conflicts that I experienced as well. It was clearly communicated (explicitly and implicitly) that the US was the land of opportunity, while the Philippines was a third world, inferior country. It was taught that Filipinos who had a Spanish last name or Spanish physical features (e.g., narrow nose, lighter skin) were preferred more than those with Filipino features (e.g., flat nose, dark brown skin). I distinctly remember an older cousin teaching my brothers and me to pinch our noses every night before we went to sleep, so that we could gain a bridge to counter our "flat" noses. I heard a lot of my friends identifying as "mixed" or "Hawaiian" because it was perceived as being "cooler" than being Filipino. But at the same time, it was also "cooler" to be American-born and speak with a perfect English accent than to be a FOB, or someone who was "Fresh-Off-the-Boat." I could name a million other messages that conveyed that being Filipino was bad and that being White or Spanish or American was better. Slowly but surely, these messages had impacts on my self-esteem, making an awkward adolescence an even more complex one.

I share these personal stories because they help me to understand why *Filipino /- American Postcolonial Psychology: Oppression, Colonial Mentality, and Decolonization* by Dr. E.J. Ramos David is an essential and innovative contribution to the literature. The concept and phenomena of colonial mentality isn't new, as Dr. David has been researching and writing about the topic for years. But to have a comprehensive text concentrating on the impact of colonial mentality on Filipinos and Filipino Americans is invaluable. Dr. David demonstrates a wealth of knowledge on the topic by examining the historical context of colonialism, as well as its manifestation in contemporary times. Throughout the text, he is able to apply salient examples of how colonial mentality may present in Filipino Americans' lives, and how it may pervasively impact psychological processes, identity, and even mental health. Most importantly, he allows the reader to think critically about the concept, in order to advocate for change on individual, group, and systemic levels.

Dr. David should really be commended for being one of the most prominent and leading researchers in ethnic minority mental health and the primary psychological scholar on colonial mentality. He especially should be applauded because of the lack of visibility, recognition, or support for Filipino American issues in the field of psychology. This lack of research focusing on our community is particularly daunting because Filipino Americans are projected to become the largest Asian American population and have been the second largest immigrant group in the US since 2000. This dearth of literature may also be due to the lack of Filipino American professors in the US. Preliminary results of a national survey that I am conducting with Dr. Dina Maramba indicate that there are less than 100 tenured or tenure-track Filipino American professors in social sciences, education, and humanities. The number of Fil-Am professors of psychology is even less—with no more than 10 known tenured or tenure-track Filipino American psychology professors in the country. Perhaps more Filipino Americans need to enter graduate school, in order for this to change. But maybe this lack of mentors, the lack of encouragement by teachers, and the colonial value that medicine is the only career path for Filipinos may all contribute to the continuation of this disparity.

But I do believe there is hope. When I first met E.J. many years ago, I instantly felt a sense of camaraderie with him. As grad students, we were both committed to giving voice to our Filipino American community and we instantly became interested and supportive of each others' works. Since then, I have admired him for a number of reasons and I have been pleased at the direction our professional relationship and friendship has taken. I genuinely believe that since we first met, we operated on the indigenous Filipino value of *kapwa* (fellow being)—we instantly connected and encouraged each other simply because we were *kababayan* (fellow countrymen) with similar passions. I have been able to notice that we operate by other values as well- including *utang ng loob* (reciprocity/generosity) and *pakisama* (togetherness/unity), which can be demonstrated by our research collaborations; our work on initiating a division of Filipino American Psychology throughout the Asian American Psychological Association; our work on creating the Filipino American Psychology student scholarship; and our many conversations and emails regarding a number of issues affecting two pinoy tenure-track professors of psychology.

I see these values operate in many of my professional relationships and friendships with a lot of other Filipino Americans professors across the United States. Perhaps there is an understanding of what each other encounters- institutional racism, lack of social support, faculty expectations and pressures, and even marginalization within the Asian American community. Perhaps we can relate to each other because we know what it's like to balance our Filipino American families, mentor young Filipino American minds, while struggling to find our identities as professors, as Filipino Americans, and as a multitude of other identities we may hold. But perhaps one of the main reasons for our unity is because we have all recognized that utilizing our indigenous Filipino values of collectivism and *bayanihan* (sense of community) are much more valuable, important, and effective than the American, colonial values of individualism and competition.

Sometimes I think we need to go back to the "Old School" way of doing things. I often reflect about how "new and improved" methods just make things more complicated and aren't as good as they may seem. For example, while technology has allowed us to be effective and expedient with our communication, perhaps there are some things that would have been better unchanged. As an American society, the increase of technology may lead to the devaluing of face-to-face conversation, warm embraces, and the actual need to speak to someone instead of sending text messages. We have learned to minimize the importance of outdoor "play" time and/or quality time with our family and friends, and instead we have become obsessed with our ipods, laptops, and DVRs. Given this, technology does have its perks but what at what cost?

In the same way, colonialism may also have its usefulness. Spanish rule resulted in Catholicism (which in many ways has been a source of hope and resilience for Filipino people), while American education systems may resulted in increased career opportunities and easier communication with the Western world. But why forget that there are several indigenous values and practices that are just as good, and in some ways even better? Perhaps if the Filipino American community recognized the value of indigenous culture, we could be more united, instead of divided. We would not be obsessed with what we think we're supposed to be or how we're supposed to look or speak, but rather we would be able to celebrate what we actually are. We would no longer uphold this competitive crab mentality of pulling each other down and instead could operate in the collectivistic, peaceful ways of our indigenous *barangays* (towns or villages). Finally, we would no longer create colonial hierarchies based on skin color, immigration status, language abilities, social class, education, and gender, but instead we would accept all Filipinos as equal members of our community and practice the spirit of *bayanihan*. I genuinely believe that if we revalued our indigenousness, even in our postcolonial world, we as Filipinos and

Filipino Americans could thrive and be more visible in the American and global society.

Kevin L. Nadal, Ph.D.
John Jay College of Criminal Justice
City University of New York

COMMENTARY

CONFRONTING A VICTIMIZING PAST

BY NILDA RIMONTE

E. J. R. David's book – *Brown Skin, White Minds* – is a first in Philippine literature, clinical or otherwise. It is first to study colonial mentality systematically, and first to openly relate this disease to the experience of colonialism—which should have been obvious from the start had previous researchers and culture critics accorded it the significance it deserved. Theorizing it as a "form of internalized oppression," he describes it as a double movement characterized by a reflexive rejection of the Filipino self and culture on one hand, while simultaneously idealizing the west on the other. Its most common form is victim-blaming that includes hypercriticism and self-bashing. What feminist nationalist Delia Aquilar (1998) likes to call "the Filipino penchant for self-denigration" finally has a historical origin that can be diced and sliced. No longer can it be ascribed simplistically and incorrectly by the self-loathing to *"Pilipino kasi!"* --implying a curse of mis-shapen genes, or dismissed as a dismaying character flaw. This penchant for self-bashing is rooted in a history of race-based systematic inferiorizing strategies, as E.J.'s book confirms, and its residual effects continue to resonate to this day.

Over a century ago, José Rizal identified this condition as feelings of shame about "their own … and …a disgust of themselves." Subtending this shame was the "paralysis" that he correctly identified as a hopelessness rooted in powerlessness, masquerading as the infamous Filipino "indolence"—a "constantly plucked soul unable to fly to the region of light."

Colonial mentality—or "CM" as E.J. conveniently refers to it – describes the nervous co-existence of two antagonistic selves in one body: one convinced of its inferiority, the other of the colonizer's superiority - a relationship that is by no means cut-and- dried. In so doing, he confirms psychologist Gordon Allport's (1958) study on oppression who wrote: "What would happen if you heard it said over and over again that you were lazy, a simple child of nature…had inferior blood ….[your] natural self-love may, under the persistent blows of contempt, turn your spirit to cringing and self-hate."

By acknowledging CM as the result of centuries of oppression, a conclusion long arrived at in studies of other cultural groups and oppressed populations, E.J. declares colonialism as a victimizing experience, something that few contemporary Filipino historians and culture critics have done.

Instead of an oppressive system, colonialism has been consistently represented as a civilizing project by historians whose works show up in the nation's educational curricula. Never mind that this project duplicitously relied on religion as a primary conquest tool; and never mind that this religion has left catastrophic legacies of intellectual backwardness and magical/miraculous thinking, a scanting of instrumental rationality, fostering habits of dependency after 350 years of life "in the convent."

I have often wondered about this reticence.

Leaving aside this religion's limitations, a critique of colonialism as an oppressive system does not equate with a critique of religion. As Rizal and his generation had demonstrated, a critique of colonial Christendom was possible without threatening the critics' faith in religion's basic tenets. By his own account, Rizal kept to his

Christian ideals, his own life exemplary of it, earning for him designation as the "Tagalog Christ" by admirers.

Growing up in Filipinas, not once did I ever encounter a definition of colonialism even as I read accounts of its coercive cultural transformations in history books. Not once did I find a definition of colonial mentality, let alone an attempt to relate it to colonialism's oppressions. The closest to it I ever found was Sen. Recto's "colonial complex," which he defined as the obsequiousness of Filipino leaders unable to separate Filipino from American interests, misbegotten by the "benevolent American's" assimilationist policies. Even today, one is hard pressed to find the word "victims" mentioned in the same line as "colonialism," or "colonialism" with "oppression" in the context of Filipino history. All that historians, culture critics and even politicians ever talked about was nationalism—the lack of it, the imperative for it. I understand nationalism as an approving view of the self—for how else can one fight for or defend one's national interests without it? Addressing colonialism's legacies of shame and self-disgust would have led to a critical understanding of colonialism as an injurious system involving unjust treatment, racism, exploitation, and extortion. Thus, might Christianized Filipinos have been empowered to confront the alien they have internalized, and to question the Spanish version of their reality?

Naturally, I refer only to my readings; others may be more fortunate, or more widely read. But like many, I came away from reading Filipino history confused about the past, suspicious of its silences, and puzzled by the present. The Filipino past, especially its Spanish aspect, has since become of enormous interest to me. As a result of this huge lacuna in their apprehension of the past, others whose accounts I read in E.J.s' book, have confessed to being perennially haunted by "some little hurt, some sense of incompleteness" --to borrow from V.S. Naipaul.

I mention colonial victimizations and I get one of three reactions: First, suppression: All that's in the past and the best way to manage the past is to keep it there. Tapós na yon, Kalimútan mo na. (That's over; all in the past; best to forget). This was exactly the priest Jesus Cavanna's reason for leading the resistance against the Recto bill in the late 50s intended to inject Rizal's critique of colonial Christendom into the nation's educational system (Constantino 1969).

Or, I hear accusing noises about "pathologizing" Filipinos. But what is CM if not a pathology? The symptoms E.J. describes, culled from his research respondents, are anything but indicators of wellness.

Then there is this wariness about "victimism." Does it make sense for Christianized Filipinos to see themselves as victims? Is there profit, if not virtue, in assuming a victim identity on top of the inferiorized identity already slapped onto them by colonialism? Is it not merely another form of reductionism to define Christianized Filipinos as victims? It may be more productive, more healing, to emphasize survival rather than victimization.

Victim-versus-survivor arguments of this nature periodically erupted in the anti-rape and anti-domestic violence movements during the time of my active involvement in Los Angeles between the late 70s and early 90s. Post-modernist insistence on survivorship was a necessary political attempt to disrupt the victim identity of women still rampant in mainstream thinking. The "survivor" label was meant to highlight women's strengths and successes and shore up their emergent sense of self. Though I recognized the necessity for such a corrective, the non-profit agency I established in Los Angeles was one of a handful that insisted, as long as I was there, on naming victimized women as victims. I saw it as an act of resistance against the patriarchalist cultures of the Pacific-Asian communities where the subordination of women was widely if tacitly accepted and violence against them legitimized as natural and normal. More, the normalization of violence was justified as consistent with the cultural requirement for familial harmony, invariably read as the submergence of the individual to the group, particularly when the individual is female. I quickly saw that my challenge was to make violence against women in this community visible by demystifying victimization; this meant de-naturalizing and de-normalizing violence as instrument of male hegemony; this meant naming violence as violence; this meant acknowledging themselves first as victims. Feminists of that time were already engaged at this task, having discovered the system of dominance at the heart of gender relations. In all my challenge, as I saw it, was to help victims see "what it meant to be a victim, how they were victimized, and that they had a choice not to be a victim any longer," as I wrote elsewhere.

A similar curtain of obfuscation and obscurantism has long descended on Filipino historical experience. Colonial conquest, particularly the Spanish kind, has been represented as the natural and inevitable fate of "low-level" cultures; we should be thankful for the improving interventions of the west.

E.J. writes that the image that has come to represent CM is that of the coconut, white heart enclosed in a brown shell. I prefer the monstrous aliens of the eponymous 1986 sci-fi film as more truly reflective of colonialism's realities. An alien monster worms its way into a human being, parasitically devouring its substance while leaving the human shape and shell intact.

Confronting the introjected alien entails the difficult work of "becoming critically aware of one's reality," Freire (1970) writes. Unfortunately, colonialism's victims often do not know that they are victims, though they behave most like victims when they are least aware, as Fanon (1965) has pointed out. Violence and oppression having been structuralized, it now lurks in every seam and vein of daily reality no longer recognizable for what it truly is. It is a measure of their oppression that they do not know, and in many ways refuse to know. E.J.'s book will significantly help colonialism's victims with this long delayed task of confronting the alien inside.

About Nilda Rimonte:

A Filipina born and raised, Nilda Rimonte was educated at the University of the Philippines. She is the founder and first executive director of the Los Angeles-based Center for the Pacific-Asian Family, a non-profit agency that operated the first, and for a long time the only, 24 -hour hotline and emergency shelter for non – English speaking Pacific-Asian victims and their families victimized by sexual assault and domestic violence. It also operated a child abuse program and "Women Entrepreneurs," a special program for former battered women. She is currently completing a book on Spanish colonialism.

COMMENTARY

DECOLONIZING THE FUTURE

BY ANDREW PHILIP PAVES

Ten. Growing up in the State of Washington in the 80s and 90s, the number 10 would probably make me think of things that most other kids my age would. Maybe the jersey number of original Seattle Seahawks quarterback Jim Zorn, or the point guard and captain of the now-departed-but-soon-to-return Seattle Supersonics who was so loved they called him "Mr. Sonic" Nate McMillan, or perhaps the iconic grunge-era album by arguably the most legendary band to come out of Seattle Pearl Jam. Ten was probably also the number of hours per day that I spent playing the Nintendo Entertainment System…and Gameboy…and Sega Genesis…and Sony Playstation. Ok, that last one might be an exaggeration. The point of my story so far is that it might seem like I was just another American kid raised by American pop culture…and throughout my childhood that was the only story I knew.

However, as I've embarked on my professional career, aka become a grown-up, the number 10 has taken new significance because the American pop culture junkie I just described happens to be a second generation Filipino American (Fil-Am) who is currently a doctoral student in clinical psychology. Ten just happens to be the estimated number of Filipino American professors in psychology across the entire U.S. (as reported by our colleague Dr. Kevin Nadal). Seeing that figure confirmed suspicions that had grown after many hours of reading, conferences, and clinical trainings: that I had entered into a field where Filipinos and Fil-Ams like me are sorely underrepresented on all sides – whether it be among the researchers, the treatment providers, the research literature, and the consumers. This alone might be enough to speak as to why I feel that Dr. E. J. R. David's *Brown Skin, White Minds: Filipino -/ American Postcolonial Psychology* is a landmark work and essential toward advancing our field. But its contributions go far beyond that.

It wasn't quite a direct path that connected me to Dr. David and his work. As an undergrad, I chose to study psychology despite having neither prior exposure nor the experiences of family and friends to draw upon. The field intrigued me because it provided a lens to make sense of my own experiences and what I had observed in others. But as much as I liked what I was learning, I hadn't quite found an area that I was passionate about. College was also the time when I actively sought to understand my Filipino heritage. Although there are over 90,000 Filipinos residing in Washington State, I did not have a single Filipino classmate until my family moved to the Seattle area when I was a teenager. I was born in Chehalis, located about halfway between Seattle and Portland, where there were maybe 3 or 4 other Filipino families at the time. We all know that teenagers aren't exactly nice to one another, but during the transition from a U.S. small town upbringing to a metropolitan area, I didn't quite act how I was "supposed" to – not white enough to be white, not brown enough to be Filipino. If college is the time where we find out who we are, I was determined to figure out: Why do we act the way we do? What does being Filipino even mean? What makes me Filipino? These questions would intertwine by the time I made it to graduate school.

While college catalyzed the search for my ethnic identity, graduate school has been an ongoing search for my academic identity. My research projects had focused on addictive behaviors, and I noticed a burgeoning line of research in alcohol and substance use amongst Asian Americans. While I was encouraged to see newer research that did not lump all Asian groups into a single category (an issue which is discussed many times throughout this book), the experience of Filipinos was relatively absent. So I had the idea: what if I could focus my dissertation and maybe future work on Filipinos? But I'd be lying if I didn't admit that there was a little hesitation; many of the theories and principles I had learned in psychology sought to explain some "universal truths" about human behavior. There is certainly a sentiment that having an ethnic-specific focus is unnecessary, inapplicable to other groups, and/or is not tenable to obtaining long-term funding and publications. I knew I had finally found an issue I was passionate about, yet I wasn't sure if it was a viable option.

Fortunately, a little digging in to the literature led me to other Filipino psychologists who had blazed the trail for future scholars to follow. Among these trailblazers was Dr. David and his research on colonial mentality (CM) and mental health. I was immediately intrigued. Here was a theory that incorporated social, historical, and political contexts, was derived from work with other ethnic groups, had implications for mental health, empirical data to support it, and made perfect sense when I looked back at my own experiences and observations. In other words, it resonated with me on both an academic and personal level. I was excited to learn more about what Filipino American psychology had to offer, and hopeful that my own work could contribute to this area. It wasn't long after that I contacted Dr. David, who has been a great mentor, colleague, friend, and supporter ever since.

Brown Skin, White Minds provides the grand stage for Dr. David's work to reach the masses, one that is well-deserved and has the potential to have a positive impact on people's lives...both directly and indirectly. For my own personal development, it has been a catalyst for reclamation, a means to help answer questions that so many young Fil-Ams have struggled with. What does it mean to be Filipino? Identifying with hip-hop music? Being Catholic? Speaking the language? I've always felt some of the answers I sought would require looking further into the past. What was it like for inhabitants of the Philippines prior to Magellan's arrival? What values and customs have been passed down and what's been lost in history? Dr. David has compiled historical events, from pre-colonial to contemporary times, and empirical studies that link past mistreatments to self-defeating attitudes of the present-day. In doing so, he challenges readers to reflect upon our own experiences and be honest with ourselves. Why didn't I idolize any Filipinos before Manny Pacquiao? Why had I heard other Filipinos tell me that the Filipino people are incapable of governing themselves? Why did I succumb to the hair-bleaching trend in the late 90s? Why did I feel like I – a Fil-Am – should receive special treatment whenever I visited the Philippines? As I came to realize, CM manifests itself in many forms. It has been present in some form or another for generations, and anyone is capable of perpetuating it. Then, the clinician in me wondered: What do we do about it? Are we expected to somehow turn back the clock on centuries of colonial history and discrimination in different parts of the world? Although a plutonium-powered DeLorean would be nice, Dr. David has also developed a thoughtful intervention that utilizes education and cognitive behavioral therapy. The initial data has been promising and should it reach that point, it can readily be disseminated to clinicians and/or adapted for communities with similar histories.

Speaking as a young psychologist, *Brown Skin, White Minds* has been fulfilling on a personal, academic, and clinical level. It addresses a glaring informational void and serves a valuable resource for scholars, practitioners, and community members alike. It is especially needed as our collective identities become more complex: a continued influx of immigrants, individuals who represent another generation removed since their family's arrival, evolving cultures in different parts of the world, or an increased number of mixed-race individuals, just to name a few. For whatever reason, our field for the most part has relied solely on an acculturation paradigm to understand the experiences of most communities of color. It is clear that that alone will be inadequate and advancements such as CM are needed to address our evolving needs. No matter what the background of readers, *Brown Skin, White Minds* can accomplish this through the following:

1.   **Reflection and acknowledgement** – It has the potential raise awareness within the Filipino/Filipino American community and educate others about the history and current conditions of Filipinos. While psychology theory and treatment has been developed by and for a European audience, another challenge has been a lack of education. Whether it is cultural mistrust, "crab mentality," or other reasons, treatment seeking is very low among Filipinos and few resources exist for treatment providers. I have personally seen similar attitudes on a broader scale, where people have said focusing on aspects of the community such as colonial mentality highlights negatives and we should only focus on the positive. But as one of my longtime mentors once told me, "if we don't acknowledge the problem, how will we address the issue?" Dr. David's message is loud and clear: it's time we: 1. be honest with ourselves and; 2. let others know.

2.   **Healing** – Dr. David has taken a courageous stand against what has been the status quo for centuries. *Brown Skin, White Minds* represents the catalyst of a healing process. Among psychologists, it passes on knowledge to the proverbial healers - the researchers and practitioners. A better understanding of the collective experience of Filipinos and colonial mentality within the field will lead to development and testing of services that meet this particular need, whether it is the intervention developed by Dr. David or others. These in turn can be applied to other forms of internalized oppression in other communities. Within the community, it can stimulate education and dialogue that can help prevent colonial mentality from being passed to future generations and move past this state of mind that has been a barrier for centuries. Last but not least,

Brown Skin White Minds can be a catalyst for decolonization within readers themselves.

3.   **Inspiration** – Finally, *Brown Skin White Minds* is an inspiration. If I think like a researcher for a moment, we've barely scratched the surface in the work that can be done on colonial mentality! How does it contribute to other health outcomes? What might influence the degree to which one holds colonial mentality? How do social interactions contribute to colonial mentality? To answer these and other questions that readers no doubt will have, Dr. David's comprehensive analyses will serve as a starting point and guide. From the ground up, perhaps it will help readers resolve issues of ethnic identity as it did for me, encourage community involvement, or perhaps even pursue a career in the field. No doubt, it will inspire action in some form or another.

Brown Skin, White Minds represents the culmination of Dr. David's hard work, and is a triumph for Filipino American, Asian American, and multicultural psychology as a whole. I am very excited and happy that colonial mentality has reached a wider audience. The best part is we are only at the beginning! The groundwork has been laid for future generations in psychology or other fields. There are opportunities and support networks for young academics like me that didn't exist but a few years ago, and for that I will forever be grateful. It's amazing how much Dr. David has been able to relate to all of our experiences. We grew up in completely different places, only drawn together by our field of study and common ancestry. Yet as I've been finding out as I get older, it doesn't matter where we were born, whom we grew up around, our hobbies and interest, our taste in music or pop culture…we all have much more in common than we realize. Decolonizing our minds will allow us to reach limits that we didn't know were possible.

About Andrew Philip Paves:

Andrew (Andy) Paves is a doctoral student in Adult Clinical Psychology at the University of Washington, and a predoctoral research assistant at the Center for the Study of Health and Risk Behaviors, His research focuses on social and cultural factors in mental and behavioral health, and integrating community-based research with evidence-based practices. He is currently completing his dissertation study examining ethnic identity, race-related stressors, coping responses, and alcohol use among Filipino Americans. He is also a clinical trainee specializing in alcohol and substance use, depression, and acculturative stress, particularly among Asian Americans. Outside of academia, Andy is a professional mixed martial arts fighter and has competed on regional events in the Pacific Northwest. He chose his ring name, "Bunso" as a nod to his heritage and a dedication to his mother. He is a native of Washington state, where his parents established their medical practices after immigrating from the Philippines. He resides in Seattle with his girlfriend, Michel, and their dog, Shinobi.

COMMENTARY

FILIPINO AMERICAN POSTCOLONIAL PSYCHOLOGY: ITS PROMISE AND POWER

BY LENY MENDOZA STROBEL

In the hands of E. J. R. David, Sikolohiyang Pilipino (SP)/Filipino Indigenous Psychology is making a mark in the field of Indigenous Psychology and Cross-Cultural Psychology, following in the footsteps of SP's founder, Virgilio Enriquez, whose important and pioneering work was cut short by his early demise in 1994. Enriquez's works bequeathed scholars with foundational theoretical framework for understanding Filipino core cultural values. As a decolonization framework, this has been the ground of my own interdisciplinary research and publications.

In *Brown Skin, White Minds*, Dr. David satisfies those who prefer quantitative measures (e.g. Colonial Mentality Scale; Colonial Mentality Implicit Association Test); these are supplemented with personal narratives of research participants – a combination that works really well in reaching a wider audience that includes not only psychologists but also social workers, mental health workers, cultural workers, public health workers, and others.

The body of knowledge on the study of colonial mentality among Filipino Americans published in the last few decades has been growing but we are yet to see its widespread accessibility by Filipino American communities and Filipinos in the diaspora. Where this knowledge has been accessible, among Filipino American college students in the Bay Area, for example, there is a visible decolonization movement. But it can also be said that it is not yet a critical mass. If decolonization discourse is accessible it will go a long way towards helping our communities think critically about the conscious and unconscious ways that imperial narratives continue to influence our lives. *Brown Skin, White Minds* is an accessible text in this regard because the author understands the need to communicate beyond the discipline of psychology even while grounding the discourse within its parameters. This book is readable and palatable, for academics and the general public, which paves the way for mass decolonization to take place.

The challenge to decolonize the dominant paradigms in the discipline of psychology, as *Brown Skin, White Minds* does, is timely and couldn't be more relevant. At this time of writing, I am reading Fareed Zakaria's The Post American World and Bill McKibben's Eaarth. Together, these two books point to the painful reality that humans have changed the planet in such radical and violent ways that what we are facing now requires an equally radical departure from our old ways of thinking in all areas: our theories of identity, nation, globalization, economics, politics, ecological limits, and many others.

In this regard, the work of decolonization, for both the colonized and the colonizer, requires the decolonization of the centers of power and master narratives. Therefore, a decolonized psychology must identify the process and framework of decolonization for the colonized while simultaneously identifying the processes and framework of decolonization for the colonizer's descendants. A Global-Community Psychology (GCP) will not be possible without such framework. This framework necessitates the focus on doing shadow work as the impact of dominant racial narratives on the descendants of colonial settlers has been rendered mute and invisible as a necessary strategy for crafting an imperial nation who deems itself as the exception. The concept of "white love" is insidious and toxic in the ways that it contributes to the pathology of whiteness and white privilege. Dr. David's book not only identifies the process and framework of decolonization among the colonized, but also addresses how the colonizing tendencies of western psychology may itself be addressed.

Also, there is a need for Filipino American postcolonial psychology (the original title of *Brown Skin, White Minds*) to be in conversation with the Sikolohiyang Pilipino (SP) in the Philippines. There has been a gap or a break in this dialogue with the demise of Enriquez in 1994. The SP that survived in the Philippines in the aftermath of his death, has focused on its "indigenization from within" discourse – as it should be. But perhaps it is time again to create the bridge between Filipino American postcolonial psychology and SP in the Philippines, and *Brown Skin, White Minds* does this by arguing that SP concepts can and should be incorporated into our understanding of Filipino American psychology, and vice versa.

In this regard, Dr. David's book should be read by SP scholars in the Philippines. One SP scholar in the Philippines in particular, Katrin de Guia, author of *Kapwa: The Self in the Other*, has already expanded SP discourse by calling attention to the relevance of Indigenous Knowledge Systems and Practices (IKSP). Through the Kapwa conferences she has been organizing since 2004 through the Heritage Arts and Academies of the Philippines: Kapwa 1 (2004), 2 (2008), and 3 (2012) and a Schools of Living Traditions consultation (2011), De Guia has been calling attention for the need to integrate IKSP into SP and other academic disciplines and institutions in the Philippines. There is an opportunity here for Filipino American Postcolonial Psychology and IKSP to dialogue on the link between decolonization and indigenization in the homeland and in the diaspora. If decolonization discourse is a counter-narrative to dominant imperial/colonial/modern narratives, then indigenization is the narrative that offers a more relevant alternative paradigm.

Brown Skin, White Minds has focused on the effects of oppression/colonialism and ways in which decolonization may be facilitated. There were also instances in the book wherein indigenization (such as in chapter 7) was advocated for. Dr. David has successfully conveyed ways for clinicians, academicians, researchers, and members of the general public to identify and address the insidious consequences of colonialism and oppression. Thus, *Brown Skin, White Minds* is sure to make an impact in both the scholarly and general community, if it hasn't already.

About Leny Mendoza Strobel:
Leny Mendoza Strobel, Ed.D., is currently a Professor and the Chair of American Multicultural Studies at Sonoma State University in California. She has authored or edited several books, including: *Coming Full Circle: The Process of Decolonization Among Post-1956 Filipino Americans* (2001, Giraffe Books); *A Book of Her Own: Words and Images to Honor the Babaylan* (2005, Tiboli Press); and *Babaylan: Filipinos and the Call of the Indigenous* (2010, Ateneo de Davao University Research and Publication Office). She is also the Director of the Center for Babaylan Studies (www.babaylan.net).

COMMENTARY

AS INDIGENOUS CHILDREN

BY "AQPAYUQ" JAMES W. LA BELLE, SR.

When western contact occurred in Alaska some 200 years ago, indigenous life and worldviews began shifting and eroding away to a decidedly European culture. In polite Alaska Native circles we call them "non-Native." Cultures rooted to land and water and possessing a relationship to animals and nature - the western insertion was fraught with upheaval and trauma. In that span of time the Alaska Native population fell 75%; decimated by genocide, disease, and forced labor inflicted by those who came to our shores. The new comers were looking for resources to exploit for economic gain, indigenous life ways be damned. A consolation prize was to impose Christianity and a Western education upon the survivors. The colonization process was deep and wide and, for a while, we thought it only happened up here. In *Brown Skin, White Minds*, it is clear that it also happened to our Filipino brothers and sisters.

As an Inupiaq, I want to share some personal experiences of being caught up in the colonization process in the Northern latitudes. While our stories may be different from those of our Filipino brothers and sisters, there is an overarching theme that my brother, Willie Hensley, has said time and again: It is a story of the powerful over the powerless. Now, however, we can collect our breath, tell our stories, and decolonize to our heart's content. In Alaska, Native educators and leaders are helping to reclaim our history, languages, and cultures. It is still a struggle in process, but moving forward nonetheless. In *Brown Skin, White Minds*, we see a pattern emerging.

Half-Breed

I was born into a bi-racial family in Fairbanks, Alaska in 1947. Fairbanks was a less tolerant community towards any Natives living in the fringes back in the 1950s and 1960s. My father was of French and Irish descent and came from Wisconsin. He died when I was seven years old. It was then that I lost a father figure and would never know how he would have dealt with my mixed-blood as I got older.

In the beginning, I did not know anything about race, let alone my own circumstance. As I got older, I started to feel the brunt of my mixed heritage. Full blood Natives would taunt me with the phrase, "half-breed." They said that half-breeds were weak. I got into many scraps over those words. I got into a lot of fights to prove them wrong. If they were bigger than me I showed them how fast I could run. It took many years to understand that, as a child, it was safe for some of the Natives to feel they could act out some measure of hostility not afforded them towards white people.

The Whites really did not see me as a mixed-blood Native; I got no favors for being a half-breed. I was still looked down on, followed around in department stores and often yelled at for no apparent reason. Not understanding the forces of colonization and interracial relationships, I lashed out towards those who taunted me. I became more insular into myself and very much shy.

Western Education and Christianity

I, along with many others in my generation, went to missionary-run and government-run boarding (BIA) schools, which were a great place to indoctrinate children into Christianity and Western worldviews. As indigenous children growing up in mission-run or BIA boarding schools in Alaska, we were never taught aspects of our culture: language, story-telling, singing, dancing or drumming and traditional values. Instead, we were immersed in a western based education: English, American and World History, Social Studies, math and science. We were infused with western values and characteristics. One recurring recreational activity I remember from the mid1950s and early 1960s were the many movie Westerns shown. They depicted the Hollywood stereotypes of American Indians as savages; stealing, pillaging, killing White women and children. A western characteristic, "divide and conquer," was learned from watching many of those cowboy and Indian movies Those of us who became astute at this method used it later in our adult life; not understanding that this attribute was contributing to the disruption in our communities, relationships and in Native politics.

At Wrangell Institute, church groups were invited each fall to the school some five miles from the town to round up children into their particular denomination. Every child had to belong to a church. Some care was given to have children enroll into the church their parents attended. On the other hand, children who spoke no English were arbitrarily assigned to some denominations on a roster of listed churches. In my case, my younger brother and I had a mother who was a Quaker (Friends). No such denomination existed in the town so we were assigned to the Southern Baptist Church. Our mother was never informed of this decision. As an eight year old, brother and I became captive of the dogma laid on us every Sunday morning and Wednesday evening.

Years later, I was taken by a conversation I overheard between two Inupiaq women about whether each were "church-goers." Both were proud to admit that they were and that they belonged to the same denomination. The denomination had been the dominant church in that area. The Native leadership that permeated all levels of society in that area was of the same denomination. It was observed by other Natives that if you were not from that congregation, you were omitted from the leadership class. Other affiliations entered the area, but still witnessed a particular church as having more political sway than others.

A story my mother told me as I was growing up was of the "second coming of Jesus." In fact, the second coming was a favorite story of the converted in the Kotzebue area. Mom paraphrased, "Jesus would come down on a golden cloud and there would be joyous noise and celebration." The story: A faint noise was heard and a strange object was seen flying low over the Kobuk River in the setting sun near the village of Noorvik, circa 1924. The setting sun made the object appear golden. As the object got closer, some fell on the ground shouting, "hallelujah, Jesus come, Jesus come!" Some of the-yet-to-be converted chose to run away, yelling in Inupiat, "Too Late, too late, Jesus come, Jesus come!" The object landed and "Jesus got out of the airplane."

In the Quaker bible, Jesus had blue-eyes, blond hair, a kindly White but bearded face. The Jesus getting out of the airplane had "bug eyes" (sun glasses), a leather jacket and blue jeans smoking a cigarette. This was the uniform of the emerging "Bush Pilot." The once rejoicing crowd was beginning to take steps backwards, never keeping their eyes off the stranger, now only whispering Jesus' name, perhaps unsure if this was indeed the "second coming."

To an Inuit community whose worldview was based on interactions with nature and the dog sled, that one solitary plane flight changed those that were present forever. For all the progress that would come from that venture it also brought in booze. Looking back, I can still recall listening to my mom's airplane story as she drank her bottle of wine.

My Internalized Oppression

It started innocently enough for me. After watching westerns on Friday nights, we would act out movie roles on the playgrounds and in the Boys dorm. Of course, no one wanted to play the "Indian." Indians were losers, menacing violent savages. And they always lost. It didn't take long for some of us boys to convince other kids to play the Indian. I and some others were almost always the white cavalry soldier or the cowboy. We enjoyed killing the Indian on the playground. Strange as it may sound, some children enjoyed playing the savage, choosing to die, with pageantry and panache. I chose to stay with the winners. Or so I thought.

When it came to a western education many of us were captive to the indoctrination. However, the quicker we were able to understand and speak English proficiently; we curried the favor of the teachers, minimized our own punishments and to use that against less able fellow students. Those of us who knew English going into boarding school had somewhat of a leg up. We keyed into the system early. We were encouraged to rat on other students for infraction of the rules by matrons who were keen to enforce sanctions. As an eight and nine year old, I became good at telling matrons that so and so was speaking his language. I must have been given some kudos and small notions for my "loyalty." To the offender, however, they became subjected to the many punishments meted out for their offenses. Some of the punishments included being spanked by a cat-o-nine tails, locked into dark closets, running through a strap line gauntlet, and the wearing the infamous dunce-cap in front of the classroom.

Early on I was a pleaser, wanting attention and perks from those adults who I viewed as substitutes for a long dead father. In many ways I became one of the kids willing to sell out fellow student for resorting back to speaking Aleut, Yupik, Inupiat, Athabascan, Suqpiaq, Tlinget, and Haida. By the time I was 12 and 13, I began to see my actions in a different light. I no longer ratted on anyone for speaking their language. In fact, I was beginning to question why I did not speak Inupiat and the never ending and senseless beatings we were subjected to, sometimes at the whim of some employees.

At the time, however, some of us still made fun of those students who struggled with the English language or could only speak Pidgin English. We would mimic their words and laugh at them. We merely added to the shame those students were already experiencing: ridicule and rounds of punishment from the adults there; be it matrons, teachers, health care workers, kitchen staff, and administrative staff. My confusions and struggles continued, and it took many years for me to figure out who I was and what my place is in both the Native and white cultures.

Parallels

In *Brown Skin, White Minds*, I see plenty of similarities between the Alaska Native and the Filipino experience. From the process of colonization, to the manifestations of internalized oppression, and up to the negative behavioral effects of colonialism and modern day oppression, it is clear that there are strong connections between the peoples of the tropics and the peoples of the north. The book talks about painful histories and contemporary realities, the immense suffering and loss. Just as importantly, this book also provides hope. By highlighting the similarly oppressed historical and contemporary conditions between peoples from different parts of the world, Dr. David is able to remind us that we are not alone in our struggles and that, together, we can all create change.

About Aqpaiyuq, James William LaBelle, Sr.

Aqpaiyuq (Fast Runner), James William LaBelle, Sr., M.A., was born to a French/Irish man and to Clara Hensley - an Inupiaq from Kotzebue/Noorvik. Among the many roles he has fulfilled during this life include being Term Instructor for the University of Alaska Anchorage's Alaska Native Studies Program, Term Instructor for the University of Alaska Fairbanks' Rural Human Services Department, Researcher for the National Resource Center for American Indian, Alaska Native, and Native Hawaiian Elders, leader in various Alaska Native corporations, and as Chair of the Alaska Federation of Natives' Wellness (Sobriety) Movement. More importantly, however, is that he is a respected leader and elder in the Alaska Native community. Jim has been married to Susan Tabios – an Alaska Native (Aleut) and Filipina – for over 40 years. They have three adult children, five grandchildren, and one great granddaughter.

COMMENTARY

Bravely Exploring and Confronting the Psychological Effects of Colonialism and its Legacies

By Martin F. Manalansan IV

Colonial mentality is a concept that pervades the scholarly literature and popular imaginings about Philippine society. Part of the persistent survival of the concept has to do with the continued misery of the Philippines after World War II and the two hundred or more years of colonial rule by Spain and the United States. "Three hundred year in the convent and 40 years of Hollywood" is a phrase attributed to the late Filipino writer Nick Joaquin as a summative statement of the historical background of the Spanish and American imperial exploits in the Philippines. Crucial to this popular understanding is the idea that such colonial experience of imperial domination also gave birth to a particular worldview or mindset at least in the Fanon-nian fashion. A mindset constituted by an intellectual and emotional enslavement to the foreign – more specifically Euro-American culture. This Westward positioned and positioning mentality is said to be the provenance of the Third Worlding of the Philippines. To borrow from Gayatri Spivak, this "worlding" of the Philippines was inscribed by colonial rulers and made manifest by present day attitudes, values, and behavior of Filipinos that directed or oriented toward the West.

Colonial mentality has always been seen as a given in traditional Philippine social science disciplines after World War II and until the present day. But it is not without its critiques. Some scholars deride the continued currency of Filipino colonial mentality as it implicitly and explicitly deny the agentive possibilities of radical democratic politics and activism to emerge out of the doldrums of economic and social misery. On the other hand, other people point to the unchanging dominance of English, Western media productions, and out-migration as "evidence" to the continued existence of colonial mentality. Be that as it may, I believe there needs to be a consistent rigorous effort from both camps to unpack and unravel the discursive category of colonial mentality. Perhaps, it is less important to know "what it is" but rather "what it does." I suggest that it is not important to say whether colonial mentality exists or not but rather to see the strength of the discourse through various disciplinary and interdisciplinary research efforts. The fact remains that colonial mentality still survives the shifts and turns in sociological, anthropological, and psychological literatures. What this ultimately means is to recognize the semantic viability of the concept in everyday ordinary talk and scholarly publications.

In this regard, Dr. E.J.R. David bravely delves into the empirical possibilities of psychological measures to illustrate the statistical viability of the concept as it is illustrated by people's seemingly random choices. How does one measure a landscape of attitudes and beliefs? In this book, Dr. David opens up a discussion to consider the materiality of this concept and how it is embodied in Filipinos' engagement with the world. Dr. David's book *Filipino -/ American Postcolonial Psychology: Oppression, Colonial Mentality, and Decolonization*, which is now revised and re-released as *Brown Skin, White Minds,* is an important contribution to the ongoing debate and discussion about the afterlife of colonialism in the lives of Filipinos and Filipino Americans. This book is bound to be a major reference and a source of inspiration for future research on the topic.

About Martin F. Manalansan IV:

Martin F. Manalansan IV, Ph.D., is an Associate Professor of Anthropology and Asian American Studies at the University of Illinois at Urbana-Champaign. His broad research interests include sociocultural anthropology, sexuality and gender, immigration and globalization, cities and modernity, food and culture, critical theory, performance, public health, Filipino diaspora, Asian Americans, North America, Southeast Asia, and the Philippines. He is the author or editor of several books, including Global Divas: Filipino Gay Men in the Diaspora and Cultural Compass: ethnographic Explorations of Asian America.

References

Adair, J. G. (1999). Indigenisation of psychology: The concept and its practical implementation. *Applied Psychology: An International Review, 48,* 403-418.

Agbayani-Siewart, P., & Enrile, A. V. (2003). Filipino American children and adolescents. In J. T. Gibbs (Ed.), *Children of Color: Psychological interventions with culturally diverse youth* (pp. 229-264). San Francisco, CA: Wiley.

Agbayani-Siewart, P., & Revilla, L. (1995). Filipino Americans. *Asian Americans: Contemporary Trends and Issues.* Thousand Oaks, CA: Sage.

Agoncillo, T. A. (1974). *Introduction to Filipino history.* Quezon City, Philippines: Garotech Publishing.

Alvarez, A. N., Juang, L., & Liang, C. T. H. (2006). Asian Americans and racism: When bad things happen to "model minorities." *Cultural Diversity and Ethnic Minority Psychology, 12,* 477-492.

Alvarez, A. N., & Juang, L. (2010). Filipino Americans and racism: A Multiple mediation model of coping. *Journal of Counseling Psychology, 57,* 167-178

Ambady, N., Shih, M., Kim, A., & Pittinsky, T. L. (2001). Stereotype susceptibility in children: Effects of identity activation on quantitative performance. *Psychological Science, 12,* 385-390.

American Psychiatric Association (2000). *Diagnostic and statistical manual for mental disorders* (4th Edition-Text Revision). Washington, DC: American Psychiatric Association.

Anderson, J. R., & Pirolli, P. L. (1984). Spread of activation. *Journal of Experimental Psychology: Learning, Memory, and Cognition, 10,* 791-798.

Aronson, E. (1969). The theory of cognitive dissonance: A current perspective. In L. Berkowitz (Ed.), *Advances in experimental social psychology* (Vol. 4, pp. 1–34). New York, NY: Academic Press.

Atkinson, D. R., Morten, G., & Sue, D. W. (1998). *Counseling American minorities: A cross-cultural perspective.* Dubuque, IA: Brown.

Baddeley, A., & Warrington, E. K. (1970). Amnesia and the distinction between long- and short-term memory. *Journal of Verbal Learning and Verbal Behavior, 9,* 176-189.

Balls Organista, P., Organista, K. C., & Kurasaki, K. (2003). The relationship between acculturation and ethnic minority mental health. In K. M. Chun, P. Balls Organista, & G. Marin (Eds.), *Acculturation: Advances in theory, measurement, and applied research* (pp. 139–162). Washington, DC: American Psychological Association.

Balota, D. A. (1983). Automatic semantic activation and episodic memory encoding. *Journal of Verbal Learning and Verbal Behavior, 22,* 88-104.

Bargh, J. A., Chaiken, S., Govender, R., Pratto, F. (1992). The generality of the automatic attitude activation effect. *Journal of Personality and Social Psychology, 62,* 893-912.

Barnes, J. S., & Bennett, C. E. (2002). *The Asian population: 2000.* Washington, DC: U.S. Bureau of the Census. Retrieved January 3, 2005, from http://www.census.gov/prod/2002pubs/c2kbr01–16.pdf

Barreto, R. M., & Segal, S. P. (2005). Use of mental health services by Asian Americans. *Psychiatric Services, 56,* 746–748.

Beck, A. T., Rush, A. J., Emery, G., & Shaw, B. F. (1979). *Cognitive Therapy of Depression.* New York, NY: Guilford.

Beck, J. S., (1995). *Cognitive therapy: Basics and beyond.* New York, NY: Guilford.

Belleza, F. S., Greenwald, A. G., & Banaji, M. R. (1986). Words high and low in pleasantness as rated by male and female college students. *Behavior Research Methods, Instruments, and Computers, 18,* 299-303.

Benet-Martinez, V., & Haritatos, J. (2005). Bicultural identity integration (BII): Components and psychosocial antecedents. *Journal of Personality, 73,* 1015-1048.

Benet-Martinez, V., Leu, J., Lee, F., & Morris, M. (2002). Negotiating biculturalism: Cultural frame-switching in biculturals with oppositional vs. compatible cultural identities. *Journal of Cross-Cultural Psychology, 33,* 492-516.

Bergano, A. L., & Bergano-Kinney, B. L. (1997). Images, roles, and expectations of Filipino Americans by Filipino Americans. In M. P. P. Root (Ed.), *Filipino Americans: Transformation and identity* (pp. 198-207). Thousand Oaks, CA: Sage.

Bernal G., & Scharron-del-Rio, M. R. (2001). Are empirically supported treatments valid for ethnic minorities? Toward an alternative approach for treatment research. *Cultural Diversity and Ethnic Minority Psychology, 7, 328-342.*

Berry, J. W. (2003). Conceptual approaches to acculturation. In K. M. Chun, P. Balls-Organista, & G. Marin (Eds.), *Acculturation: Advances in Theory, Measurement, and Applied Research.* Washington, DC: American Psychological Association.

Beveridge, A. J. (1900). In Support of an American Empire *Congressional Record, 56 Cong., I Sess., 704-712.*

Bhatia, S., & Ram, A. (2001). Locating the dialogical self in the age of transnational migrations, border crossings and diasporas. *Culture & Psychology, 7, 297–309.*

Blascovich, J., & Tomaka, J. (1993). Measures of self-esteem. In J. P. Robinson, P. R. Shaver, & L. S. Wrightsman (Eds.), *Measures of Personality and Social Psychological Attitudes (3rd Edition).* Ann Arbor, MI: Institute of Social Research.

Blount, J. H. (1913). *American Occupation of the Philippines, 1898/1912.* New York: The Knickerbocker Press.

Bornstein, R. F. (1992). Subliminal mere exposure effects. In R. F. Bornstein and T. S. Pittman (Eds.), *Perception without awareness: Cognitive, clinical, and social perspectives* (pp. 191-210). New York: Guilford.

Brands, H. W. (1992). *Bound to Empire: The United States and the Philippines.* New York. NY: Oxford Press.

Brave Heart, M. Y. H. (1998). The return to the sacred path: Healing the historical trauma and historical unresolved grief response among the Lakota. *Smith College Studies in Social Work, 68,* 287-305.

Brillantes, G. C. (2008). *The Cardinal's Sins, The General's Cross, The Martyr's Testimony, and Other Affirmations.* Manila, Philippines: Ateneo de Manila University.

Bulhan, H. A. (1985). *Frantz Fanon and the psychology of oppression.* New York: Plenum.

Bulosan, C. (2002). *America is in the Heart: A Personal History.* Seattle: University of Washington Press.

Cabezas, Y. (1982). *In Pursuit of Wellness*. San Francisco, CA: California Department of Mental Health.

Carter, R. T. (2007). Racism and psychological and emotional injury. Recognizing and assessing race-based traumatic stress. *The Counseling Psychologist, 35*, 13-105.

Camic, P. M., Rhodes, J. E., & Yardley, L. (Eds.) (2003). *Qualitative Research in Psychology: Expanding Perspectives in Methodology and Design*. Washington, DC: APA.

Chambless, D. L., & Hollon, S. D., (1998). Defining empirically supported therapies. *Journal of Consulting and Clinical Psychology, 64*, 497-504.

Chambless, D., Sanderson, W. C., Shoham, V., Johnson, S. B., Pope, K. S., Crits-Christoph, P., et al. (1996). An update on empirically validated therapies. *The Clinical Psychologist, 49*, 5-14.

Church, A. T. & Katigbak, M. S. (2002). Indigenization of psychology in the Philippines. *International Journal of Psychology, 37*, 129-148.

Cimmarusti, R. A. (1996). Exploring aspects of Filipino-American families. *Journal of Marital & Family Therapy, 22*, 205-217.

Clark, L. A., & Watson, D. (1991). Tripartite model of anxiety and depression: Psychometric evidence and taxonomic implications. *Journal of Abnormal Psychology, 100*, 316-336.

Clark, L. A., Watson, D., & Reynolds, S. (1995). Diagnosis and classification of psychopathology: Challenges to the current system and future directions. *Annual Review of Psychology, 46*, 121-153.

Codina, G. E., & Montalvo, F. F. (1994). Chicano phenotype and depression. *Hispanic Journal of Behavioral Sciences, 16*, 296-306.

Collins, A. M., & Loftus, E. F. (1975). A spreading-activation theory of semantic processing. *Psychological Review, 82*, 407-428.

Combs, D. R., Penn, D. L., & Fenigstein, A. (2002). Ethnic differences in subclinical paranoia: An expansion of norms of the paranoia scale. *Cultural Diversity & Ethnic Minority Psychology, 8*, 248–256.

Constantino, R. (1975). *The Philippines: A past revisited Vol. 1 (Pre-Spanish-1941)*. Quezon City, Philippines: Tala.

Constantino, R. (1982). *The miseducation of the Filipino*. Quezon City, Philippines: The Foundation of Nationalist Studies.

Cordova, F. (1973). The Filipino American: There's always an identity crisis. In S. Sue, & N. Wagner (Eds.), *Asian Americans: Psychological perspectives* (pp. 136-139). Palo Alto, CA: Science and Behavior Books.

Cordova, F. (1983). *Filipinos: Forgotten Asian Americans.* Dubuque, Iowa: Kendall/Hunt.

Crocker, J., & Luhtanen, R. (1990). Collective self-esteem and in-group bias. *Journal of Personality and Social Psychology, 58,* 60-67.

Crocker, J., Luhtanen, R., Blaine, B., & Broadnax, S. (1994). Collective self-esteem and psychological well-being among White, Black, and Asian college students. *Personality and Social Psychology Bulletin, 20,* 503-513.

Cross, W. E., Parham, T. A., & Helms, J. E. (1991). The stages of Black identity development: Nigrescence models. In R. L. Jones (Ed.), *Black psychology (3rd ed.)* (pp. 319-338). Berkeley, CA: Cobb & Henry Publishers.

David, E. J. R. (2006). Biculturalism. In Y. Jackson (Ed.), *Encyclopedia of Multicultural Psychology (pp. 66-68).* Thousand Oaks, CA: Sage.

David, E. J. R. (2008). A colonial mentality model of depression for Filipino Americans. *Cultural Diversity and Ethnic Minority Psychology, 14,* 118-127.

David, E. J. R. (2009). Internalized oppression, psychopathology, and cognitive-behavioral therapy among historically oppressed groups. *Journal of Psychological Practice, 15,* 71-103.

David, E. J. R. (2010a). We have colonial mentality: An honest call to the Filipino American community. In K.L. Nadal (Ed.) *Filipino American Psychology: A Collection of Personal Narratives.* (pp. 97-106). Bloomington, IN: AuthorHouse.

David, E. J. R. (2010b). Testing the validity of the Colonial Mentality Implicit Association Test (CMIAT) and the interactive effects of covert and overt colonial mentality on Filipino American mental health. *Asian American Journal of Psychology, 1,* 31-45.

David, E. J. R. (2010c). Cultural mistrust and mental health help-seeking attitudes among Filipino Americans. *Asian American Journal of Psychology, 1,* 57-66.

David, E. J. R. (2010d). Afterword: Research, Clinical, and Community Directions in Filipino American Psychology. In

K.L. Nadal (Ed.) *Filipino American Psychology: A Collection of Personal Narratives.* (pp. 321-326). Bloomington, IN: AuthorHouse.

David, E. J. R. (2011). Cultural conflicts within and outside the family among Filipino American adolescents. *Journal of Filipino Studies, 3*, 1-3.

David, E. J. R., & Nadal, K. L. N. (under review). The colonial context of the Filipino American immigration experience.

David, E. J. R., & Okazaki, S. (2006a). Colonial Mentality: A Review and recommendation for Filipino American psychology. *Cultural Diversity and Ethnic Minority Psychology, 12*, 1-16.

David, E. J. R., & Okazaki, S. (2006b). The Colonial Mentality Scale for Filipino Americans: Scale construction and psychological implications. *Journal of Counseling Psychology, 53*, 241-252.

David, E. J. R., & Okazaki, S. (2010). Activation and automaticity of colonial mentality. *Journal of Applied Social Psychology, 40*, 850-887.

David, E. J. R., Okazaki, S., & Giroux, D. (in press). A Set of Guiding Principles to Advance Multicultural Psychology and its Major Concepts. In F. T. L. Leong, L. Comas-Diaz, G. N. Hall, V. McLoyd, & J. Trimble (Eds.) *Handbook of Multicultural Psychology (Vol. 1).* Washington, DC: American Psychological Association.

David, E. J. R., Okazaki, S., & Saw, A. (2009). Bicultural self-efficacy among college students: Initial scale development and mental health correlates. *Journal of Counseling Psychology, 56*, 211-226.

de Guia K. (2005). *Kapwa: The Self in the Other. Worldviews and Lifestyles of Filipino Culture-Bearers.* Pasig City, Philippines: Anvil Publishing.

dela Cruz, F. A., Padilla, G. V., & Agustin, E. O. (2000). Adapting a measure of acculturation for cross-cultural research. *Journal of Transcultural Nursing, 11*, 191–198.

dela Cruz, F. A., Padilla, G. V., & Butts, E. (1998). Validating a short acculturation scale for Filipino Americans. *Journal of the American Academy of Nurse Practitioners, 10*, 453-460.

del Prado, A. M., & Church, A. T. (2010). Development and validation of the Enculturation Scale for Filipino Americans. *Journal of Counseling Psychology, 57*, 469-483.

Devos, T. (2006). Implicit bicultural identity among Mexican American and Asian Amercan college students. *Cultural Diversity and Ethnic Minority Psychology, 12,* 381-402.

Diaz-Loving, R. (1999). The indigenisation of psychology: Birth of a new science or rekindling of an old one? *Applied Psychology: An International Review, 48,* 433-449.

Diener, E., Emmons, R. A., Larsen, R. J., & Griffin, S. (1985). The Satisfaction With Life Scale. *Journal of Personality Assessment, 49,* 71-75.

Draine, S. C., & Greenwald, A. G. (1998). Replicable unconscious semantic priming. *Journal of Experimental Psychology: General, 127,* 286-303.

Duran, E. (2006). *Healing the soul wound: Counseling with American Indians and other Native Peoples.* New York, NY: Teachers College Press.

Duran, E., & Duran, B. (1995). *Native American Postcolonial Psychology.* Albany, NY: State University of New York.

Ebbinghaus, H. (1964). *Memory: A Contribution to experimental psychology.* New York, NY: Dover. (Original work published 1885).

Enriquez, V. G. (1977). Filipino psychology in the third world. *Philippine Journal of Psychology, 10,* 3-18.

Enriquez, V. G. (1993). Developing a Filipino psychology. In U. Kim, & J. W. Berry (Eds.), *Indigenous Psychologies: Research and Experience in Cultural Context* (pp. 152-169). Newbury Park, CA: Sage.

Enriquez, V. G., (1994). *From Colonial to Liberation Psychology: The Philippine Experience.* Manila, Philippines: De La Salle University Press.

Espina, M. (1988). *Filipinos in Louisiana.* New Orleans, LA: A. F. Laborde.

Espiritu, Y. L. (2003). *Home bound: Filipino American lives across cultures, communities, and countries.* Los Angeles, CA: University of California Press.

Fanon, F. (1965). *The Wretched of the earth.* New York, NY: Grove.

Fazio, R. H., Jackson, J. R., Dunton, B. C., & Williams, C. J. (1995). Variability in automatic activation as an unobtrusive measure of racial attitudes: A bona fide pipeline? *Journal of Personality and Social Psychology, 69,* 1013-1027.

Fazio, R. H., Sanbonmatsu, D. M., Powell, M. C., & Kardes, F. R. (1986). On the automatic activation of attitudes. *Journal of Personality and Social Psychology, 50,* 229-238.

Festinger, L. (1957). *A theory of cognitive dissonance.* Evanston, IL: Row, Peterson, and Company.

Freire, P. (1970). *The Pedagogy of the oppressed.* New York, NY: Continuum.

Freud, S., & Breuer, J. (1960). Studies on hysteria. New York: Avon Books. (Original work published 1895).

Fuks, S. I. (1998). Systems theory perspective and community psychology. *Journal of Community Psychology: Special Issue, 26,* 243-252.

Gardner, W. L., Gabriel, S., & Lee, A. Y. (1999). "I" value freedom, but "we" value relationships: Self-construal priming mirrors cultural differences in judgment. *Psychological Science, 10,* 321-326.

Gaston, M. (2003, March). Big C Little M. *Filipino American Herald*, p. 9.

Gawronski B., & Bodenhausen, G. V. (2006). Associative and propositional processes in evaluation: An integrative review of implicit and explicit attitude change. *Psychological Bulletin, 132,* 692-731.

Gawronski, B., Hofmann, W., & Wilbur, C. J. (2006). Are "implicit" attitudes unconscious? *Consciousness and Cognition, 15,* 485-499.

Gawronski, B., LeBel, E. P., & Peters, K. R. (2007). What do implicit measures tell us? Scrutinizing the validity of three common assumptions. *Perspectives on Psychological Science, 2,* 181-193.

Go, J. (2003). The chains of empire: State building and "political education" in Puerto Rico and the Philippines. In J. Go, & A. L. Foster (Eds.), *The American colonial state in the Philippines: Global perspectives* (pp. 182-216). Duke University Press.

Gomez Borah, E. (1995). Filipinos in Unamuno's California expedition of 1587. *Amerasia Journal, 21.*

Gone, J. P. (2009). A community-based treatment for Native American historical trauma: Prospects for evidence-based practice. *Journal of Consulting and Clinical Psychology, 77,* 751-762.

Gong, F., Gage, S. L., & Tacata, L. A. (2003). Helpseeking Behavior Among Filipino Americans: A Cultural Analysis of Face and Language. *Journal of Community Psychology, 31,* 469-488.

Gong, F., Takeuchi, D. T., Agbayani-Siewart, P., & Tacata, L. (2003). Acculturation, distress, and alcohol use: Investigating the effects of ethnic identity and religiosity. In K. M. Chun, P. Balls-Organista, & G. Marin (Eds.), *Acculturation: Advances in theory, measurement, and applied research* (pp. 189–206). Washington, DC: American Psychological Association.

Gosling, S. D., Vazire, S., Srivastava, S., & John, O. P. (2004). Should we trust web-based studies? A comparative analysis of six preconceptions about internet questionnaires. *American Psychologist, 59*, 93-104.

Graf, P., & Mandler, G. (1984). Activation makes words more accessible, but not necessarily more retrievable. *Journal of Verbal Learning and Verbal Behavior, 23,* 553-568.

Greenwald, A. G., & Banaji, M. R. (1995). Implicit social cognition: Attitudes, self-esteem, and stereotypes. *Psychological Review, 102*, 4-27.

Greenwald, A. G., Draine, S. C., & Abrams, R. L. (1996). Three cognitive markers of unconscious semantic activation. *Science, 273,* 1699-1702.

Greenwald, A. G., & Farnham, S. D. (2000). Using the Implicit Association Test to measure self-esteem and self-concept. *Journal of Personality and Social Psychology, 79,* 1022-1038.

Greenwald, A. G., Klinger, M. R., & Liu, T. J. (1989). Unconscious processing of dichoptically masked words. *Memory and Cognition, 17,* 35-47.

Greenwald, A. G., Klinger, M. R., & Schuh, E. S. (1995). Activation by marginally perceptible ("Subliminal") stimuli: Dissociation of unconscious from conscious cognition. *Journal of Experimental Psychology: General, 124*, 22-42.

Greenwald, A. G., McGhee, D. E., & Schwartz, J. L. K. (1998). Measuring individual differences in implicit cognition: The Implicit Association Test. *Journal of Personality and Social Psychology, 74*, 1464-1480.

Greenwald, A. G., Nosek, B. A., & Banaji, M. R. (2003). Understanding and using the implicit association test: I. An improved scoring algorithm. *Journal of Personality and Social Psychology, 85*, 197-216.

Gregory, R. J. (2001). Parallel themes: Community psychology and Maori culture in Aotearoa. *Journal of Community Psychology, 29,* 19-27.

Hagborg, W. J. (1993). The Rosenberg Self-Esteem Scale and Harter's Self Perception Profile for Adolescents: A concurrent validity study. *Psychology in the Schools, 30,* 132-136.

Halagao, P. E. (2004). Holding up the mirror: The complexity of seeing your ethnic self in history. *Theory and Research in Social Education, 32*, 459-483.

Halili, M. C. N. (2004). *Philippine History.* Manila, Philippines: Rex Bookstore.

Hall, G. N. (2001). Psychotherapy research with ethnic minorities: Empirical, ethical, and conceptual issues. *Journal of Consulting and Clinical Psychology, 69,* 502-510.

Hall, R. E. (1994). The "bleaching syndrome": Implications of light skin for Hispanic American assimilation. *Hispanic Journal of Behavioral Sciences, 16*, 307-314.

Harrell, C. J. P. (1999). *Manichean psychology: Racism and the minds of people of African descent.* Washington, DC: Howard University Press.

Hatzenbuehler, M. L. (2009). How does sexual minority stigma "Get under the skin"? A psychological mediation framework. *Psychological Bulletin, 135,* 707-730.

Hays, P. A., & Iwamasa, G. Y. (Eds.) (2006). *Culturally-Responsive Cognitive-Behavioral Therapy: Assessment, Practice, and Supervision.* Washington, DC: American Psychological Association.

Heras, P. & Revilla, L. A. (1994). Acculturation, generational status, and family environment of Pilipino Americans: A study in cultural adaptation. *Family Therapy, 21*, 129-138.

Hoeffel, E. M., Rastogi, S., Kim, M. O. & Shahid, H. (2012). The Asian population: 2010. Washington, DC: U.S. Bureau of the Census. Retrieved September 29, 2012, from http://www.census.gov/prod/cen2010/briefs/c2010br-11.pdf

Hong, Y., Chiu, C., & Kung, T. M. (1997). Bridging culture out in front: Effects of cultural meaning system activation on social cognition. In K. Leung, U. Kim, S. Yamaguchi, & Y.

Kashima (Eds.), *Progress in Asian Social Psychology* (Vol. 1, pp.139-150). Singapore: Wiley.

Hong, Y., Morris, M. W., Chiu, C., & Benet-Martinez, V. (2000). Multicultural minds: A Dynamic constructivist approach to culture and cognition. *American Psychologist, 55*, 709-720.

Howarth, C. S. (2001). Toward a social psychology of community: A social representations perspective. *Journal for the Theory of Social Behavior, 31*, 223-238.

Ignacio, A., de la Cruz, E., Emmanuel, J., & Toribio, J. (2004). *The forbidden book: The Philippine-American war in political cartoons.* San Francisco, CA: T'boli Publishing.

Israel, B. A., Schulz, A. J., Parker, E., & Becker, A. B. (1998). Review of community-based research: Assessing partnership approaches to improve public health" *Annual Review of Public Health, 19*, 173-202.

Jacoby, L. L. (1988). Memory observed and memory unobserved. In U. Neisser & E. Winograd (Eds.), *Remembering reconsidered: Ecological and traditional approaches to the study of memory* (pp. 145-177). Cambridge, England: Cambridge University Press.

Karnow, S. (1989). *In Our image: America's empire in the Philippines.* New York, NY: Random House, Inc.

Kelly, J. G. (1990). Changing contexts and the field of community psychology. *American Journal of Community Psychology, 18*, 769-792.

Kim, J. (1981). The process of Asian American identity development: A study of Japanese-American women's perceptions of their struggle to achieve personal identities as Americans of Asian ancestry. *Dissertation Abstracts International, 42*, 1551A.

Kim, T. E. & Goto, S. G. (2000). Peer delinquency and parental social support as predictors of Asian American adolescent delinquency. *Deviant Behavior, 21*, 331-347.

Kim, U. (2000). Indigenous, cultural, and cross-cultural psychology: A theoretical, conceptual, and epistemological analysis. *Asian Journal of Social Psychology, 3*, 265-287.

Kim, U., & Berry, J. W. (1993). Introduction. In U. Kim & J. W. Berry (Eds.), *Indigenous Psychologies: Research and Experience in Cultural Context (pp. 1-29).* Newbury Park, CA: Sage.

Kim, U., Park, Y. S., & Park, D. (1999). The Korean indigenous psychology approach: Theoretical considerations and empirical applications. *Applied Psychology: An International Review, 48,* 451-464.

Kinoshita, S. & Lupker, S. J. (2003). *Masked Priming: State of the Art.* New York: Psychology Press.

Klonoff, E. A., Landrine, H., & Ullman, J. B. (1999). Racial discrimination and psychiatric symptoms among Blacks. *Cultural Diversity and Ethnic Minority Psychology, 5,* 329-339.

Kraut, R., Olson, J., Banaji, M., Bruckman, A., Cohen, J., Couper, M. (2004). Psychological research online: Report of Board of Scientific Affairs' Advisory Group on the Conduct of Research on the Internet. *American Psychologist, 59,* 105-117.

Kuo, W. H. (1984). Prevalence of depression among Asian-Americans. *Journal of Nervous and Mental Disease, 172,* 449–457.

LaFromboise, T., Coleman, H. L. K., & Gerton, J. (1993). Psychological impact of biculturalism: Evidence and theory. *Psychological Bulletin, 114,* 395-412.

Landrine, H., & Klonoff, E. A. (1996). The Schedule of Racist Events: A measure of racial discrimination and a study of its negative physical and mental health consequences. *Journal of Black Psychology, 22,* 144-168.

Lawson-Te Aho, K., & Liu, J. H. (2010). Indigenous Suicide and Colonization: The Legacy of Violence and the Necessity of Self-Determination. *International Journal of Conflict and Violence, 4,* 124-133.

Legarda, Jr., B. (2001). Cultural landmarks and their interactions with economic factors in the second millennium in the Philippines. *Kinaadman (Wisdom): A Journal of the Southern Philippines, 23,* 40.

Leong, F. T. L., Inman, A., Ebreo, A., Yang, L., Kinoshita, L., & Fu, M. (Eds.) (2002). *Handbook of Asian American Psychology* (2nd Ed.). Thousand Oaks, CA: Sage Publications.

Leong, F. T. L., Okazaki, S., & David, E. J. R. (2006). The history, present, and future of Asian American psychology. In F. Leong, A. Inman, A. Ebreo, L. Yang, L. Kinoshita, & M. Fu

(Eds.), *Handbook of Asian American Psychology* (2nd Ed.) (pp. 11-28). Thousand Oaks, CA: Sage Publications.

Leung, K., & Wu, P. K. (1997). *Indigenous and cross-cultural orientations should not be incredulous of each other.* Institute of Ethnology Academia Sinica.

Liebkind, K. & Jasinskaja-Lahti, I. (2000). Acculturation and psychological well-being among immigrant adolescents in Finland: A comparative study of adolescents from different cultural backgrounds. *Journal of Adolescent Research, 15,* 446-469.

Lott, J. T. (1976). Migration of a mentality: The Pilipino community. *Social Casework,* 165-172.

Luhtanen, R., & Crocker, J. (1992). A Collective Self-Esteem Scale: Self-evaluation of one's social identity. *Personality and Social Psychology Bulletin, 18,* 302-318.

Major, E. F. (1996). The impact of the Holocaust on the second generation: Norwegian Jewish Holocaust survivors and their children. *Journal of Traumatic Stress. 9,* 441-454.

Markus, H. R. and Kitayama, S. (1991) *Culture and the self: Implications for cognition, emotion and motivation.* Psychological Review, 98, p. 224-253.

Marsella, A. J. (1998). Toward a "Global-Community Psychology": Meeting the needs of a changing world. *American Psychologist, 53,* 1282-1291.

McBride, B. A. (2002). Aspects of community healing: Experiences of the Sault Sainte Marie tribe of Chippewa Indians. *American Indian & Alaska Native Mental Health Research, 11,* 67-83.

McWilliams, C. (2002). Introduction. In C. Bulosan's *America is in the Heart: A Personal History.* University of Washington Press: Seattle.

Memmi, A. (1965). *The colonizer and the colonized.* Boston, MA: Beacon.

Meyer, I. H. (2003). Prejudice, social stress, and mental health in lesbian, gay, and bisexual populations: Conceptual issues and research evidence. *Psychological Bulletin, 129,* 674-697.

Miller, D. B., (1999). Racial socialization and racial identity: Can they promote resiliency for African American adolescents? *Adolescence, 34,* 493-501.

Milner, B., Corkin, S., & Teuber, H. L. (1968). Further analysis of the hippocampal amnesic syndrome: 14-year follow-up study of H. M. *Neuropsychologica, 6,* 215-234.

Nadal, K. L. (2000). F/Pilipino American substance abuse: Sociocultural factors and methods of treatment. *Journal of Alcohol and Drug Education, 46,* 26-36.

Nadal, K. L. (2004). Pilipino American Identity Development Model. *Journal of Multicultural Counseling and Development, 32,* 44-61.

Nadal, K. L. (2009; 2011). *Filipino American Psychology: A Handbook of Theory, Research, and Clinical Practice.* New York, NY: Wiley.

Nadal, K. L. (2010). *Filipino American Psychology: A Collection of Personal Narratives.* Bloomington, IN: AuthorHouse.

Nadal, K. L., Escobar, K. M., Prado, G., David, E. J. R., & Haynes, K. (2012). Racial Microaggressions and the Filipino American Experience: Recommendations for counseling and development. *Journal of Multicultural Counseling and Development, 40,* 156-173.

Nagata, D. K., & Cheng, W. J. Y. (2003). Intergenerational communication of race-related trauma by Japanese American former internees. *American Journal of Orthopsychiatry, 73,* 266-278.

Nagata, D. K., Trierweiler, S. J., & Talbot, R. (1999). Long-term effects of internment during early childhood in third-generation Japanese Americans. *American Journal of Orthopsychiatry, 69,* 19-29.

Napoleon, H. (1996). *Yuuyaraq: The Way of the Human Being.* Fairbanks, AK: Alaska Native Knowledge Network, University of Alaska Fairbanks.

Neely, J. H. (1977). Semantic priming and retrieval from lexical memory: Roles of inhibitionless spreading activation and limited-capacity attention. *Journal of Experimental Psychology: General, 106,* 226-254.

Newcomb, M. D., & Bentler, P. M. (1988). Impact of adolescent drug use and social support on problems of young adults: A longitudinal study. *Journal of Abnormal Psychology, 97,* 64-75.

Norcross, J. C., Hedges, M., & Prochaska, J. O. (2002). The face of 2010: A Delphi poll on the future of psychotherapy.

Professional Psychology: Research and Practice, 33, 316-322.

Nosek, B. A. (2005). Moderators of the relationship between implicit and explicit evaluation. *Journal of Experimental Psychology: General, 134,* 565-584.

Nosek, B. A., Greenwald, A. G., & Banaji, M. R. (2005). Understanding and using the Implicit Association Test: II. Method variables and construct validity. *Personality and Social Psychology Bulletin, 31,* 166–180.

Okamura, J. Y. (1998). *Imagining the Filipino American Diaspora: Transnational Relations, Identities, and Communities.* New York: Garland.

Okamura, J. Y., & Agbayani, A. R. (1997). Pamantasan: Filipino American higher education. In M. P. P. Root's (Ed.) *Filipino Americans: Transformation and Identity* (pp. 183-197). Thousand Oaks, CA: Sage.

Okazaki, S. (2002). Beyond questionnaires: Conceptual and methodological innovations in Asian American psychology. In G. C. N. Hall, & S. Okazaki (Eds.), *Asian American psychology: The science of lives in context* (pp. 13-39). Washington, DC: American Psychological Association.

Okazaki, S., David, E. J. R., & Abelman, N. (2007). Colonialism and the psychology of culture. *Social and Personality Psychology Compass, 1, 90-106.*

Okazaki, S., & Tanaka-Matsumi, J. (2006). Cultural considerations in cognitive-behavioral assessment. In P. A. Hays, & G. Y. Iwamasa (Eds.), *Culturally responsive cognitive-behavioral therapy* (pp. 247-266). Washington, DC: American Psychological Association.

Ongel, U. & Smith, P.B. (1999). The search for indigenous psychologies: Data from Turkey and the former USSR. *Applied Psychology: An International Review, 48,* 465-479.

Owens, T. J. (2001). *Extending Self-Esteem Theory and Research.* Cambridge, MA: Harvard University Press.

Padesky, C. A., & Greenburger, D. (1995). *Clinician's guide to mind over mood.* New York, NY: Guilford Press.

Pavot, W., & Diener, E. (1993). Review of the Satisfaction With Life Scale. *Psychological Assessment, 5,* 164-172.

Peirce, R. S., Frone, M. R., Russell, M., Cooper, M. L., & Mudar, P. (2000). A longitudinal model of social contact, social support, depression, and alcohol use. *Health Psychology, 19,* 28-38.

Pe-Pua, R. & Protacio-Marcelino, E. (2000). Sikolohiyang Pilipino (Filipino psychology): A legacy of Virgilio G. Enriquez. *Asian Journal of Social Psychology, 3,* 49-71.

Perdue, C. W., Dovidio, J., F., Gurtman, M. B., & Tyler, R. B. (1990). Us and them: Social categorization and the process of intergroup bias. *Journal of Personality and Social Psychology, 59,* 475-486.

Perez, M. P. (2005). Colonialism, Americanization, and indigenous identity: A research note on Chamorro identity in Guam. *Sociological Spectrum, 25,* 571-591.

Peterson, C., & Seligman, M. E. P. (1984). Causal explanations as a risk factor for depression: Theory and evidence. *Psychological Review, 91,* 347-374.

Phinney, J. (1992). The Multigroup Ethnic Identity Measure: A new scale for use with adolescents and young adults from diverse groups. *Journal of Adolescent Research, 7,* 156-176.

Phinney, J., Chavira, V., & Williamson, L. (1992). Acculturation attitudes and self-esteem among high school and college students. *Youth & Society, 23,* 299–312.

Pido, A. J. A. (1997). Macro/Micro dimensions of Pilipino immigration to the United States. In M. P. P. Root (Ed.), *Filipino Americans: Transformation and identity* (pp. 21-38). Thousand Oaks, CA: Sage.

Plested, B. A., Edwards, R. W., & Jumper-Thurman, P. (2005). *Community readiness: A handbook for successful change.* Fort Collins, CO: Tri-Ethnic Center for Prevention Research.

Poortinga, Y. H. (1999). Do differences in behaviour imply a need for different psychologies?_*Applied Psychology: An International Review, 48,* 419-432.

President's Advisory Commission on Asian Americans and Pacific Islanders (2001). *Asian Americans and Pacific Islanders: A People looking forward.* Retrieved December 20, 2001, from http://www.aapi.gov/

Prilleltensky, I., & Gonick, L. (1996). Polities change, oppression remains: On the psychology and politics of oppression. *Political Psychology, 17,* 127-148.

Prochaska J. O., & Velicer, W. F. (1997). The transtheoretical model of health behavior change. *American Journal of Health Promotion, 1,* 38-48.

E. J. R. DAVID, PH.D.

Radloff, L. S. (1977). The CES-D scale: A self-report depression scale for research in the general population. *Applied Psychological Measurement*, 1, 385-401.

Rajaram, S., & Roediger, H. L. III (1993). Direct comparison of four implicit memory tests. *Journal of Experimental Psychology: Learning, Memory, and Cognition, 19*, 765-776.

Rappaport, J. (1977). *Community Psychology: Values, Research, and Action.* Orlando, FL: Holt, Rinehart and Winston, Inc.

Rappaport, J. (2005). Community psychology is (Thank God) more than science. *American Journal of Community Psychology, 35*, 231-238.

Rappaport, J. & Seidman, E. (Eds.) (2000). *Handbook of Community Psychology.* Dordrecht, Netherlands: Kluwer Academic.

Revilla, L. A. (1997). Filipino American identity: Transcending the crisis. In M. P. P. Root (Ed.), *Filipino Americans: Transformation and identity* (pp. 95-111). Thousand Oaks, CA: Sage.

Rimonte, R. (1997). Colonialism's legacy: The inferiorizing of the Filipino. In M. P. P. Root (Ed.), *Filipino Americans: Transformation and identity* (pp. 39-61). Thousand Oaks, CA: Sage.

Roberts, R., Phinney, J., Masse, L., Chen, Y., Roberts, C., & Romero, A. (1999). The structure of ethnic identity in young adolescents from diverse ethnocultural groups. *Journal of Early Adolescence, 19,* 301-322.

Roccas, S., Horenczyk, G., & Schwartz, S. H. (2000). Acculturation discrepancies and well-being: The moderating role of conformity. *European Journal of Social Psychology, 30,* 323-334.

Rodriguez, F. I. (1997). Filipino Americans and ecology: New challenges in the global future. In M. P. P. Root (Ed.), *Filipino Americans: Transformation and identity* (pp. 316-323). Thousand Oaks, CA: Sage.

Rodriguez, W. C., Bravo, M., & Moreno, M. A. (1999). Psychological research in Puerto Rico. *Applied Psychology: An International Review, 48,* 497-509.

Roediger, H. L. III (1990). Implicit memory: Retention without remembering. *American Psychologist, 45,* 1043-1056.

Roediger, H. L. III, Weldon, M. S., Stadler, M. L., & Riegler, G. L. (1992). Direct comparison of two implicit memory tests: Word fragment and word stem completion. *Journal of*

Experimental Psychology: Learning, Memory, and Cognition, 18, 1251-1269.

Roesch, R. & Carr, G. (2000). Psychology in the international community: Perspectives on peace and development. In J. Rappaport & E. Seidman (Eds.), *Handbook of Community Psychology (pp. 811-831).* Dordrecht, Netherlands: Kluwer Academic

Rogers, C. (1980). *A Way of Being.* Boston: Houghton Mifflin

Root, M. P. P. (1997a). *Filipino Americans: Transformation and Identity* . Thousand Oaks, CA: Sage Publications.

Root, M. P. P. (1997b). Contemporary mixed-heritage Filipino Americans: Fighting colonized identities. In M. P. P. Root's (Ed.), *Filipino Americans: Transformation and Identity* (pp.80-94). Thousand Oaks, CA: Sage Publications.

Root, M. P. P. (2002). Methodological issues in multiracial research. In G. C. N. Hall, & S. Okazaki (Eds.), *Asian American psychology: The science of lives in context* (pp. 171-193). Washington, DC: American Psychological Association.

Rosenberg, M. (1965). *Society and the Adolescent Self-Image.* Princeton, NJ: Princeton Press.

Rudkin, J. K. (2003). *Community psychology: Guiding principles and orienting concepts.* Upper Saddle River, NJ: Pearson.

Rudmin, F. W. (2003). Critical history of the acculturation psychology of assimilation, separation, integration, and marginalization. *Review of General Psychology, 7,* 3–37.

Rusling, J. (1903). Interview with President William McKinley. *The Christian Advocate, 22*(17).

Rusling, J. (1987). Interview with President William McKinley. In D. Schirmer and S. Rosskamm Shalom (Eds.), *The Philippines Reader* (pp. 22-23). Boston: South End Press.

Ryder, A. G., Alden, L. E., & Paulhus, D.L. (2000). Is acculturation unidimensional or bidimensional?: A head-to-head comparison in the prediction of personality, self-identity, and adjustment. *Journal of Personality and Social Psychology, 79,* 49-65.

Said, E. W. (1979). *Orientalism.* New York: Vintage.

Said, E. W. (1983). *Culture and imperialism.* New York: Knopf.

Sanchez, F., & Gaw, A. (2007). Mental health care of Filipino Americans. *Psychiatric Services, 58,* 810–815.

Sanchez, L. M. (1999). Psychology in Venezuela: Perceptions and opinions of research psychologists. *Applied Psychology: An International Review, 48,* 481-496.

Sands, E. A., & Berry, J. W. (1993). Acculturation and mental health among Greek-Canadians in Toronto. *Canadian Journal of Community Mental Health, 12,* 117–124.

San Juan, Jr., E. (2005). We Charge Genocide: A Brief History of US in the Philippines. http://www.politicalaffairs.net/article/articleview/2274/1/134/. Retrieved August 25, 2010.

Santiago, C. E., & Enriquez, V. G. (1976). Tungo sa makapilipinong pananaliksik (Toward a Filipino-oriented research). *Sikolohiyang Pilipino: Mga ulat at balita, 1,* 3-10.

Shams, M. (2002). Issues in the study of indigenous psychologies: Historical perspectives, cultural interdependence and institutional regulations. *Asian Journal of Social Psychology, 5,* 79-91.

Sibley, C. G. (2010). The dark duo of post-colonial ideolgy: A model of symbolic exclusion and historical negation. *International Journal of Conflict and Violence, 4,* 106-103.

Sinha, D. (1997). Indigenizing psychology. In J. W. Berry, Y. H. Poortinga, & J. Pandey (Eds.), *Handbook of Cross-Cultural Psychology: Vol. 1: Theory and Method* (pp. 129–169). Boston: Allyn & Bacon.

Smith, L. T. (1999). *Decolonizing Methodologies: Research and Indigenous Peoples.* London, England: Zed Books

Solomon, R., & Liefeld, C. P. (1998). Effectiveness of a family support-center approach to adolescent mothers: Repeat pregnancy and school drop-out rates. *Family Relations, 47,* 139-144

Sorscher, N., & Cohen, L. J. (1997). Trauma in children of Holocaust survivors: Transgenerational effects. *American Journal of Orthopsychiatry, 67,* 493-500.

Speight, S. L. (2007). Internalized racism: One more piece to the puzzle. *The Counseling Psychologist, 35,* 126-134.

Steele, C. M. (1997). A threat in the air: How stereotypes shape intellectual identity and performance. *American Psychologist, 52,* 1613-1629.

Steele, C. M., & Aronson, J. (1995). Stereotype threat and the intellectual test performance of African Americans. *Journal of Personality and Social Psychology, 69,* 797-811.

Steir, M., Lasota, M., & Christensen, C. (2007). Empirically validated treatments. *Journal of Psychological Practice, 14,* 56-66.

Steptoe, A., Wardle, J., Pollard, T. M., Canaan, J., Davies, G. J. (1996). Stress, social support, and health-related behavior: A study of smoking, alcohol consumption and physical exercise. *Journal of Psychosomatic Research, 41,* 171-180.

Stevenson, H. C., (1994). Validation of the Scale of Racial Socialization among African American adolescents: Steps toward multidimensionality. *Journal of Black Psychology, 4,* 445-468.

Strobel, L. M. (1997). Coming full circle: Narratives of decolonization among post-1965 Filipino Americans. In M. P. P. Root (Ed.), *Filipino Americans: Transformation and identity* (pp. 62-79). Thousand Oaks, CA: Sage.

Strobel, L. M. (2001). *Coming full circle: The process of decolonization among post-1965 Filipino Americans.* Quezon City, Philippines: Giraffe Books.

Sue, D. W. (2010). *Microaggressions in Everyday Life: Race, Gender, and Sexual Orientation.* Hoboken, NJ: Wiley and Sons.

Sue, S., & Zane, N. (2006). Ethnic minority populations have been neglected by evidence-based practices. In J. C. Norcross, L. E. Beutler, & R. F. Levant (Eds.), *Evidence-Based Practices in Mental Health: Debate and Dialogue on the Fundamental Questions* (pp. 329-337). Washington, DC: American Psychological Association,

Sue, S., & Zane, N. (1987). The role of culture and cultural techniques in psychotherapy: A critique and reformulation. *American Psychologist, 42, 37-45.*

Tajfel, H., & Turner, J. C. (1986). The social identity theory of intergroup behavior. In S. Worchel & W. Austin (Eds.), *Psychology of intergroup relations.* Chicago, IL: Nelson-Hall.

Tanaka-Matsumi, J., Seiden, D., & Lam, K. (1996). The Culturally Informed Functional Assessment (CIFA) interview: A strategy for cross-cultural behavioral practice. *Cognitive and Behavioral Practice, 3,* 215-233.

Tatum, B. (1994). The colonial model as a theoretical explanation of crime and delinquency. In A. T. Sulton (Ed.), *African American perspectives on crime, causation, criminal justice administration, and crime prevention* (pp. 33-52). Woburn, MA: Butterworth-Heinemann.

Taylor, D. M. (1997). The quest for collective identity: The plight of disadvantaged ethnic minorities. *Canadian Psychology, 38,* 174-189.

Terrell, F., & Terrell, S. (1981). An inventory to measure cultural mistrust among Blacks. *Western Journal of Black Studies, 5,* 180–185.

Tewari, N., & Alvarez, A. N. (Eds.) (2009). *Asian American Psychology: Current perspectives.* New York, NY: Psychology Press.

Thomas, C. W. (1971). *Boys no more: A Black psychologist's view of community.* Beverly Hills, CA: Glencoe.

Tirona, C. (1995). Sometimes, I am not sure what it means to be an American. In Y. L. Espiritu (Ed.), *Filipino American lives* (pp. 65–80). Philadelphia: Temple University Press.

Tompar-Tiu, A., & Sustento-Seneriches, J. (1995). *Depression and other mental health issues: The Filipino American experience.* San Francisco, CA: Jossey-Bass/Pfeiffer.

Trafimow, D., Silverman, E. S., Fan, R. M.-T., & Law, J. S. F. (1997). The effects of language and priming on the relative accessibility of the private self and the collective self. *Journal of Cross-Cultural Psychology, 28,* 600-625.

Trafimow, D., Triandis, H. C., & Goto, S. G. (1991). Some tests of the distinction between the private self and the collective self. *Journal of Personality and Social Psychology, 60,* 649-655.

Triandis, H. C. (2001). Individualism-Collectivism and Personality. *Journal of Personality , 69,* 907-924.

Trickett, E. J. (1991). *Living an idea: Empowerment and the evolution of an alternative high school.* Boston: Brookline Books.

Trickett, E. J. (1996). A future for community psychology: The contexts of diversity and the diversity of contexts. *American Journal of Community Psychology, 24,* 209-229.

Tsai, J. L., Chentsova-Dutton, Y., & Wong, Y. (2002). Why and how researchers should study ethnic identity, acculturation, and cultural orientation. In G. C. N. Hall & S. Okazaki (Eds.), *Asian American psychology: The science of lives in context* (pp. 41–66). Washington, DC: American Psychological Association.

United States Department of State (2006, October). *U.S.-Philippines Relations*. Retrieved February 27, 2007 from http://www.state.gov/r/pa/ei/bgn/2794.htm.

Varas-Diaz, N., & Serrano-Garcia, I. (2003). The challenge of a positive self-image in a colonial context: A psychology of liberation for the Puerto Rican experience. *American Journal of Community Psychology, 31*, 103-115.

Villa, D. (1995). I offended many Filipinos because I was an FOB. In Y. L. Espiritu (Ed.), *Filipino American lives* (pp. 169–180). Philadelphia: Temple University Press.

Volpato, C., & Licata, L. (2010). Collective memories of colonial violence. *International Journal of Conflict and Violence, 4,* 4-10.

Walker, R. L., Wingate, L. R., Obasi, E. M., & Joiner, T. E. (2008). An empirical investigation of acculturative stress and ethnic identity as moderators for depression and suicidal ideation in college students. *Cultural Diversity and Ethnic Minority Psychology, 14, 75-82.*

Wallerstein, N., & Duran, B. (2003). The conceptual, historical and practical roots of community based participatory research and related participatory traditions. In M. Minkler, & N. Wallerstein (Eds.) *Community Based Participatory Research for Health (pp. 27-52).* San Francisco, CA: Jossey-Bass.

Watson, D., Weber, K., Assenheimer, J. S., Clark, L. A., Strauss, M. E., & McCormick, R. A. (1995). Testing a tripartite model: I. Assessing the convergent and discriminant validity of anxiety and depression symptom scales. *Journal of Abnormal Psychology, 104,* 3-14.

Whaley, A. L. (2001). Cultural mistrust: An important psychological construct for diagnosis and treatment of African Americans. *Professional Psychology: Research and Practice, 32,* 555–562.

Williams, W. L. (1980). United States Indian Policy and the Debate over Philippine Annexation: Implications for the Origins of American Imperialism. *The Journal of American History, 66,* 810-831.

Williamson, I. (2000). Internalized homophobia and health issues affecting lesbians and gay men. *Health Education Research, 15,* 97-107.

Wingenfeld, S., & Newbrough, J. R. (2000). Community psychology in international perspective. In J. Rappaport & E. Seidman

(Eds.), *Handbook of Community Psychology (pp. 811-831).* Dordrecht, Netherlands: Kluwer Academic.

Wolf, D. L. (1997). Family secrets: Transnational struggles among children of Filipino immigrants. *Sociological Perspectives, 40,* 457-482.

Yang, K. S. (2000), Monocultural and cross-cultural indigenous approaches: The royal road to the development of a balanced global psychology. *Asian Journal of Social Psychology, 3,* 241-263.

Ying, Y.-W. (1995). Cultural orientation and psychological well-being in Chinese Americans. *American Journal of Community Psychology, 23,* 893–911.

Ying, Y-W, & Hu, L. (1994). Public outpatient mental health services: Use and outcome among Asian Americans. *American Journal of Orthopsychiatry, 64,* 448-455.

Young, B. B., & Kinzie, J. D. (1974). Psychiatric consultation to a Filipino community in Hawaii. *American Journal of Psychiatry, 131,* 563–566.

Zane, N., Hall, G. N., Sue, S., Young, K., & Nunez, J. (2003). Research on psychotherapy with culturally diverse populations. In M. J. Lambert (Ed.), *Bergin and Garfield's handbook of psychotherapy and behavior change (5th ed., pp. 767-804).* New York: Wiley.

E. J. R. David, Ph.D.
300

Glossary Of Terms

Acculturation – the process of adjusting to a new culture, or a culture that is different from one's heritage culture (Chapters 7, 8, and 9)

Baybayin – the indigenous form of written language by the indigenous Taos, or the indigenous inhabitants of the Philippines (Chapters 1 and 2)

Assimilation – one way to acculturate, in which a person adopts and adheres to a new culture while forgetting or separating from his or her heritage culture (Chapters 7, 8, and 9)

Babaylan – leaders, mostly women, who were regarded as spiritual and psychological healers in indigenous Tao culture and society (Chapter 1)

Bagong Bayan or Bagumbayan – the site of Jose Rizal's execution by the Spanish; now called Luneta (Chapter 2)

Balangay or Baranggay – the smallest unit of government in indigenous and modern Filipino society (Chapters 1 and 2)

Balikbayan – a term used to refer to Filipinos who live or work outside the Philippines as they return to visit the country (Chapter 8)

Bayanihan – helping or assisting others willingly, without being asked and without an expectation of getting something in return (Chapters 7 and 8)

Benevolent Assimilation – an American concept that refers to the idea that Americans need to get involved in international affairs simply because they want to help other peoples in other parts of the world (Chapters 1 and 2)

Bicultural or Biculturalism – a concept that refers to individuals who are comfortable in, competent in, and positively regard two cultures simultaneously (Chapters 8, 9, 10, and 11)

Bleaching Syndrome – a phenomenon common among many historically and contemporarily groups wherein individuals use bleach or other skin-whitening products to whiten their skins (Chapters 5 and 6)

Cognitive Behavioral Therapy – a popular form of therapy that conceptualized many psychological problems as caused by maladaptive, distorted, or inaccurate thoughts or beliefs (Chapters 10 and 11)

Cognitive Dissonance Theory – a theory about the human desire to make our thoughts, attitudes, and behaviors consistent with each other; when they are inconsistent, it is easier to change our thoughts and attitudes to make them consistent with our behaviors, than the other way around (Chapter 9)

Collective Empowerment – raising a group of people's sense of power or control over their lives, as well as over their group's lives (Chapter 11)

Collective Self-Esteem – the extent to which individuals positively regard or evaluate the characteristics of the groups they belong to (Chapter 9)

Collectivism or Collectivistic – terms often used to refer to cultures or societies that place more importance on group goals rather than individual goals (Chapter 7)

Colonial Debt – a form of colonial mentality wherein individuals view historical colonialism as absolutely positive and necessary; may lead individuals to also view contemporary oppression as the price they have to pay for civilization (Chapter 2, 3, 5, 6, and 8)

Colonialism – a specific form of oppression wherein one group forcibly enters a new territory to exploit its resources, including the territory's original inhabitants (Chapters 1-12)

Colonial Mentality – a specific form of internalized oppression wherein individuals regard anything of their heritage as inferior to anything of their colonizers or oppressors (Chapters 1-12)

Community Based Participatory Research or Participatory Action Research – a research approach that is characterized by an equal collaboration or partnership between professionals and community members as they attempt to conduct work that is important, relevant, and empowering to the community (Chapter 12)

Community Psychology – a subfield of psychology that emphasizes the importance of context, systemic and institutional influences, diversity of worldviews, social change, and strengths of individuals and communities (Chapter 12)

Conscientization – or critical consciousness, is a psychological state wherein an individual becomes aware of the social and political inequalities in the world and how such oppression affects people (Chapter 11)

Covert Colonial Mentality – a category of colonial mentality that is composed of accepting one's alleged inferiority and feeling ashamed or embarrassed of one's heritage culture or ethnicity (Chapters 5, 6, 7, 8, and 9)

Crab Mentality – a term often used in the Filipino and Filipino American community to refer to the tendency of many of its members to pull successful members down (Chapter 8)

Cultural Mistrust – a psychological construct that refers to the general suspicion that many minorities have toward mainstream or dominant peoples and institutions that are controlled or governed by such peoples (Chapters 9 and 10)

Cultural Shame and Embarrassment – a specific type of colonial mentality that refers to feeling ashamed or embarrassed of one's heritage ethnicity or culture (Chapters 5 and 6)

Datu or Rajah – in indigenous Tao culture, the leader or king of the baranggay or the tribe (Chapters 1 and 2)

Decolonization – the process developing a critical consciousness and ridding colonial mentality (Chapters 10, 11, and 12)

Distorted Core Belief – in Cognitive Behavioral Therapy, an inaccurate belief that is predicted to be the root of psychological problems (Chapter 10)

Dynamic-Constructivist Approach to Culture and Cognition – an approach to understanding how individuals may be able to competently switch between two or more cultural knowledge systems depending on what the context requires (Chapter 6)

Dysfunctional Self-Schema – a general system or set of beliefs about one's abilities and traits that is inaccurate or maladaptive (Chapter 10)

Empirically-Supported Treatments – treatments of therapies that conventional psychology considers to be effective and efficacious based on scientific evidence (Chapters 10 and 11)

Enculturation – the extent to which an individual adheres to, is competent in, and positively regards his or her heritage culture (Chapters 8 and 9)

Ethnic Identity – the extent to which an individual positively regards, identifies with, and is involved in his or her ethnic heritage (Chapters 8, 9, and 11)

Externally-Driven Over Colonial Mentality - a type of the overt colonial mentality category that is driven by factors outside the person such as pressure from other people to behave in a certain way (Chapter 9)

Factor Analysis – a type of statistical analyses often used in psychology when developing tests or measurement tools (Chapter 5)

Filipino – a term that was originally reserved for Spanish individuals who lived in the Spanish colony of the Philippines (Chapter 2)

Fresh-Off-the-Boat or FOB – a derogatory term used to tease or berate individuals who are recent immigrants or those who may still speak English with an accent (Chapters 5, 6, 7, 8, and 11)

Golden Legend – the belief that indigenous Taos needed American and Spanish colonialism in order to become civilized; that the indigenous Taos had nothing worth keeping prior to western colonialism (Chapters 2, 3, 5, 6, and 8)

Hindi Ibang Tao – a term used to regard someone who is no longer considered to be an outsider (Chapter 12)

Hiya – is best translated into the English term of shame, which is a surface Filipino value that indicates collectivism (Chapters 7 and 8)

I am Spanish-Chinese-Filipino (SCF) Syndrome – a phenomenon in the Filipino and Filipino American community that is an attempt by many to dilute their Filipino-ness (Chapter 7)

Ibang tao – a term used to regard someone who is considered to be an outsider or not part of the group (Chapter 12)

Implicit Activation – a concept in psychology that refers to the notion that thoughts and attitudes may become activated without people's awareness or intention (Chapter 6)

Implicit Association Test – a tool commonly used in psychology to measure people's implicit or automatic thoughts and attitudes (Chapters 6 and 9)

Implicit Learning – a concept in psychology that refers to the notion that people learn or remember without intention or even outside of their awareness (Chapter 6)

Indigenization From Within or Cultural Revalidation – a term used by Sikolohiyang Pilipino to describe one manner in which the field of psychology in the Philippines may be indigenized; refers to developing psychological knowledge using concepts, methods, and theories developed by Filipinos themselves (Chapter 12)

Indigenization From Without – a term used by Sikolohiyang Pilipino to describe one manner in which the field of psychology in the Philippines may be indigenized; refers to modifying or translating foreign psychological concepts, methods, and theories to fit the Filipino experience and context (Chapter 12)

Indigenous Psychology - an international movement in the field of psychology that recognizes the limitations of Western theories, concepts, and methods when applied to non-Western peoples; calls for more culturally and indigenously appropriate practice of psychology (Chapter 12)

Indio – a terms used by Spanish colonizers to refer to the indigenous Taos (Chapter 2)

Individualism or Individualistic - terms often used to refer to cultures or societies that place more importance on individual goals rather than group goals (Chapter 7)

Integration – a specific way in which a person may acculturate; refers to positively regarding, being competent in, and being comfortable in two cultures simultaneously; theorized to lead toward biculturalism (Chapters 8 and 9)

Internal Colonialism – an oppressive condition that has all the components of classical colonialism without the recent forced entry of a foreign group into a new territory (Chapters 4 and 5)

Internalized Ethnic and Cultural Inferiority – a specific type of colonial mentality wherein individuals come to accept the alleged inferiority of their heritage culture and ethnicity (Chapters 5, 6, and 9)

Internalized Homophobia – a specific form of internalized oppression wherein homosexual individuals come to hate themselves for being homosexual (Chapter 5)

Internalized Oppression or Internalized Colonialism – a condition wherein oppressed individuals or groups come to hate themselves for being of a certain ethnicity, culture, race, sex, sexual orientation, and other group membership (Chapters 5 and 6)

Internally-Driven Over Colonial Mentality – a specific type of the category of over colonial mentality that is driven by factors within the person such as perceiving one's heritage culture or ethnicity as inferior; strongly related to psychological distress and poorer mental health (Chapter 9)

Kapampangan – the people of the river bank; now used to refer to people who are from the Philippine province of Pampangga (Chapter 2)

Kapwa or Kapwa-Tao – in indigenous Filipino worldview, the core and the most importance part of the Filipino personhood that drives all other Filipino values (Chapters 7, 8, 9, 10, and 11)

Learned Helplessness – in psychology, a condition that develops when an organism has learned that there is nothing one can do to change or influence one's undesired situation or environment (Chapter 10)

Lexical Decision Priming Technique – a method commonly used in psychology to measure people's implicit or automatic thoughts and attitudes about certain things (Chapter 6)

Magnification of Negatives – in Cognitive Behavioral Therapy, a form of distorted thinking that emphasizes the negative aspects of one's life (Chapter 10)

Maladaptive General Beliefs – in Cognitive Behavioral Therapy, a view of the world and of one's self that is inaccurate and, therefore, not beneficial to one's mental health (Chapter 10)

Manifest Destiny – an American belief that it is their right or destiny to expand and propagate their beliefs to the rest of the peoples of the world in order to save or civilize them (Chapters 2 and 3)

Manong – a term used to refer to the early Filipinos in America during the early 1900s; a respectful term used to call older gentlemen (Chapter 4)

Marginalization – a specific way in which one can acculturate, wherein an individual is not involved in, competent in, or comfortable in both his or heritage culture and the mainstream culture (Chapters 7, 8, and 9)

Maynila or Maynilad – the name of the prosperous part of the island archipelago now known as the Philippines; currently the capital of the Philippines (Chapter 2)

Minimization of Positives – in Cognitive Behavioral Therapy, a form of distorted thinking wherein individuals pay less attention to the positive aspects of one's life (Chapter 10)

Neocolonialism – a term used to refer to the current conditions of many societies around the world that resembles the oppressive structures of colonialism (Chapter 4)

Oppression – when one group of people imposes its beliefs, ways of life, and values on another group of people (Chapters 1-12)

Overt Colonial Mentality – a category of colonial mentality that includes discriminating against others who are recent immigrants or are perceived as FOBs, as well as wanting to change one's physical characteristics to look more White or European (Chapters 5, 6, 8, and 9)

Pacification Campaign – the years that followed the Philippine-American War in the late 1800s to early 1900s when Filipinos continuously fought to keep their independence from the United States (Chapter 3)

Pagkatao – in English, refers to personhood (Chapter 7)

Pakikisama – a Filipino surface value that refers to the tendency to go along with group goals and decisions even if such goals and decisions may not be consistent with one's personal goals and decisions (Chapters 7 and 8)

Pakiramdam – a core Filipino value that refers to the heightened sense of empathy and sympathy of Filipinos; an ability to sense subtle, non-verbal cues (Chapters 7 and 8)

Pasalubong – a term used to refer to things that are brought home, usually by a balikbayan, to give away to his or her friends and family (Chapter 8)

Pensionados – Filipinos who studied in prestigious American universities under American scholarship funds (Chapter 3)

Personal Empowerment - raising an individual's sense of power or control over his or her own life (Chapter 11)

Personal Self-Esteem – the extent to which individuals positively regard or evaluate the characteristics of the groups they belong to (Chapter 9)

Pessimistic Explanatory Style – a general pattern of explaining what happens to one's self in a negative, self-defeating manner (Chapter 10)

Philippine-American War in 1899 – a war between the United States and the Philippines that was sparked by Americans' desire to colonize the Philippines and the Filipinos' desire to keep the independence they fought for against Spain (Chapter 3)

Pilipino American Identity Development (PAID) Model – a theoretical model of how second-generation Filipino Americans may regard themselves, other Filipinos, other Asians, other minority groups, and the dominant White population (Chapters 8 and 11)

Postcolonialism – a scholarly field that analyzes the effects and legacies of historical colonialism and contemporary oppression (Chapter 4)

Prime or Priming Paradigm – a method commonly used in psychology wherein individuals are prepared or led to think a certain way, often times in very subtle techniques or strategies (Chapter 6)

Protective Factor – things that may serve as buffers or a shields against negative or undesired psychological conditions (Chapter 9)

Racial Microaggressions – a modern form of racism that is more subtle and sometimes not intentional (Chapter 4)

Racism – a general belief that some racial or ethnic groups are superior than others; these beliefs may be expressed through behaviors and institutional policies (Chapter 4)

St. Louis World's Fair in 1902 – an event staged by the United States government to showcase to the American people the United States' successful conquest and civilization efforts throughout the rest of the world (Chapter 3)

St. Malo, Louisiana – the place of the first Filipino settlement in the United States (Chapter 4)

Sanduguan – blood compact; in indigenous Tao life, different tribes used this ceremony to symbolize their partnership (Chapter 1)

Self-Defeating Cognitions – in Cognitive Behavioral Therapy, inaccurate or distorted negative thoughts about one's self and one's abilities (Chapter 10)

Separation – a specific way in which one can acculturate, wherein an individual may only be comfortable in or competent in one's heritage culture but not with the mainstream or dominant culture (Chapter 9)

Sikolohiyang Pilipino – indigenous Filipino psychology that emphasizes the importance of using indigenous Filipino language, concepts, worldview, and methods (Chapter 12)

Spreading Activation Theory – a theory in psychology that refers to the notion that the human mind is composed of a network of concepts; once a concept is activated by something in the environment, other concepts that are linked to the activated concept may automatically be activated as well (Chapter 6)

Structural Equation Modeling – a form of statistical analyses often used in psychology to describe the relationships between multiple variables of psychological constructs (Chapter 9)

Tagalog – people of the river; also used to refer to a group of Filipinos who live in Manila; also used to refer to the common language of Filipinos (Chapter 2)

Tao – the people; Tagalog word for person (Chapters 1, 2, 7, and 8)

Thomasites – American educators who came to the Philippines during the early 1900s as part of the Pacification campaign; teachers who came to the Philippines to teach and administer the newly established public school system (Chapter 3)

Transnationalism – a term used to describe the current cultural condition of many Filipinos and Filipino Americans today because of the high level of intercultural contact between the Philippines and the United States historically and contemporarily (Chapter 8; Epilogue)

Treaty of Paris in 1898 – an agreement between the United States and Spain that ended the Spanish-American War, but also gave the United States ownership of the Philippines, Puerto Rico, Guam, and Cuba (Chapters 2 and 3)

Utang na Loob – a Filipino surface value that is similar to reciprocity; the need or desire to want to repay another for the person's goodwill and generosity (Chapters 7 and 8)

Vicarious Learning – in psychology, the notion that we learn not just from direct experience but also through the experiences of other people (Chapters 5 and 8)

Vicarious Racism – experiences of racial discrimination that did not directly happen to one's self, but instead to others (Chapter 4)

Within-Group Discrimination – a specific form of colonial mentality wherein Filipinos may discriminate against other Filipinos because they are not Americanized enough or because they are perceived as FOBs (Chapters 5, 6, 7, 8, 9, and 11)

CONTRIBUTIONS

Foreword: Sumie Okazaki, Ph.D., *Associate Professor of Psychology, New York, University*

Afterword: Kevin Nadal, Ph.D., *Assistant Professor of Psychology, John Jay College of Criminal Justice, City University of New York*

Commentaries: Nilda Rimonte
                       Andrew Philip Paves
                       Leny Mendoza Strobel
                       Martin F. Manalansan IV
                       James LaBelle Sr.

Peer Reviewers: Christine Marasigan, M.A., *Trustee, Filipino American National Historical Society*
                       Mariecris Gatlabayan, M.S., *Assistant Professor and Archivist, University of Alaska Anchorage*
                       Anne Saw, Ph.D., *Associate Director of the Asian American Center on Disparities Research, University of California - Davis*
                       Gabriel Garcia, MPH, Ph.D., *Assistant Professor of Public Health, University of Alaska Anchorage*
                       Matthew R. Lee, Ph.D., *Assistant Professor of Psychology, James Madison University*
                       Dinghy Sharma, M.A., *Doctoral Student in Clinical-Community Psychology, University of Alaska Fairbanks*

Reviewer and
Back Cover Quote: Alvin Alvarez, Ph.D., *Professor of*
                       Counseling, San Francisco State University

Baybayin Consultant: Jacob Ira Azurin Vijandre

Cover Photography
and Design: Vicente T. Capala III

Cover Photo Credits: Anthony Cruz
                       Melissa Salazar-Blake
                       Diego Brown
                       Edwin Brown
                       Elli Ebue
                       Vilma Rollins
                       Benjo Holganza
                       Kriselle Cadiz
                       Melanie Marasigan
                       Kawika Hepa
                       Chester Mainot
                       Kristine Rollins
                       Karla Phillips
                       Nicholas Foote

Front Cover Model: Billy Vallejo

ABOUT THE AUTHOR

Dr. E. J. R. David was born in the Philippines. His first home was in Pasay City, where he shared a one-bedroom shack with his mother, father, and older sister. When he was about 5-years-old, his father left the Philippines to work in the United States and, a year later, his family was able to save enough money to build a house in the Las Piñas suburb of B.F. Homes. While in the Philippines, E.J. attended Don Bosco Technical Institute, an all-boys catholic school in Makati.

In 1994, he moved to Barrow, Alaska, a small Inupiat village of about 5,000 people and is the northernmost point in the United States. He struggled with his identity and with cultural clashes between the Filipino, Inupiat, and mainstream American cultures. At that time, E.J. negotiated such difficulties and confusions by focusing on basketball, where he was a four-year starter for the Barrow High School Whalers as a point guard. He was given All-State Basketball honors during his junior and senior years.

After high school, E.J. enlisted in the United States Army because he had no other option. However, a few months before he was supposed to begin Basic training, he was awarded a scholarship to attend the University of Alaska Anchorage (UAA). Despite working full-time at a local mental health agency and spending a summer working in the oil fields of Kuparuk near Prudhoe Bay, E.J. obtained his B.A. in psychology in three years with departmental and university honors.

Afterward, E.J. attended the University of Illinois at Urbana-Champaign, where he obtained a Masters Degree and a Ph.D. in Clinical-Community Psychology. Currently, E.J. is an Assistant Professor of Psychology at UAA, with his primary duties being with the University of Alaska PhD Program in Clinical-Community Psychology that has a Cultural and Indigenous emphasis. His father still lives in Barrow, Alaska, his older sister and two nieces still live in the Philippines, and his younger brother and mother now live with him in Anchorage, Alaska. E.J. is also blessed to have a beautiful Koyukon Athabascan wife, Margaret, with whom he has three amazing "Filibascan" children – Malakas (strong), Kalayaan (freedom), and Kaluguran (love).

E.J. has traveled to various cities and states as an invited workshop facilitator, speaker, and presenter on colonial mentality or internalized oppression, and other Ethnic Minority, Asian American, and Filipino American psychological issues. He has published theoretical and empirical works on such topics. His work on colonial mentality led to him being awarded the Distinguished Student Research Award by the American Psychological Association (APA) Division 45 (Society for the Psychological Study of Ethnic Minority Issues) for "his significant contribution in psychological research related to ethnic minority populations." Most recently, due to the impact of his work in only five years since obtaining his Ph.D., E.J. was honored by the APA Minority Fellowship Program with the 2012 Early Career Award in Research for Distinguished Contributions to the Field of Racial and Ethnic Minority Psychology, citing his "outstanding scientific contributions and the application of this knowledge toward the improved mental and physical well-being of people of color."

SUBJECT INDEX

psychopathology   148, 160, 165-6, 174-5
Puerto Ricans   60-2

R

racism   40, 46, 48, 58, 63, 129, 148, 171, 251
recreation, cultural   57, 64
religion   11, 193, 250
research, implicit memory   81-2, 84, 87

S

savages   28-9, 31, 55, 269, 271
schizophrenia   148, 160
schools   33, 68, 85, 126, 130-1, 185, 268-9
science   42-3, 162, 215, 224, 269
self   12, 52, 74, 109-10, 115-17, 119, 127, 141-2, 159, 163, 169, 171, 251-2, 265
  personal   126, 128, 141
self-blame   167, 169, 198-9
self-concept   141-2, 156
self-esteem   65, 77, 141, 145, 147, 152, 159, 165, 243
  personal   141-5
self-government   26-7, 35
self-report   84, 97-8
sensitivity, cultural   154, 160, 177
service providers   172, 175-7, 201
shame   62, 66-7, 75, 86, 98, 107-8, 112, 117, 123, 150, 152, 181, 190, 197, 249
Sikolohiyang Pilipino (SP)   203, 205, 212-13, 215-16, 224, 227-8, 234, 263, 265

social action   180-1, 183, 194
social anxiety   145, 165, 169-72
social cognition paradigms   81, 98
social group   53, 117-18, 141, 167-8, 171, 237
social interactions   214-15, 260
society, colonial   47, 55-6, 237
Spain   1, 15-17, 19-22, 25-6, 29, 35, 38, 42, 47, 54-5, 61-3, 66, 241-3, 273
Spanish   17, 19, 21, 27, 34, 63, 243, 251, 253
Spanish and American colonialism   14, 49, 61, 70, 80, 155-6
Spanish colonialism   8, 12-13, 21, 55, 254
Spanish colonies in Latin America   21
Spanish colonizers   15, 17, 20
Spanish culture   17, 19-20, 60
Spanish occupation   11, 14, 16, 20
Spanish rule   1, 15, 18-20, 35, 37, 246
spiritual beliefs   8-9, 17, 21
spreading activation theory   83, 86, 94, 96
St. Louis World   31
stress, acculturative   58, 139, 261
subjugation, cultural   22, 48-9, 165
suicide   58-60, 137, 139, 145, 147, 152, 182
superiority   31, 47, 55, 58, 63, 80, 86, 94, 96-7, 99-101, 126, 130, 164

Made in the USA
Las Vegas, NV
30 March 2022